The Saints Show Us Christ

Daily Readings on the Spiritual Life

RAWLEY MYERS

The Saints Show Us Christ
Daily Readings
on the Spiritual Life

IGNATIUS PRESS   SAN FRANCISCO

Cover art: Fra Angelico,
The Last Judgement (details)
Museo San Marco,
Florence, Italy
Erich Lessing/Art Resource, N.Y.

Cover design by Roxanne Mei Lum

ISBN 0–89870–542–8
Library of Congress catalogue number 95–75665
Printed in the United States of America ∞

Dedicated to
Tim and Priscilla
and
Miles and Marilyn,
whom I admire

CONTENTS

PREFACE

This book is the spiritual life according to the saints. A saint is a story of God's love. As Christ's closest friends, they know him best. They have the wisdom of Heaven, and are our tried and true guides to Heaven, for the saints take us to the feet of Christ. Today too many self-appointed experts in religion tell us about the spiritual life, but their books are mostly amateur psychology and sociology, having little about true religion. Most of these modern authors do not pray as the saints did and so do not truly know Christ. These experts tell us *about* Christ, but the saints introduce us *to* Christ, whom they have loved so much. The wise will listen to the saints, while those in love with novelty will run after every new guru who comes along.

To know Jesus is the heart of our faith. No one has known him better than the saints.

DAILY READINGS

St. Francis de Sales *January 1*

St. Francis de Sales said a soul that knows its misery can still have great confidence in God. Many of the great saints began their prayers with the confession of their own unworthiness. The more we acknowledge ourselves to be poor spiritually, the more we must put our confidence in the goodness and mercy of God. God's mercy can be exercised only toward the merciful.

St. Francis said, we have nothing in ourselves in which we can trust. In fact, we must mistrust ourselves and look to our heavenly Father for help. Jesus came to rescue us.

We wait for the mercy of God. Humility helps us ascend to God.

We are confused and must look to God with love. We are unclothed and God must clothe us. We must not let our confusion be attended with sadness and we must not be upset: this comes from self-love. We are troubled because we are not perfect. Our pride is hurt.

If we lack confidence, Francis said, we should pray, "Although, dear Lord, I have no feeling of confidence in thee, I know all the same that thou art my God, and that I am wholly thine, and that I have no hope but in thy goodness; therefore, I abandon myself, with all that I am, into thy hands."

St. Francis said that we must offer this prayer even though we pray without fervor and without feeling satisfaction. We must not distress ourselves about our weakness. Even in difficulties we should show our fidelity to Christ.

Having put your faith in God, you must, he said, be at peace and not dwell upon your troubles. Think of helping others.

St. Teresa of Avila *January 2*

The great St. Teresa of Avila reformed the Carmelite order in Spain and made convents more prayerful and penitential. She said that though she was weak and despicable, she worked for the Lord. She prayed constantly, pleading tearfully with Jesus, begging him to cure the evils in the land. She said she would gladly give her life just to save one soul. St. Teresa prayed that since God had so many enemies and so few friends, the friends should at least be good ones. She resolved to do the "very little within my power" to try to improve the spiritual life in the convent. She wrote, "I trusted in the great goodness of God, who never fails anyone."

St. Teresa said, "O my Redeemer, it breaks my heart to know how thou art persecuted by those who wish to fasten thee to the cross once more. What has happened to Christians? Are there always to be people who offend thee? They for whom thou hast worked thy greatest favors, who owe thee the most, whom thou hast chosen for thy friends, among whom thou dost give thyself in the Sacraments, and suffered torments and afflictions—they are so often indifferent to thee. O Lord of my soul, save us."

She said that many Christians seem to have so little loyalty to Christ. "It breaks my heart. Help to beg Jesus to save souls. We must long for, weep for, pray for souls."

St. Teresa wrote, "The world is on fire; once more men seemingly would wish to put Christ to death, for they bring a thousand false witnesses against him and seek to overthrow his Church." She said we must pray for them and the salvation of their souls, not for trivial things.

St. John of the Cross   *January 3*

St. John of the Cross, a devout Carmelite priest, helped St. Teresa of Avila reform the Church in Spain. He said that the relationship between the rational creature and Creator is based on love. Let us unite our souls with God. It is faith, hope and charity that are the foundation of this union.

Some souls are lazy. They want a close friendship with God but will not labor for it.

We were made for the Beatific Vision, which we will enjoy in heaven. On earth we are to prepare for this glorious event. The reason for the many trials and troubles through which the soul must pass to divine union is that these purify the soul. They prepare the spirit for higher things.

The one thing, the saint said, upon which the salvation of the soul depends is love, love for God and for our neighbor in God. St. John repeatedly insisted on this. He said, "Love is the inclination of the soul, the strength and power by which it goes to God, for by means of love the soul is united to God." At judgment we will be examined on our love.

With love you walk toward heaven. It is necessary for salvation. Because of love the soul sees God in heaven, "some more fully, some less, but all see God and are content, since the capacity of each is satisfied". What does the soul see? The unveiled vision of God.

All souls are called to heaven. God leads the soul. He humbles us with trials, so we will pray to him and more purposely walk in his way. We must beg God to help us. For without external assistance we can do nothing.

St. John said that it is providence that orders all things wisely. The soul passes through darkness on its journey to God, but if we trust him, he leads us.

St. Thomas Aquinas *January 4*

St. Thomas Aquinas was one of the most brilliant thinkers in the Middle Ages. He was of the noble Aquino family, born in the Castle of Rocca Secca, high in the mountains of Italy in the Kingdom of Naples. His father, Count Aquino, was a nephew of the Emperor Frederick I. His mother was a countess in her own right.

Thomas was a gentle child with deep lustrous eyes and a thoughtful expression even though his father and brothers were warriors. When Thomas was only six he was sent to study with the monks at Monte Cassino. After that he attended the University of Naples. His parents would have preferred him to remain at Monte Cassino and eventually become the abbot. They were very ambitious, especially since he was of royal blood. But

Thomas wanted none of that. It was in Naples that he met members of the newly formed Dominican order. He wished to become a Dominican. As far as his parents were concerned, this was beneath the dignity of a noble family. The Dominicans were a band of poor friars.

In the Dominican church in Naples, Thomas was often seen absorbed in prayer. In time he told the prior that he wished to give himself to the order, and he was accepted. When word reached Rocca Secca, a storm of rage broke out. His mother especially was angry. Thomas was told to accompany some other Dominicans on a journey to Paris to study. His mother, however, had his brothers kidnap him and bring him to Rocca Secca. There he was locked in his room until he would give up this silly idea. Thomas would not budge.

Once his brothers even bribed a prostitute to enter his room. But Thomas grabbed up a burning stick from the hearth and chased her away, branding a cross on the door.

Eventually his family gave in. They saw they could not break his will. Finally he was able to escape, and they let him go. He went on to Paris to study, and, in time, came to be one of the greatest professors at the University of Paris, then the greatest center of learning in the world.

St. John of the Cross   *January 5*

St. John of the Cross was a very small man with a very great soul.

He stated that there are three ways God can be in the soul. There is the first, which applies to every soul, "even in that of the greatest sinner in the world". The Creator must sustain each soul or it would cease to exist.

The second way is the union of grace accomplished by God in baptism "wherein man is made partaker of the divine nature, i.e., of the divine life and activity raised to the supernatural state, which is the preparation for the Beatific Vision of God in heaven".

The third way is a union and transformation of the soul with God, when there is a "likeness of love; and the wills, that of the soul and that of God, are conformed together in one, the one having nothing repugnant to the other". He wrote, "God is a fountain from which each one draws water according to the vessel he carries."

Someone said, "A great part of St. John's mission was to convert Christians to Christianity."

He wrote that we are to put on the mind of Christ. It is a growing up into Christ, a conforming of the mind and will to the divine mind and will. Unfortunately, many Christians who have a minimum of religion ignore this.

St. John was especially devoted to Mass and to our Lady. His devotion inspired the devotion of others. At Mass, God conveys his purifying and illuminating streams of truth and grace to our intellects and wills, St. John said.

A commentator in our day has written of St. John, "No one has ever more completely exposed the emptiness of that emotional slush of the feelings which runs riot today under the name of Christianity than he does."

St. Francis de Sales   *January 6*

St. Francis de Sales was born into a noble family. He studied with brilliant success. His father wanted Francis to be a lawyer so that he could take his place as a senator from the French province of Savoy. Francis wanted to be a priest and, after a time, he was able to enter the seminary. As a student he went through a period of near despair, but he prayed lovingly to the Blessed Mother and found peace of soul.

As a priest he was in the Diocese of Geneva where most people were Calvinist Protestants. Francis preached beautifully but he wanted to do more. He wrote and passed out pamphlets. It was a thankless task, as he went door to door, for most people were prejudiced and many doors were shut in his face. The people often not only rejected him but threatened and insulted him. But he persevered, and soon his writings became well known.

The zealous priest reminded himself that St. Augustine was always gentle. We too, he said, should bear with the imperfections of others, as God bears with our imperfections. He said, "Jesus on the Cross, with a heart full of tenderness and love, prayed for others. We should strive to forget injuries others cause us, as Jesus in agony on the Cross asked that those who nailed him there be forgiven for their evil and outrage."

Like children we ought to share our joy. We will be more cheerful if we are humble. The proud are too pompous to laugh, especially at themselves.

We are humble when we do not dwell on the faults of others but on their virtues, mindful of our own sins. Humility makes us think less of ourselves. It makes us very much aware of all our gifts from God.

St. Thomas Aquinas   *January 7*

St. Thomas Aquinas studied at Paris and Cologne. In the churches of Cologne and Bonn, he poured out his rich thoughts; people loved to hear him preach. He spoke to the heart because he prayed so much. The people instinctively knew he was a holy man who did more than utter platitudes. They came under his spell. His sermons were well-reasoned. One writer said, "He was heard by the people as if his discourse came from God."

He was soon called back to study and teach at Paris, and he renewed his friendship with the great Franciscan friar St. Bonaventure.

Thomas, in time, took part in the public disputes and debates at the University. Again his clear mind and logical presentations won over the crowd. He was writing a great deal. He composed treatises "On Man", "On Eternity", "On Thought", "The Power of the Soul", and "The Essence and Dimensions of Matter".

Soon there arose a bitter battle over whether religious orders had a right to exist. He and Bonaventure together won this debate. Also, Thomas was summoned to Rome by the Dominican

Master General to refute a book of impiety and false mysticism, which he did eloquently.

Back in Paris, Thomas wrote masterful manuscripts including the *Summa Contra Gentiles.* St. Louis IX, King of France, held Aquinas in the highest esteem. He often consulted him about matters of state.

The beauty of his writing rested on sublimity of thought, subtlty of argument, simplicity of style, and a pleasing spirit. His masterpiece, of course, is the *Summa Theologica.* Few, if any, greater works in theology have ever been written. This magnificent study covers almost the whole field of theological thought. With his masterful mind Thomas seems like an oracle sent from God. He had such a mastery of his subject that there has been no one to equal him. And yet Thomas always remained a simple, humble, meek, and mild friar.

St. Augustine   *January 8*

"The very countenance of creation is a great book", said St. Augustine. Read this book well. God in nature places before your eyes all that he has made. "Why do you seek greater testimony? Heaven and earth cry out to you, 'God made me.' Gaze with reverence upon heaven and earth."

Do not be too busy to see the beauty all about you or to honor its author. Augustine quotes St. Paul who wrote, "Although they knew God, they did not glorify him."

St. Augustine said that to glorify God is to give thanks to him. "For one who has been created in the image of God, what can be worse than ingratitude toward God?" he asked.

The proud do not often think of God. Senseless minds do not honor him. Vain individuals are too preoccupied with self. As St. Paul wrote, "For while professing to be wise, they have become fools." St. Augustine said that by claiming as their own what has been given by God, the proud are untruthful. Thus does God hide himself from the proud and reveal himself as the sole Creator to those who search for him in creation. "Thou didst hide these things from the wise", St. Matthew wrote.

The humble know God, and they are happy. The humble look to Christ who said, "Come to me and I will give you rest." Learn from him. "You will not be humble unless you fix your attention on Jesus who was made humble because of you." Listen to Christ for he will teach you what you cannot learn from man. In him is the true meaning of humility. He who draws near to Jesus is first molded according to this humility.

St. Gertrude   *January 9*

St. Gertrude lived in the thirteenth century. She became an illustrious Benedictine Abbess in Germany. She had profound intellectual gifts. Our divine Savior frequently conversed with her.

The *Revelations* of St. Gertrude tell of frequent and familiar visits with Jesus. He was tender and familiar with his loving daughter. And Gertrude rested with mystic rapture upon his bosom. Hers was a free spirit, bright, joyous. There was in her none of the narrow mistrust that mediocre souls have. A loving heart, always grateful, was within her. A continual incense of thanksgiving ascended from her heart. Gertrude's love for Christ burned daily deeper and brighter.

She entered the Benedictine abbey at an early age. In time her Spouse, Jesus, began speaking to this devoted soul. She listened attentively to his whispers. At the first visit Jesus came as she was performing an act of humility and obedience. Jesus told her that he dearly loved her, and she was filled to overflowing with love for him. She trusted the Sacred Heart of Jesus entirely.

Gertrude said of death, "It is indifferent to me whether it be slow or sudden, provided that it is pleasing in God's sight, him to whom I hope it will bring me; for I trust, in whatever manner I die, that I shall not be deprived of the mercy of my God, without which my eternal ruin would be inevitable."

In all that she did Gertrude had a happy manner. In one vision she saw Jesus seated on a throne and she walked around him, "never taking her eyes off him". He was so magnificent, so wondrous.

It was her habit to have recourse to her heavenly Spouse in every trial. And it almost seemed that Jesus so loved Gertrude that he was pained to refuse a request. And yet he did so at times for her sake. He told her, "Our wills are so closely united by the sacred tie of grace that you desire nothing but what I myself desire." Thus when refused in prayer, she changed her mind.

St. Augustine   *January 10*

St. Augustine asks, "What is Christ?" He is the Lamb of God, he who died for us with great humility. Crucifixion was a death regarded among the Jews as a terrible disgrace. Jesus humbled himself so that he might destroy our pride. "Are you ashamed to be humble for him in whom the nature of God was humbled?" asked Augustine. Jesus said, "Learn of me." You are troubled in heart but once you find Jesus whom your heart has been seeking, you at last find repose.

"My yoke is easy", Jesus said. If you have feared his yoke, learn from him and you will rejoice, Augustine wrote. When one seeks human things and temporal gains he is bound by chains. The yoke of Christ is not like that. Do not fear. Take it up, for it is light. It brings no hardship with it. It puts chains only on that freedom which brings misery.

Jesus' yoke does not weigh you down; it lifts you up, the saint said. "It encumbers you, not with a burden but with honor. When you have his burden, you are in no way oppressed by it. You should think of this as a burden, only if you think the wings of a bird are a burden to it.

"What can be heavy for one who loves? Do you not see how the hunter toils? So much does a man endure that he may come upon a wild deer, and yet he shirks the burden that he may come upon God."

St. Augustine comments that "men say, 'How can the burden of Christ be light?' It is because of love. Many have suffered for him but have rejoiced. Love for him bore them through all adversity. This is the burden of Christ, which he lays upon us. It is given in the name of love. Because of love all things that once were toilsome are made easy. All things that were heavy are made light."

Take up this burden. It does not weigh you down. It will be as wings for you. Before you have these wings you are earthbound. Receive this burden and you will find peace of soul. Take these wings and fly to the heights.

St. Francis de Sales   *January 11*

St. Francis de Sales in time became the Bishop of Geneva. He was in great demand as a preacher. His essays on the Church came to be read everywhere. Francis was very clear both in the pulpit and in his writings. He was most sincere and convinced many.

Though he was from the noble class, he sought no honors. But his fame brought him in contact with many of the leaders of Europe. He was a godsend in this post-reformation time, and he counselled them wisely. Francis wrote of Christianity in an attractive way, and since he himself led a deeply spiritual life, he spoke with authority, for he spoke so often to Jesus. His kind of sanctity—quiet, gentle, kindly, cheerful—does not frighten people. A man of tranquility and moderation, he won many souls to Jesus.

Even as a bishop he continued to teach religion to the children. He visited every parish, no matter how remote, teaching and preaching there. His gentle character was greatly loved. As he said, "A spoonful of honey attracts more flies than a barrel of vinegar."

A generosity of spirit makes us like Jesus. And we esteem our gifts with humility, knowing that all have been given us by God. Generosity was the spirit of the saints. St. Paul wrote, "I can do all things in him who strengthens me." Humility makes us mistrust ourselves and trust in God.

"Do not deceive yourself with a false and foolish humility that will not admit the real good which God implants in you", Francis urged. "The gifts that God gives us ought to be recognized and esteemed, and credit given to him. They are given us to glorify the divine goodness."

St. Thérèse of Lisieux   *January 12*

St. Thérèse of Lisieux is known and loved all over the world as the Little Flower. She was an unknown Carmelite nun in France who died at the age of twenty-four. Under obedience she wrote her spiritual autobiography. She said, "Before taking up my pen I knelt before our Lady's statue, the one that so often assures us that the Queen of Heaven looks on our community with special favor. My prayer was that she would guide my hand."

Little Thérèse wrote, speaking of her vocation to the Carmelites of Strict Observance, that God doesn't often seem to call the most talented people. There are some Jesus chooses, however; little people Jesus sees fit to hold in his arms from the cradle to the grave. These he calls.

Thérèse wrote that all the flowers that God has made are beautiful. Some are large, some are small, but none robs the other of its fragrance and charm. The variety gives gaity to the garden, and so God has great saints and small saints. But all can become saints.

Our Lord's love is in the simplest soul as it is in great souls. In fact, she said, the whole point of love is making one's self small. "If we were all like the great Doctors who shed luster on the Church by their brilliant teaching, there wouldn't be much condescension on God's part. But no, he has created little children who have no idea what is going on and like a baby can only express themselves by helpless crying." We are infants in the Church. God is content to forget his dignity and to come into our little hearts too. It is by such condescension that God shows his infinite greatness.

Jesus takes a special interest in each soul, as if there were no other like it. God is so merciful.

We are exiles in this world, still on alien shores. May Jesus be merciful to us. Soon we shall bloom as beautiful flowers in heaven.

St. John of the Cross   *January 13*

St. John of the Cross saw the things of religion as those that bind the mind and will to God. Sentiments and feelings do not endure. He held that a spirituality that is not rooted in reason is the most dangerous of delusions, and that the one test of Christian belief and practice is laid down in the words of Jesus, "Not everyone that says unto me, 'Lord, Lord', shall enter into the Kingdom of Heaven, but he who does the will of my Father who is in heaven."

The task of the Christian is to change from his unlikeness to God to a likeness to him. St. John wrote, "Even as in the consummation of marriage according to the flesh the two become one flesh, as Scripture says, so when this spiritual marriage between God and the soul is consummated there are two natures in one spirit and love of God."

Following St. Thomas Aquinas, this Carmelite saint makes it clear that while the intellect is the highest faculty of the soul, since it is by it, aided by faith, that the soul apprehends God in this life and sees him in the *Lumen Gloria* in heaven, yet the will plays a foremost part on earth, since it lays hold of that which the mind perceives by an act of love. On earth this is of more value than an act of knowledge, for it completes and perfects it.

For union with God we clear the garden of weeds.

St. John said that many in the spiritual life lose their way or turn back because they do not understand. And they do not understand because they do not pray faithfully.

The spiritual life begins when the soul is awakened and sees Christ in a new light. Through prayer it rouses itself from apathy and sees that we are not called to mediocrity but to walk in life with Jesus.

St. Thérèse, the Little Flower, said that we are like a flower that can lift its head after the storm passes, because of God's mercy. "The Lord is my shepherd; how can I lack anything?" To each of us the Lord is "pitying and gracious, patient and rich in mercy".

If a flower could talk it would tell openly about all that God has done for it. In like manner God has given us so very many undeserved gifts. All things come from him. Anything good in us is because of his mercy.

Thérèse frequently thanked God for her good parents, who were a gift from him. They trained her well. Their home was filled with love, which made the family rich, richer than the wealthy.

Thérèse wrote of the day she entered the enclosed Carmelite convent. She related that she and her family went to Mass in the convent chapel, the part that is open to the public, and received Communion. "There was sobbing all around me, nobody but myself was dry-eyed. My own sensation was a violent beating of the heart." Then the members of the family kissed her, and she knelt for her father's blessing. (Her mother had died.) He too knelt down, and he blessed her with tears in his eyes. She wrote, "I think the angels smiled down on us, rejoicing at the sight of an old man giving up his daughter." She continued, "A few moments more, and the doors of God's Ark shut behind me, and I was being embraced by all those dear nuns inside whose example I was to henceforth take as my rule of living."

Thérèse felt refreshed and at peace, and this interior certitude was to be deep and lasting, even amid her trials.

Little Thérèse, still in her early teens, was then taken to make a visit to Christ in the Blessed Sacrament. She prayed to him with all her heart, for he was the reason for her life.

St. Thérèse of Lisieux *January 15*

St. Thérèse found that, as her convent life went on, "our Lord let me see clearly that if I wanted to win souls I must do so by bearing a cross." Her cross was anxieties of heart. A holy priest helped her by saying, "My child, there is only one superior— Jesus Christ."

God's grace is always there to help us, Thérèse said. Nearness to God makes us simple. She said that in the strict convent life she survived because of the crucifix. She knelt often in the shadow of the cross "watered by our Lord's tears, and his Precious Blood, with the adorable Face for its sun, the Face overcast with sorrow".

Thérèse said that in the world people want to be known, but in the spiritual life it is glory to be unknown by the world.

Then a most severe trial came to her. Her father had a nervous breakdown. It was a difficult cross, and she suffered a great deal for his sake. His sufferings pierced her heart like a sword. For three years this cruel torment lasted, and then the good man died. She was certain he was in heaven, away from the heartaches of the world.

Thérèse grew in soul. She said that we must give ourselves over to the Lord to do as he wishes. He illumines our minds little by little.

She wrote, "I tried my best to do good on a small scale, having no opportunity to do so on a large scale."

At times Thérèse felt a dryness at prayer, without consolation. She said it was as if Christ were asleep in the boat. But she kept on trying. She said, "God knows the stuff of which we are made, and he can't forget that we are only dust." Thérèse wrote that even in her dryness, "I felt God was showing me the right way to do his will."

St. John of the Cross *January 16*

St. John of the Cross, the great Spanish Carmelite mystic, said that our prejudices and passions all turn us away from God. They destroy the spirit of Christ within us.

If the world perishes from lack of vision, he said, blame Christians who are dying of complacency and insipidity. They obscure Christ who is supposed to shine through them.

St. John compares the soul to a window that, if stained by dirt, the light cannot penetrate. Only if it is clean can the sun's rays pass through. God's goodness shines through the purified window of the soul.

Selfishness, he states, keeps us from union with the unselfish Christ. Our attachment to childish things keeps us from him. We must give up the less important for the more important.

Christ did not seek to please himself, and we must be Christlike. We must know Christ so we can imitate him. We then are lifted up in mind and heart, determined to shake off our slothfulness and to strive to be like Jesus.

St. John of the Cross wrote, "In order to conquer all lesser desires, the love and affection which inflame the will to seek enjoyment in them, it is necessary for the soul to be set on fire by another and a greater love, having its delight in God, and then it will have the courage and constancy to deny itself all else with ease."

Unless the soul is drawn to and enkindled with the desire for God, this saint wrote, it is unable to throw off the natural yoke and the desire for self-centered pleasure.

Not only must the End (God) be seen, but the Way must be known. Christ is the Way. John of the Cross said, "Progress is possible only through the imitation of Christ." Jesus said, "I am the door; by me if any man enter he shall be saved." To be a Christian is to be "another Christ". Jesus said, "Follow me."

St. Thomas More   *January 17*

St. Thomas More had a gifted mind. He was lord chancellor of England under King Henry VIII. But when Henry declared himself the head of the Church in England in order to give himself a divorce, Thomas would not endorse this false measure; and Henry had St. Thomas' head cut off.

Sir Thomas More, who was a brilliant man, always put God first. He prayed, "My Sweet Saviour Christ, whose own disciple, entangled with the devil because of vile and wretched greed, betrayed you, inspire me to marvel at your majesty and to have the love of goodness deep in my heart, that I may please you and may always set this world as nought."

He wrote, "When I was Chancellor of the realm, it was very well known what manner of favour I bore toward the clergy and that I loved and honoured the good, and was not remiss nor slack in providing for the correction of those who were not and were vexatious to good people and slandered their own order. They had little favour with me."

Thomas said, "Whoever will mark the devil and his temptations shall find him much like an ape. For like an ape, not well looked upon, he will be busy and bold to do mischievous turns of all kinds. Finding a man idle, the devil tempts him and deceives him because he is not ready to resist." On the other hand, he said, if the devil sees a man diligent in persevering to oppose temptations, he will try to make him weary and weak.

"The devil is of such high pride he cannot abide to be mocked." So laugh at him.

St. Thomas wrote, "He who bids others to do well and gives a bad example himself is like a foolish weaver who weaves a part with one hand and unweaves it as fast with the other."

St. Vincent de Paul   *January 18*

St. Vincent de Paul reformed the Church in France and in a large part of Europe, and he sent his spiritual sons as missionaries to many places in the world. His priests were called the Congregation of the Mission, or Vincentians. He established seminaries and his priests preached missions. His Sisters were the Daughters of Charity.

Vincent and his companions were known for their great charity and were beloved by the poor. Vincent saw his work prosper and in his humility said they were "contrary to my deserts". It was his humility that enabled God to use him as an instrument for good in the world. He lived in a time when the poor were greatly neglected and the rural people knew little about the faith. He helped change this.

St. Vincent had been a mediocre priest when, on a ship, he was captured by pirates and sold into slavery in North Africa. The misery of this life changed him. As a slave he learned to depend entirely on God, who was all he had.

Vincent wrote, "God always kept alive in me the conviction that I would be freed because of my unceasing prayers to him and to the Blessed Mother, through whose sole intercession I firmly believed I would be delivered."

At length he did escape and he and another man crossed the Mediterranean Sea in a tiny ship and returned home. Vincent, back in France, was a changed man. He said that our Lord leads us in life, and we must always wait patiently for the "manifestation of his holy and adorable will".

Later, he wrote to one of his priests about humility. The priest was very popular as a preacher. Vincent said, "We are all greatly consoled by this. And because we recognize that this abundant grace comes from God, a grace that he keeps on giving only to the humble who realize that all the good done through them comes from God, I beg him with all my heart to give you more and more of the spirit of humility in all your duties. You must believe most assuredly that God will take this grace away from you as soon as you allow vain complacency to enter your mind, attributing to yourself what belongs to God alone."

St. Vincent de Paul   *January 19*

St. Vincent de Paul advised his priests, "Humble yourself greatly then at the thought that Judas had far more graces than you, but in spite of that he was lost. What would it profit the greatest apostle in the world, endowed with the most eminent talents, to have made his words resound with applause throughout the entire province and even to have converted thousands of souls to God, if, in spite of all that, he were to lose his soul!"

Vincent said Jesus loved the ordinary and abject of life and so should we. He spent his days helping the needy. When he preached he used simple language. He said that our Lord gives us the spirit of humility, if we ask him and are faithful to his grace and careful to put it into practice.

"How fortunate we are to honor the poor", he said, "by helping them and living in poverty with them. I am the son of a poor farmer, I have looked after pigs."

In one letter he thanked most humbly a woman for the rosaries and holy pictures she sent. He wrote, "I beg God that they may be profitable to those to whom we shall distribute them, and that he may be your glory as he is the One who gave you this devotion."

St. Vincent said, "I praise God that he is so good as to raise up in this century so many good and holy souls for the assistance of the poor common people." He continued, "I beg him with all my heart to bless the programs of these holy people and grant them success for his glory."

He remarked that some were divided as to how to do the work for the needy. There was often disorder. He stressed that it was very important for people to unite and have the same spirit so they could accomplish more.

To a person in trouble, St. Vincent de Paul wrote, "Blessed be God for the difficulties he is pleased that you should encounter. You must remember the difficulties his Son had on earth. Many were adverse to him for his holy teachings. People made fun of him and scoffed at him and spit in his face. Let us, like him, bear the contradictions that befall us. Let us rejoice in the good that will come from them."

St. Ignatius Loyola   *January 20*

St. Ignatius Loyola, a Spanish soldier, founded the Jesuits.

He said that Jesus shows us that we must pray. In remaining

behind in the temple, Jesus displayed his eagerness, at the early age of twelve, to tell people of the love of his heavenly Father.

Jesus wishes all men to love and honor God and to serve others. Satan, Ignatius said, seeks to let anger, hatred and hostility enter into our hearts. He tempts men with a lust for riches and the empty honors of the world. Unbounded pride ruins many. Our Lord begs all his servants and friends to be loving and to spread love and kindness in the world. We are to urge others to follow Christ and be humble.

St. Ignatius said we should speak to our Lady and ask her to obtain from her Son the grace to imitate him.

A good person wishes to save his soul: if he stood in the presence of God and all his saints and asked to know what is most pleasing to his Divine Goodness, God would tell him to free himself from the attachments he has to money in order to find peace in the Lord.

Let the Lord inspire you to give glory to God, said the saint. This Jesus did. When he left Nazareth to go to John the Baptist at the Jordan, Jesus set out to serve the Father. After his baptism he went into the desert to pray and do penance. Jesus was humble. Following him in that humility is necessary for salvation, St. Ignatius Loyola wrote. A servant of the Lord does not seek honors. He serves God and saves souls. He praises and gives glory to God. In order to be more like Christ he does not seek riches or fame. He is willing to be considered a fool for Christ, who suffered such treatment before us. The Christ-follower implores our Lord to bless him and help him be humble.

St. Ignatius wrote, "I must look only to the end for which I am created, that is, for the praise of God, our Lord, and for the salvation of my soul." My first desire cannot be to be honored or to be wealthy, for then God is second.

St. Charles Borromeo   *January 21*

St. Charles Borromeo, the reforming Cardinal of Milan, renewed the Church in his diocese, following the Reformation and after the Council of Trent. He was a leader of compelling personality and dramatic zeal. When St. Charles entered Milan for the first time, he was such a striking figure the crowd cried out, "A second St. Ambrose".

Charles, a young churchman, was a gifted thinker but even more he was deeply devout. He was the distinguished scion of a noble family. If he had been so inclined he could have been rich, famous and powerful. But he wished to do God's will and he felt called to the priesthood. He wished to walk closely with Christ. During his entire life of heroic sanctity he was a stimulus and an inspiration.

His mother was the sister of the Pope and Charles rose quickly to a high ecclesiastical career. He was a cardinal at the age of twenty-two. But because he had a good mind and a holy soul, he served the Vatican well. And after that he was sent to Milan.

As a student, Charles was said to be "always most serene and friendly". He was liked and respected. As a cardinal he won the admiration and praise of the people for his prayer life and his energy and accomplishments and for his sterling character.

He accepted the appointment to Milan with the words, "We begin reform by first reforming ourselves."

Charles disposed of all his rich benefices, giving a great amount to charity and the rest to education and the Holy See.

In Milan Charles began his reform by reducing his staff and living simply. He had two small rooms, a bedroom and study, in the residence near the chapel. He led his household in the spiritual exercises of St. Ignatius Loyola. The proud were given the most menial tasks to make them humble.

His austerity was a protest against the almost universal carelessness and luxury of the wealthy clergy.

St. Charles Borromeo   *January 22*

St. Charles Borromeo was the Cardinal of Milan during the post-reformation period, and he was most influential in reforming the Church.

St. Charles knew that his primary weakness was pride, and so he constantly practiced humility.

To look out on the corrupt Church of his times might have made a lesser person despair. Instead he prayed. He knew that real reform is beyond human power. He begged God for divine assistance. He made himself God's instrument. The work must be done, yes, but only with grace. "Not I but Christ in me", he said, was the source of his strength.

Two Scripture texts especially inspired him. "Jesus began to do and to teach", and "I chastise my body and bring it into subjection lest perhaps when I have preached to others I myself should become a castaway", as St. Paul said.

Though a cardinal, he slept on bare boards and did daily penances. He was very thin because he ate so little. Self-control, he knew, was of the greatest importance.

Another cardinal cautioned him, "Save yourself; do not work so madly. Less work or your body will be completely broken." But he never stopped working for Jesus. His enthusiasm for reform drove him.

Among other things, he drew up a scheme for reform for Rome, beginning with the curia. He sent it to the Pope saying, "It is useless for us to make decrees for reforms unless we ourselves observe them." He added, "It will be a long and difficult task, for among the cardinals are few who are spiritually minded and detached from the world."

All around were lazy priests who lived well and did not do their duties, and monks and friars who were fat and idle. But it was not long before their worst fears were realized. St. Charles began a reform and started with his cathedral. He abolished frivolous and irreverent music. He did away with the overly pretty in the church and substituted the beautiful. And many, many more people came to church.

St. Elizabeth Seton

January 23

St. Elizabeth Seton was the first American-born saint to be canonized. Mother Seton was the founder of the parochial schools in this country and of the American Sisters of Charity.

She had been born a Protestant and married into a wealthy family. She and Will Seton had five children. Elizabeth was a bright girl. Her father was the city doctor in New York City. He opened his library to her and her mind was curious and she read many books, something few young women of wealth or position did in those days.

Elizabeth was charming, beautiful, popular, and she and Will attended all the great social events in the city. She played the piano beautifully, loved to dance and sing and laugh and go to parties. But even in her busy life she found time to go with other women to take food and medicine to the poor.

Later William Seton's father died suddenly, and Will had to take over his business, which began to fail. Worse, William became seriously ill with tuberculosis. The doctors told him he needed a change of climate. Elizabeth and Will and their daughter Anna sailed for Italy and sunshine. The crossing was difficult because of many storms, but it was worse when they got to Italy. Because of an epidemic of Yellow Fever which had broken out in New York, the passengers had to be placed in quarantine for a month.

The old building where they stayed was drafty, damp and cold, a miserable place, the worst possible for one with tuberculosis. It was not only wretched but confining, like a jail, a frightening experience. Will got worse. All poor Elizabeth could do was pray. The dreary, cold wind came through every crack. Often Elizabeth knelt beside her husband and held his hand, watching as his health daily deteriorated. He was in terrible pain. She could only kiss his poor, pale face. And soon he died.

St. John Vianney, the Curé of Ars, was all his life a simple parish priest in France in the last century. When he arrived at Ars he found that the people did not pray. He said, "I will pray for them." And he did so tirelessly. Through prayer and penance in time he attracted not only the people of the parish but many others from near and far. A holy priest does this.

In the beginning of his days at Ars he was seen kneeling before the Blessed Sacrament with tears running down his cheeks as he said, "My God, convert my parish!"

When he had been sent to this French village he was told, "There is no great love of God in this parish; it will be your job to make it grow there." He did. His many prayers eventually won over the people.

The Curé provided for the poor. There was an orphanage crowded with children. One day he brought in a girl whom he found wandering and homeless. He said to the director, "Here, Catherine, take in this child sent us by God." She replied, "But there is no bed for her." As he was leaving, he said, "There is always yours."

He told someone, "I had a great number of orphans to feed and in the storehouse there was only a handful of wheat. It occurred to me that St. Francis Regis, who had fed the poor miraculously, might well do it again. I had the relic of the saint and I placed it among the wheat which remained. And I had the children pray. And the storehouse room was full."

The village of Ars was not an attractive place but people came for miles around to hear this holy man and go to confession to him. He heard confessions for endless hours, day after day.

One woman was forever pestering St. John. He prayed, "Lord, deliver me from this lady. She is to be pitied, but she is too much for me." But most often he visited with whoever came to him. And he helped so many.

St. John Vianney, the Curé of Ars, is the patron of parish priests.

At a dinner presided over by the bishop at the conclusion of a mission, one man observed that the Abbé Vianney did not wear a sash with his cassock. Another replied, "Even without a sash he is a much better priest than most who wear them." The bishop agreed. Although St. John wore old clothes and carried a battered hat, he was always clean.

He received a letter that stated, "You are said to be a saint, and yet not everyone who goes to see you is converted. You would do better to moderate your ill-judged zeal, otherwise we shall be obliged to inform the bishop." The Curé replied, "I thank you sincerely for the charitable advice that you have been good enough to offer me. I acknowledge my ignorance and my incapability. If people from neighboring parishes have not been converted after receiving the sacrament at my hands I am deeply sorry for it. If you think it a good thing you can write the bishop, who, I hope, will be kind enough to move me. Please pray to God that I do less evil and more good."

Another priest nearby was very angry when he found out that some lay people were taking up a collection in his parish and sending it to Ars. He told the Curé of Ars that he was very displeased and that men with so little theology, like him, had no right to set foot inside the confessional. St. John responded, "I have every reason to love you, for you are the only one who really knows me. Since you are so kind and charitable as to take interest in my poor soul, please help me to obtain the favor that I have been asking for a long time past so that, being moved from a post for which I am unworthy on account of my ignorance, I can retire to some corner and weep over my poor life. I have many tears to shed."

But the bishop had different ideas. He appointed him to be one of the confessors at the priests' retreat.

St. Elizabeth Seton January 26

After the death of Will, Elizabeth Seton was distraught and she wanted to go to church to pray. But there were no Protestant churches, so she went to a Catholic church with the Italian family with whom she was staying. The first thing that surprised her was that it was so beautiful. The churches she attended in New York were very bare, like meeting halls. Then at Mass one day the daughter of the family whispered to Elizabeth that Catholics believed Christ was present in the Eucharist. Elizabeth could not comprehend this but the thought was so beautiful that she put her head in her hands and began to weep. She also loved the Catholic devotion to the Blessed Mother. Later she was to say that it was the Blessed Sacrament and the Blessed Mother that brought her into the Church.

Back in New York Elizabeth found that the Setons had lost their money. She would have to provide for her five children. She courageously set out to do so. She said in some ways poverty was much better. Now that she did not have to attend all the social events, she could spend more time with her children.

When her Protestant family and friends learned she was interested in the Catholic Church, it was a great shock to them. Almost everyone of importance in New York was Protestant. Some thought she had lost her mind, for Catholics there in that day were a rag-tag little group of poor immigrants. Some of her friends and some of her family turned away from her. But she continued to go to the Catholic church, old St. Peter's, to pray. There, though the people were very poor, the Mass and the statues were as they had been in Italy.

She struggled for months with the notion of becoming a Catholic. The cold, impersonal Protestant services had lost their appeal for her after the warm devotions and beauty of the Catholic churches in Italy.

But she could not make up her mind. She could only pray. She prayed and prayed.

Elizabeth Seton taught in a private school, but when the parents learned she prayed in a Catholic church, they threatened to take their children away unless she was let go. She resigned.

Round and round in her mind she argued about whether she should become a Catholic. Then she learned there was a very holy priest in Boston. She was told to write him. He was Father John Cheverus, a very intelligent and holy French priest who later became the first Bishop of Boston.

She wrote to him, and he told her that she was a Catholic in heart already. It was the very encouragement that she needed. So she was received into the Church. She left for her entrance into the Church, she said, with "a light heart and with a clearer head than I have had these many long years". She begged our Lord to bury her heart deep in the wound in his Sacred Side. And then when she received Holy Communion for the first time, Elizabeth exclaimed, "At last, God is mine. Now let all earthly things go as they will. I have received him."

Elizabeth said that she felt like "a poor shipwrecked mariner on being restored to his true home". Her former friends shed tears for "the poor deluded Mrs. Seton". They "deplored her aberrations". But she had never been happier. It was worse with her family. Her sister-in-law, young Cecilia Seton, wanted to become a Catholic too. The Setons were up in arms. They were certain Elizabeth had corrupted the mind of the girl. They even threatened to have Elizabeth expelled from New York. And when Cecilia did join the Church it was like the eruption of a volcano. But through it all Elizabeth remained calm and was happy, for she had a new peace within.

St. Elizabeth Seton *January 28*

St. Elizabeth Seton was rescued from New York City by the pastor of a parish in Baltimore, where there were more Catholics. He met her at a parish in New York and invited her to come to

Baltimore to start a school in his parish, the first parochial school in this country.

Father William DuBourg offered Mass at old St. Peter's and had noticed her. When she received Communion her face was aglow with devotion. After Mass he met Elizabeth when she came to the sacristy to ask for his blessing, as she did with all new priests. Later, by accident, or providence, he met her again in the hall in the parish house and they visited. He told her of his dream to start a school in his parish. He had been told she was a teacher. He asked, "Would you come?" Elizabeth said at once that she would. In Baltimore a house was rented and a good number of children attended. In time other young women came to help teach.

It was then that they decided to form a religious community. There was no American Sisterhood at the time. Land was given them for a motherhouse at Emmitsburg, a Catholic village in a mountain valley fifty miles from Baltimore. They went there by covered wagon, most of the Sisters walking alongside. Thus began the American community of the Sisters of Charity. Mother Seton was in charge.

The little Sisterhood struggled and suffered much, but they were devoutly prayerful and God saw them through their many troubles. Mother Seton was the sterling example. When they built their small convent she arranged it so that her room was directly across from the chapel and she left both doors open so she could pray to Jesus as she worked.

St. Benedict   *January 29*

St. Benedict was the founder of Western monasticism. He was the son of a well-to-do family and was sent to Rome to study. But the wickedness of the city made him flee to the hills where he lived and prayed in a cave. Other young men joined him and they established a farm, the first monastery in the West. He wrote them a masterful rule. This sixth-century rule was so brilliant it has remained to this day the rule of the Benedictines and other orders as well. His motto was, "Pray and work." He was, first of all, a man of great prayer. The work in between was to help the monks pray better and to provide for their food, clothing, shelter and books. His first monastery was at Subiaco. Then he and some of the monks moved to Monte Cassino. One day, we are told, the community was on the brink of starvation. Benedict, the abbot, told them not to worry but to trust God. All would be well. The next morning a load of corn was found at the abbey gate. No one was ever able to discover who left it.

So often the kindness of St. Benedict was shown in what he did. He often gave gifts to the poor and helped the sick and counselled the doubtful.

Nearby his sister Scholastica had founded a convent of nuns who used his rule. The day came when she visited with her brother Benedict for the last time. They spent the day in pious discussions, especially speaking about the joys of heaven. She wanted Benedict to continue talking with her, so delightful was their conversation, but he said that he must go. She clasped her hands before her on the table and prayed. There had not been a cloud in the sky, but suddenly a hard rain fell and Benedict was unable to leave. She was very happy that he could stay longer, for she seemed to know she would never see him again in this world.

After he returned to Monte Cassino three days later he looked out the window and saw a dove winging its way heavenward. He knew St. Scholastica had died.

St. Philip Neri   *January 30*

St. Philip Neri is called the Apostle of Rome. He reformed that city and other areas after the reformation in the sixteenth century. He was far from being a Puritan. Philip was always cheerful, always pleasant, many times joking. He loved to play the fool and make jokes for the love of God. Philip was God's jester. After all, God made laughter. This saint's laughter was contagious; it showed his humility and his sanity.

The love of God waxed strong in Philip's heart. He did many

penances and labored long for the glory of God. He lived eighty. Philip founded the Fathers of the Oratory. "Oratory" means a place of prayer. (Cardinal John Henry Newman was an Oratorian.)

Philip looked upon himself as the least of God's flock, and yet popes and cardinals asked his advice. He embraced all.

Someone wrote, "He was the most human of humans, an incomprehensible saint, an impossible saint." He was so incomprehensible because he in no way acted as people think saints should.

He was very attractive, though not handsome. Many fell under his spell, and he could direct them to Jesus.

Philip said he was "useless and foolish for Christ's sake". But he could touch hearts for Jesus. He had a peculiar charm, a winsome nature, a happy eagerness. Few have been so beloved by so many. The fire of divine love burned in his heart.

Frequently, in his early days in Rome, before he became a priest, Philip visited the churches to pray. In between churches he walked along "so humble and so poor, alone, rapt in meditation". Few suspected the love hidden in his heart. Some, however, asked him to pray for them.

A favorite place of prayer for Philip was down in the caves of the catacombs, where the early, holy Christian martyrs were buried. He often went there and prayed for a long time.

St. Gertrude   *January 31*

Jesus appeared to St. Gertrude and said, "Some rebel against my will, and I am obliged to make them seek me in prayer, since they come to me only when they have no other resource. When I refuse you, however, in your desires, you know your prayers have not failed, for I grant you in return some other spiritual favor."

As St. Gertrude prayed for light on an important matter, our Lord said, "Fear nothing. Be consoled, take courage and be at rest. I am the Lord thy God; I am thy Beloved, who has created thee out of pure love; I have chosen thee to make thee my abode by my grace and to take my delight in thee. I will answer thee and those who seek me through thee with fervor and humility. Send forth prayers in greatest security. For your sake I will excuse none from my paternal affection; rather, I will embrace them in the tenderest charity and refuse them not my sweetest kiss of peace."

Gertrude reflected in amazement at how such a beautiful promise could be made to one so unworthy.

Jesus told her that his clemency prevailed and people would repent of their sins.

Gertrude said that her words seemed to have so little effect on some people, even though she had a most ardent desire that they be saved and led to glory. Jesus replied, "Marvel not if your words are sometimes fruitless and produce no effect, since, when I dwelt among men, my own words, though uttered with the fervor and power of the Godhead, produced not the fruit of salvation in the hearts of all. It is through Providence that all things are arranged and perfected in the fitting time, as appointed by me."

St. Catherine of Siena   *February 1*

St. Catherine of Siena was born in 1347 in Italy. She was both a mystic and a peacemaker. Even as a girl her wisdom and prudence were admired. And she had such a love of God that when a person conversed with her he could no longer be sad. Mental weariness departed and a tranquility of soul took its place. Not a few marveled and felt a new kind of joy.

As a child Catherine delighted many. She was joyful and cheerful and loving. She had a special, great devotion to the Blessed Mother.

In later life Christ appeared to her often and smiled upon her and blessed her. She loved silence, fasted frequently and prayed fervently.

When Catherine was a teen, her family sought to find her a husband. She objected and they thought she was obstinate, but she had taken a vow of virginity. Her Dominican confessor allowed it. The Dominican Fathers in her city, amid all the ecclesiastical corruption that surrounded them, were men of solid faith and prayer.

Catherine's room was taken from her and she was forced by the family to do all the menial drudgery of the house. She had to work so long and hard she had little time for formal prayer, but she prayed as she worked. The family tried desperately to break down her "stubbornness", but in vain.

Finally they gave in to her. She became a third order Dominican and wore the habit while remaining at home. She did charitable work at the hospital.

Catherine prayed, "How could I be content, Lord, if anyone of those who have been created to thy image and likeness should perish. I want the Old Enemy to lose them all and thou to gain them, to the greater glory and praise of thy name." She added, "I am fain to offer thee my body in sacrifice, and to bear all the world's sins, that thou mayest spare it and change its ways." And when she said these words she was rapt in ecstacy. And when she returned to herself, she said, "Love, Love, I have conquered thee with thyself. For thou dost wish to be besought for what thou canst do of thine own accord."

St. Catherine of Siena   *February 2*

St. Catherine of Siena lived in a little cell in her family home. There she had visions. She smelled the fragrance of celestial lilies and heard the ineffable melodies of paradise. Christ appeared to her and instructed her in divine things. He conversed with her as friend to friend and kissed her with "the mysterious kiss that infused into her spirit the sweetness of tremendous delight". Jesus said, "Know, my daughter, that you are she who is not, and I am he who am. If you know this in your soul, the enemy will never be able to deceive you, and you will escape from all his snares; and every grace, every truth, with clearness, you will acquire without difficulty."

Catherine said, "The soul that already sees her own nothingness and knows that all her good is in her Creator, entirely abandons herself with all her powers and all creatures, and immerses herself utterly in her Creator, in such wise that she directs all her activity primarily and entirely toward him; nor would she in any way go out of him, in whom she perceived she had found every good, and all perfection and happiness. And from the vision of love, which daily increases in her, she is in a manner so transformed into God that she cannot think or understand, or love, or remember anything save God and what concerns him. She sees no creature except in God; even as one dives down into the sea, and is swimming under the waters, neither seeing nor touching anything except the waters of the sea and the things that are in those waters; he sees nothing outside those waters, touches nothing, feels nothing. And this is ordered and right love for creatures, in which we cannot go wrong, because of necessity it is governed by divine rule; neither by it is anything desired outside of God, because it is ever exercised in God."

She said we must hate sin. "Woe to that soul in whom is not this holy hatred, for self-love will reign, which is the cesspool of all sins and the root cause of all evil greed."

St. Dominic   *February 3*

St. Dominic, the founder of the Order of Preachers, the Dominicans, said to one of his friars, "Go confidently, the Lord will be with you." And this is the way this Spanish saint lived all his life. It was said of his Dominicans, "Their souls were united by the bonds of charity." A writer wrote of this thirteenth-century saint, "The blessed Dominic was of medium height, slight build and his countenance was of fair complexion, with light hair and beard and luminous eyes; a kind of radiance shone from his brow, inspiring love and reverence. Full of joy, he seemed ever ready to smile, unless moved to pity by the affliction of his neighbor. His hands were long and shapely, his voice strong, noble and sonorous."

His greatness was that he took his many God-given talents and did not hide them or devote them to worldly gain. He used them for the sake of God and God made them greater. Born to be a leader and a guide of souls, he always did more himself than he asked of others. He was a true apostle, great and powerful in words and works. Faith and charity animated his soul. His fellow workers all mentioned his spirit of joy and also his tears at the sight of suffering. Dominic was generous, living for others. He was great in compassion and consolation. This saint denied himself daily with mortification, fasting and penance; like an athlete in training, he ever practiced self-discipline. He was an athlete of Christ.

Gentle, strong, ardent, radiating inner courage, his power of persuasion was forceful, for Christ was always at his side. A great part of his nights he passed in prayer in churches. One companion said, "He was either speaking to God or about God."

Most of the clergy of his day were sterile, inert and engrossed in temporal concerns. Dominic and his group prayed diligently and did a great deal to renew the faith in their area. Dominic himself led the way. He exhausted himself preaching and praying.

St. Charles Borromeo   *February 4*

St. Charles Borromeo was himself present at all religious functions in his cathedral. This example brought many more to church. In addition, he was seen praying before the Blessed Sacrament for long hours.

His motto was, "To do and to teach". He provided good seminaries where new priests could be trained and learn the spiritual life. He knew nothing would accomplish more. He provided for a future generation of good priests. He organized courses of study for the priests of his diocese, many of whom were lax and lacking in learning.

There was so much to do. And the situation seemed so bleak. Anyone but a saint would have shrunk from the seemingly impossible task.

At a later provincial council St. Charles was able to say,

"Three years ago we began the work and now we have been able to give milk to our people. Now they need more solid food. Let us not be the shadows but the living incarnation of that Christian discipline which by the help of God we are going to establish. You know by what troubles the Christian world is engulfed, what violent revolutions, what massacres, what struggles. Churches are destroyed, consecrated places robbed of the most precious statues and ornaments. Sacred vessels are stolen, priests and religious are murdered, holy virgins deflowered, holy places defiled. All is ruin and desecration." But he was determined to continue the fight. To encourage his priests he visited every parish. In spite of illness and fatigue he journeyed on. When he arrived, no matter how late and even though he had been travelling all day, he went straight to the church to hear confessions. One of his priests was sent on ahead to tell the people he was coming. His Masses on these visits were crowded and, with simple sermons, he explained the faith. The Communions were many. Everyone sensed that he was a saint.

St. Francis de Sales   *February 5*

St. Francis de Sales, a gifted spiritual director, tells us that Christ inspires us and urges us so that we will help others, as he desires. We are frequently so concerned about ourselves that we put off helping the needy because we are afraid it might interfere with our repose and indolence. We let Jesus knock again and again at the door of our heart, and we do not answer.

He quoted the great St. John Chrysostom who said, "O man, you who are so much disquieted because all things do not succeed according to your wishes, are you not ashamed to see that what you want Christ does not want?"

Consider the great peace and serenity of mind the Blessed Mother had in all her many problems and trials, he said. A great number of difficulties befell her, but she prayed and prayed and would not let her heart be troubled.

We should pray to our Guardian Angel. How highly we

ought to esteem the angels with whom God encompasses us in order to help us walk on the path to paradise.

He quoted St. Gregory who said that in this difficult world, in order to remain firm in the faith, we must pray. We must pray for each other, thus taking each other by the hand and holding up one another on the journey. For all about us there are dangers. We can easily slip and fall. We need to pray so as not to become discouraged, but to keep steadfastly climbing on the road to heaven.

St. Francis stated that prayer helps us so that melancholy does not invade the soul and convince us that we can never do any good and so give up. Unreasonable passion tries to pull us down.

Jesus blesses us with grace. How grateful we should be that he blesses us. We do not deserve it. It is his grace that gives us new hope and defends us against evil.

St. John of the Cross   *February 6*

St. John of the Cross said the Christian life is a growing into Christ. He wrote, "O, if the spiritual person did but know how much good and abundance of spirit they lose through not seeking to raise their desires above childish things."

God is Love and the soul can do nothing greater than to love God with heart and soul. St. John frequently spoke of the Christian life as a journey with God as our guide. We must leave our own way and do things God's way. "Upon his road we must journey to attain our goal", he wrote. Otherwise we wander around, going nowhere.

That for which man was created is our goal, and that goal is God himself. The perfection of our human nature takes us to him. Only in heaven will our destiny be fulfilled. As the Apostle John wrote, there "we shall be like God because we shall see him as he is." There we will be happy, for there will be the perfect harmony of the faculties of our nature with the being of God, so that there is nothing in that nature which in any way or degree is contrary to God. This union with God surpasses both that of nature and grace. It is a union, this Carmelite monk stated, of the human mind and will with the divine, eternal Mind and Will of God, a union of the human spirit with God who is Pure Spirit, a union of human personality with the Personal God. The future life must be thought of not in terms of a place, but in terms of God.

Man on earth is on a pilgrim journey. Not on his own can he attain the high estate of union with God. But our ever-loving Father will always help us.

The dignity of the soul consists in that it was created for union with the Creator. Its misery comes from turning aside from this great prize. St. John of the Cross wrote, "All the affections the soul has for creatures is pure darkness before God." We are earthbound, pleasure-seeking individuals who walk in darkness and "darkness cannot receive the light". God must help us. We must pray.

St. John of the Cross   *February 7*

St. John of the Cross teaches us the way by which the disordered nature of man may be restored to unity, to the divine order in which it was created. God became man in order to reestablish that unity, so that the whole man might go forward to his end. He wrote, "Having been reformed and purified and brought into conformity, the soul is ready to receive spiritual blessings, since it already participates in those which it possesses according to its capacity."

We free ourselves from undue attachment to the things of the world. The way of detachment is not the way of destruction and death, but the way of life and light and freedom, as our Lord declared in the Gospel, "He that follows me shall not live in darkness but shall have the light of life." And he said, "If the Son shall make you free, you shall be free indeed."

St. John's doctrine of detachment comes from Christ's command to love God with all your heart and soul and mind and strength. Our being is united to him by an act of our mind and will.

God is most deserving of our love and more. He has done everything for us and continues to do so. And he is God and God is Love and he is the most lovable. With him nothing created can compare.

St. John of the Cross wrote, "All the beings of creation, compared with the infinite being, are nothing."

All the beauty and attractive grace, wrote this saint and mystic, all the goodness, wisdom and knowledge, all dominion and freedom of the world, all delight and pleasures of will, all the wealth and glory of the created universe is less than nothing compared with God.

He wrote, "The affection and attachment which the soul has for creatures causes it to be like the creatures, for love causes likeness, and love makes the lover subject to the object loved." But our Lord said, "You cannot serve God and mammon." When men love creatures too much, God seems far away. But man is created to be happy with God. This is his greatest joy.

St. Thomas Aquinas   *February 8*

St. Thomas Aquinas, the gifted theologian of the thirteenth century, said that all things tend to God as their last end, to acquire the greatest good for them. The last end is to be like unto God.

All creatures, he said, are images of the First Agent, the Creator. And the perfection of the creature consists in being as like the Creator as possible. Therefore, he wrote, all things exist for the purpose of acquiring a likeness to God, as for their last end. Each thing by its movement or action tends to some good as its end. Now a thing partakes of good insofar as it is like to the first good, which is God, who is also their last end.

St. Thomas tells us that Jesus Christ came to us to be our Savior, to save us from our sins. He revealed himself as the road to truth that will lead us to the endless happiness of eternal life. As John Damascene said, "By the mystery of the Incarnation God wed his goodness and his wisdom." He became man to rescue

God's very nature is goodness; goodness by its very definition
is self-giving. Perfect Goodness gave himself to us. In the Incarnation he in a new way united himself with that which he created.
Just as all creation began to exist after first not having done so,
so, appropriately, after first not having been united to God, it
later became united. Creation depended on God's goodness and
his wisdom, as does the Incarnation, and on his mercy.

With Christ we have a high priest who has entered into the
heavens: Jesus, the Son of God. Of Christ, Aquinas said that he
acts as a go-between between God and his people, handing on to
the people the things of God, and offering to God the prayers of
the people, and making amends for their sins. He reconciled
mankind to God; he is the font of all graces. He with his blessings
preserves us in God's grace, where our peace and welfare lie.
Through Christ we have received grace in abundance.

The willful slaying of Christ was freely accepted by him,
making him the Lamb of God, a sacrificial victim for us. In his
acceptance of death, Christ gained the graces to turn our hearts
back from sin to God.

St. Thérèse of Lisieux   *February 9*

St. Thérèse, the Little Flower, said she derived a good deal of
consolation from God by reading the Holy Scripture and the
Imitation of Christ. She said, "There you have solid, wholesome
nourishment. But above all it is the Gospel that occupies my
mind when I am at prayer." In these books she found fresh
insights. In the Gospels, Christ is our teacher. He guides us,
inspires us, just when we need it the most. So with the psalmist
Thérèse said, "Give thanks to the Lord; he is gracious and his
mercy endures forever." Then she had no fear. "For me his
infinite mercy is the quality that stands out most in my life", she
said. God wonderfully takes all our weakness into consideration;
he knows our frail nature for what it is. He who graciously

pardoned the prodigal son will help us, especially if we are faithful in prayer.

Love is what our Lord really wants. He is merciful love. Happiness can not be found in creatures. We must throw ourselves into the arms of Jesus, where there is infinite tenderness, where our hearts are on fire with divine life. Let his love pierce us through and wrap us round. The Little Flower said that no merits of ours can win God's love. But it is always there.

How are our lives going to end? We do not know, but we do not have to know as long as we love God. We do know that the mercy of God will always be with us. And for all eternity we will rejoice, for all eternity we will sing his glory, a song of love that can never lose the freshness of its inspiration.

In the Gospel, she said, we gather up the threads of divine teaching. Our goal is to follow Jesus.

Thérèse said that in prayer she experienced periods of dryness and difficulty. But these are tests. We must persevere in prayer. Passing through these arid periods shows our love. She wrote, "It is only love that makes us what God wants us to be."

St. Ignatius Loyola   *February 10*

St. Ignatius Loyola was a Spanish soldier who was one of the defenders of Pamplona in Spain against the French. He refused to surrender even though the other officers were in favor of it. As he stood upon the ramparts, his right leg was hit by a cannon ball which completely shattered the bone, while the other leg was wounded by flying masonry. When Ignatius fell, the resistance was broken. The French and their Navarrese allies streamed into Pamplona. From then on, even after his recovery, Ignatius walked with a limp.

On his sickbed Ignatius became bored. He was a man of action. The dreary weeks of lying in bed while his fractured bone mended were dull for him. As he was most often alone, he asked for books to read. There were few to be found. One was a life of Christ, another was on the lives of the saints. These were very unlike the romances which Loyola liked to read. But because the days were dull he picked them up and read them. Anything to get his mind off the slow passing of the hours. These books made him think of spiritual things. Stirred especially by the lives of St. Francis and St. Dominic, he began to think that he could become a soldier of Christ.

He had outstanding courage. When the surgeon set his broken leg, the operation was very painful but he endured it with fortitude. Then because it was found that some of the bone still protruded, he told them they must fix this. The doctor said that to saw away this scrap of bone would be more painful than the operation. Ignatius insisted and suffered the agony stoically.

Then on our Lady's feast of the Assumption, she appeared to him as he lay awake at night and in her arms was the Infant Jesus. (He gave an account of this vision years later to Father Gonzales de Camara.) This changed his life. He would be a soldier of Christ.

St. Ignatius Loyola   *February 11*

After reading of Christ and the saints while recovering from the wound he had received in battle, Ignatius Loyola began to pray more devoutly. Before, he had been a soldier of the king. Now his thoughts turned to being a soldier of Christ.

Following his recovery Ignatius made a pilgrimage to a shrine of Mary at Montserrat. There he made a general confession and gave his handsome clothing to the poor. He put on a garment of sackcloth and spent a night of watching in prayer at the altar.

He next planned to make a pilgrimage to Jerusalem, but since this was delayed, he spent many months in a town called Manresa. There he lived by begging his bread and practicing many penances. He was sheltered in a hospice for the poor and at times in a cell made available to him by the Dominican friars in the monastery where he daily went to Mass. Not far away there was a cave in the craggy cliffs, and he went there to meditate undisturbed. In solitude he drew closer to Christ. He relates that before he found the peace of Christ which he sought, he was severely troubled by terrible temptations, even the thought of suicide.

The former soldier for a time contemplated joining the Carthusians, for he felt a strong attraction to the contemplative life. But he decided against it. Perhaps then he began to envisage, in dimmest outline, what eventually came into being as the Company of Jesus, the Jesuits.

At Manressa, praying in the cave, Ignatius bent his energies on perfecting himself and expressing his love for Jesus. And he sought to learn God's will for his life. He was convinced it did not matter what work he did as long as it was the work to which he was called. As with all the saints his primary desire was God's will be done.

St. Ignatius Loyola   *February 12*

St. Ignatius Loyola asks us to reflect on the scenes in the life of Christ. How, for instance, there was no room for the Baby to be born in Bethlehem. The birth took place in a cold and humble cave. Look at the poor shepherds kneeling before the crib. We are like the shepherds. We see the love of Mary for the Child, and the devotion of Joseph, and the Baby's warmth and love and goodness. Despite all the hardships, the Infant is happy, and so is his Mother.

After so many difficulties, Mary feels peace and joy. And this Child will spend his lifetime helping others. He in manhood endured hunger and thirst, heat and cold, insult and injuries, rejection and false charges to bring the message of heaven to earth. And he died in agony on the Cross—for us. When we picture these things, as St. Ignatius urges us to do, they mean more to us.

When the Child was presented in the temple Simeon foretold hardships. And almost at once the Holy Family was forced to flee into Egypt and live in exile.

They returned to Nazareth. As we reflect on Jesus as a youth think about him at prayer there, and we profit from his example.

When he remained behind in the temple at the age of twelve, he manifests his eagerness, even at such an early age, to tell people of the love that his heavenly Father has for them.

Ignatius wants us to think about these scenes and all the others in the Gospels in order to see how Jesus loved all men and wants us to do so also. We are to be of service to one another in order to make God's love known. Satan seeks to let anger, hatred and hostility enter the heart and overcome us. He tempts men with a lust for riches and unbounded pride and the empty honors of the world, St. Ignatius wrote. But our Lord begs all his disciples to spread his Kingdom.

St. Francis of Assisi   *February 13*

St. Francis of Assisi, the little poor man, was a great reformer of the Church. He was a true reformer, for he changed hearts.

He tried in every act to conform to Christ. He was mighty in humility and holiness. Often in prayer he conversed with Jesus.

Francis did penance, mortifying himself so he could more closely conform to Christ. He was ridiculed as a madman, but he only smiled. He accepted all insults patiently and went down the road singing a song. It was evident that he walked with Christ.

Francis frequently raised his hands to heaven and with heartfelt feeling said over and over, "My God, my God!" Sometimes he remained on his knees all night. He knew that praising God is our greatest prayer. He knew that, if he but praised God and thanked him, the Father would have pity on his poor soul and the souls of many others. Prayer is the best way to save souls. God can accomplish great things if we pray. Frequently Francis called to the Lord for help for souls. In prayer this holy man rejoiced in spirit.

Francis prayed to please the Lord and to know his will. He was well aware that Jesus was the only one who could direct us on the right road to travel.

When someone gave money to this man, who wore a gunny-sack with a rope around his waist, Francis gave the coins away to the next poor person he saw. He did not want money or possessions to clutter up his mind. He wanted to think about Jesus. Francis was one of the happiest persons who ever lived. And he had nothing. Advertisements constantly try to tell us that we can buy happiness. This first Franciscan, who lived in poverty, puts the lie to that notion.

St. Francis of Assisi   *February 14*

St. Francis of Assisi, with a happy heart, would walk down dusty roads from village to village to tell people how much Jesus loved them. And, as Jesus' ambassador, he was most loving. When he saw an old widow who needed her wood chopped, he would stop and chop it; when he saw an old man who needed his house painted, he would paint it; when he saw a mother with so many children she didn't know what to do, he would take them to an open area, play games with them, and tell them stories about Jesus, so that the mother would have some time to do her work at home.

Francis was a true servant of Jesus. He spoke to him as a friend. And as a friend he spoke of him to the people. St. Francis said, "If it were to please God that the Little Brothers should give everywhere a great example of holiness and edification—this would not be perfect joy. If the Little Brothers were to make the lame walk, if they should make the crooked straight, gave sight to the blind, hearing to the deaf, speech to the speechless, and even greater works, if they should raise the dead to life, this would not be perfect joy.

"If the Little Brothers were very learned and could explain all Scripture and could prophesy and make known all future things and could read souls, this would not be perfect joy." He continued saying that if the Little Brothers could speak with the tongues of angels and could convert infidels, this still would not be perfect joy. He then was asked what *was* perfect joy. He replied that if, in the rain and icy sleet, when he was exhausted and hungry and covered with mud he knocked on a door for shelter and was refused and was yelled at angrily and chased away—and he stood in the rain and snow, suffering cold and hunger, and if he accepted such injustice and cruelty without murmuring—that would be perfect joy, for he would show Jesus how very much he loved him. He said, "Accept all with patience, joy and charity, thinking of the sufferings of our Blessed Lord, which we share out of love for him."

St. Bonaventure   *February 15*

St. Bonaventure was a great teacher who became the head of the Franciscan order and was later made a cardinal. It was said that when he was a child he was gravely ill. His mother carried him to St. Francis of Assisi, who cured him.

A commentator has said of Bonaventure, "His writings are incredibly rich in the knowledge of Christ." Bonaventure said that God is beyond comprehension. In his great goodness he sent us Christ. "To know Christ is our goal. We discover the wealth and meaning of Christ's message in prayer, and we reap the fruits of intimacy with him. Then do we know light and sweetness", he said. Then we are guided rightly on the road to heaven, for the whole soul is converted to Christ. Beside this, worldly wisdom is vain and foolish.

He quoted St. Bernard of Clairvaux, "As long as a man does not fear or love God, no matter how great his reputation for wisdom may be, I shall never consider him wise."

All who knew Bonaventure said that he was always gentle, affable and humble. His writings reflect this: they draw the heart to desire Christ. As we read this Franciscan saint we receive some of his calm and beauty of spirit.

He wrote, "Draw near with loving steps to Jesus wounded for you, to Jesus crowned with thorns for you, to Jesus nailed to the wood of the Cross for you. Gaze at the prints of the nails in his hands and the scar of the spear in his heart. Be not satisfied with putting your fingers into his hands and your hand into his side, but enter into the very heart of Jesus burning with love for you, and be transformed into Christ."

St. Augustine   *February 16*

The great St. Augustine wrote, "All things belong to God, who is Love. We are his creatures. There is no man who does not love. It need only be asked what he loves. We are not urged to forebear from loving, but only that we choose with care that which we do love. But what are we to choose unless we are first chosen? What are we to love, unless we are first loved?" God first loves us. Because of this Augustine tells us, let us sing a new canticle to the Lord. A canticle is a song of joy and a thing of love. He who knows how to love knows how to sing a new song.

Augustine said, "God is the source of all love. We who are frail love God who is merciful because God gives us love." He quotes St. Paul who said, "He whom we love gives us love. The love of God is poured forth into our hearts." He also quoted St. John, "In this is love, not that we have loved God, but that he has first loved us."

Emboldened by this gift of love from God, let us love God. St. John wrote, "God is love, and he who abides in love abides in God, and God in him."

It is not enough to say love is from God. St. Augustine said, "I urge upon your love of God to love your neighbor." Love God and you will possess him. See Christ in your neighbor and you will love him.

St. Augustine reminds us of the words of St. Paul, "Do you not know that your bodies are members of Christ?" Paul goes on to tell us that Christ is our head, his body is the Church. With this in mind, "Whither do you wish to hurl yourself?" asks Augustine. "Know the Christ whose member you are. Listen to the Church, for Christ speaks through the Church.

57

"Wherever you may go God Jesus sees you: Jesus who made you and redeemed you when you were lost; he who died for you when you were dead."

St. Augustine

St. Augustine was one of the greatest thinkers who ever lived. He wrote, "God never turns his eyes from you. Some say, 'I shall do as I wish, for God would not trouble himself to notice my offenses.' But this is false. All our actions are seen."

He wrote, "Do you think there is another's life by which your soul itself has life?" At death we enter eternal life when the soul is judged. The life of the body is the soul; the life of the soul is God.

Therefore let the enemy rage against you and threaten you with death, he said. Let him carry out his design if he can. God will protect your soul if you pray. It is empty fear that grips all men who fear the loss of temporal things and death. Let us find a fruitful fear in this empty fear. Let us fear sin.

There is something that you can do so that you will never die. If you fear death, then love life, the great saint said. Your life is God, your life is Christ. Never will you please him by acting basely. God does not dwell in a fallen temple. Cry out to him that he build up your temple. Let him build up what you have torn down, ask him to restore that which you have destroyed. Ask him to erect that which you have cast down. Call upon God, cry out within yourself.

Seek after the love of God, said Augustine, and let it enter into you. Make way for a love that does not sin, make way for a love that enables you to live virtuously. Make this love enter into you and fear departs. St. John said, "Perfect love casts out fear."

Augustine noted that the more a man adds to the adornment of his outer aspect, the more the inner self declines. If one prays, God does not leave the inner man impoverished. He enriches the invisible self with invisible wealth, and he adorns the unseen man with unseen wealth.

58

The remarkable St. Bonaventure seems to have learned the very secrets of the Heart of Jesus. He asked, "Do your thoughts tend toward pleasure and pride? Are you angry, impatient, unkind, lukewarm?" He pointed out the great need for humility. St. Bonaventure wrote, "To try to excel in virtue and yet not have humility is simply to carry dust before the wind." We should say, "All the good we do, Lord, is your work."

Humility renders one pleasing to God. So lowly did Christ make himself, he was considered a vile criminal. "Can a follower of Christ see his Master ridiculed and humiliated and himself be proud?" asks Bonaventure.

This noble Franciscan refers to Augustine, who asks, "Why are you puffed up? How dare a lowly disciple be proud when Christ was humble? You are here today and gone tomorrow. We are beggars before God. We have nothing. Humility helps make up for our sins. As the Scripture states, 'Be humble, and you shall find grace before God.'"

The Blessed Mother found favor because of her humility. She said, "He has regarded the humility of his handmaid." St. Augustine said, "The less the pride, the more the love." Just as water flows to the low places, so grace flows to the humble. Ecclesiasticus says, "The prayer of him that humbles himself shall pierce the clouds." And the psalmist wrote, "The Lord will do the will of them that fear him, and he will hear their prayers."

Bonaventure continued, "Humility is perfected by patience." Said St. Augustine, "It is easy to wear poor clothes and walk with the head cast down, but it is patience that proves a person to be truly humble."

The proud are unbearable, pompous, stiff-necked, harsh and stern, ever on the lookout for the first place, boastful and wishing to be honored. This Bonaventure pointed out. He said that we must not love riches. Jesus became poor for our sake. Should we seek many possessions? Spiritual treasures come to those who do not pile up temporal treasures.

The humble St. Francis of Assisi said, "Above all the graces which Christ grants to his friends is the grace of overcoming oneself and willingly accepting, out of love for Christ, suffering and injury, discomfort and contempt. In all other gifts of God we cannot glory because they proceed not from ourselves but from God. But in the cross of tribulation we may glory for, as St. Paul said, 'I will not glory save in the cross of our Lord Jesus Christ.'"

Francis with many sighs and tears said, "O Lord of heaven and earth, I have committed against thee so many sins that I deserve to be condemned." Striking his breast he cried out these same words again and again.

A Brother told St. Francis that the world was following him, but the Brother could not figure out why since Francis was not learned, handsome or a great orator. At this Francis greatly rejoiced. He lifted up his eyes to heaven and thanked God that the other had seen his littleness. And he said to the Brother, "Do you know why men come after me? It is because of the Lord, who is in heaven, who sees the evil and the good in all places—because his holy eyes have found among men no one more lowly and more imperfect than I am, to accomplish the wonderful work which he intended to do. He has found no creature more worthless than me; for which reason he has chosen me to confound all the strength, greatness, beauty and knowledge of the earth in order that people may learn that every virtue and every good gift comes from him, and not from any creature, and that no one can glory before him, for they must glory in the Lord, to whom all glory belongs."

One day when St. Francis was traveling with a Brother, they came to a fork in the road. "Which way shall we go?" the Brother asked Francis.

Francis answered, "The one which God chooses."

"Which way is that?" he was asked. Francis told the Brother to turn around and around, until the Brother was dizzy and had to stop. He faced toward Siena.

Francis said, "This is the road." They went there and did great good.

St. Ignatius Loyola *February 20*

St. Ignatius Loyola said, "Let a man use his reason to think of the advantages and benefits that would accrue if his first concern is to praise God. Think of the dangers and disadvantages of doing otherwise. Act then upon the strong judgment of reason and not on the inclinations of the senses. From reason let a person come to a decision about how to live. And then pray diligently."

He said, "Consider that if I were at the point of death, what decision I would wish I had made. . . . Consider how I shall be on the day of judgment, to think how I shall then wish to have made my decision."

He said that we should think of Jesus and his last days and ask for sorrow for our sins, for he suffered and died because of them.

At the Last Supper see Jesus washing the feet of the Apostles, he wrote. Think how gracious and generous he was in giving us the great and wonderful gift of the Holy Eucharist.

Then Jesus took the apostles to the Garden of Gethsemane. He began to pray and his sweat became drops of blood. Then Judas came and gave him the kiss of peace in betraying him. Jesus was seized as a malefactor. Think of his grief, his brokenheartedness, his tears and deep suffering.

Jesus endured the false trial before the Sanhedrin and then endured the unjust trial of Pilate, and the humiliation at the court of Herod, and the scourging and crowning with thorns. He was made to carry his Cross, was nailed to the wood and died in agony on the Cross for love of us, all for love of us.

But on Easter there was great gladness. He appeared first to his Mother. The divinity of Christ which hid itself during the Passion now appears and manifests itself miraculously in the Risen Christ. The Risen Christ is our wonderful comfort.

St. Ignatius Loyola *February 21*

St. Ignatius Loyola said that our love is to be manifested in deeds, not in words. The lover gives himself to the beloved. There is an exchange in which they share their love. Christ loves us beyond words; we want to show him our love.

We have been blessed abundantly and more. There is the great gift of life given us; there is the great gift of redemption; there are the countless daily graces. God supports us day and night. Surely we should return his love. Reflect on your blessings and be filled with gratitude. In all things love and serve the Lord, the saint said.

God created us to his image and likeness. God gives us here on earth a wonderful garden that provides for our well-being. We men are very limited, but help always comes from Almighty God. We are like little children and our gracious, generous heavenly Father takes care of us; he is very merciful. His goodness descends upon us just as the rays of the sun nourish the flowers.

St. Ignatius said we must ask questions: Where am I going? For what purpose? Reflect on how you keep the Ten Commandments, and ask for the grace to do better in the future and to give greater praise and glory to God. One can see Ignatius' military background at work in his orderly thinking. He wrote that we must strive to imitate Jesus and that Jesus was a man of prayer. Therefore, we must pray.

In prayer one can think about each phrase of a memorized prayer or a read prayer and reflect upon it. In prayer a person may be kneeling or sitting, whatever suits his disposition at the time and whichever is more conducive to devotion. Let him say, "Our Father", and then reflect upon this as long as he finds meaning, compassion, relish and consolation in its consideration. Then he should go on to the next phrase and contemplate it. And he can do this with other prayers as well.

St. Ignatius Loyola   *February 22*

St. Ignatius Loyola founded the Jesuits. The little community prayed and lived together. In so simple a fashion was started this great religious order.

In time they became the most outstanding force in saving the faith during the counter-reformation. They were a company of soldiers for Christ. Starting with only seven who bound themselves with vows in a little chapel on Montmartre in Paris, their numbers increased and they came to be known everywhere, either loved dearly or fiercely feared. The author Balzac said he could not help but admire this first extraordinary group of seven who turned to heaven and consecrated themselves to the good of their fellow men.

While still a handful, they set about working for Christ. They assisted the needy. One wrote of those early days of working in hospitals, "We tend the patients, make the beds, sweep the floors, scrub the dirt, wash the pots, dig the graves, carry the coffins, and read the service to bury the dead."

The group decided to make a pilgrimage to the Holy Land. When they got to Italy, however, they found that this was then impossible, so they went to Rome. There they visited the Holy Father and put themselves in his hands. They would be the apostles of the pope, doing whatever he directed them to do. Among other things, he asked that they instruct the boys in a school in Rome. The Jesuits have been teachers ever since.

That year was a terrible time in the Eternal City. There was famine, cold and disease. Ignatius and his company were heroic. Wherever one looked they were nursing the sick, begging food for the hungry and sheltering the homeless. So great was their effort that the Holy Father, previously a bit skeptical, gave them his whole-hearted blessing.

It was an auspicious beginning.

St. Ignatius Loyola   *February 23*

St. Ignatius Loyola urges that we reflect on events in the life of Jesus. He gave examples to show what he meant. Palm Sunday: (1) Jesus sends for the ass and colt, saying, "Loose them and bring them to me, and if anyone says anything to you, you shall say that the Lord has need of them and immediately he will send them." (2) He rides on the donkey which is covered with the garments of the apostles. (3) The people come out to meet him, spreading their garments and waving branches along the way, saying, "Hosanna to the Son of David! Blessed is he who comes in the name of the Lord, hosanna in the highest!"

The Last Supper: (1) At the meal with the Twelve, Jesus foretells his death, saying, "Amen I say to you, one of you is about to betray me." (2) He washes the feet of the apostles, even the feet of Judas. When he comes to Peter, this apostle, considering the greatness of the Lord and his own lowly state, will not permit it. He says, "Lord, will you wash my feet?" Peter did not understand that Jesus was giving them the example of humility. Jesus therefore said to him, "I have given you an example, that as I have done, you also should do." (3) He instituted the most Holy Mass as the greatest proof of his love for us; he said, "Take and eat." Before that, Judas went out into the darkness to sell Christ for thirty pieces of silver.

The agony in the garden: (1) They left the upper room and went to the garden. The disciples were full of fear. Jesus asked them to pray with him. (2) With Peter, James and John Jesus went farther. He prayed, "Father, if it be possible, let this cup pass me by; yet not as I will, but as you will it." He fell into an agony and prayed more earnestly. (3) Fear possessed him and he said, "My soul is sad, even unto death." He sweat blood. As St. Luke wrote, "His sweat became as drops of blood running down upon the ground."

St. Ignatius Loyola   *February 24*

St. Ignatius Loyola gives us other examples of how we can reflect on the events in the life of Jesus.

Judas' betrayal of Jesus: (1) Jesus allowed the traitor Judas to kiss him, and Jesus was seized like a thief. He said, "As against a robber you have come out with swords and clubs to take me. I sat daily with you teaching in the temple, and you did not lay a hand on me." (2) St. Peter cut off the ear of the servant of the High

Priest, but Jesus said, "Put back the sword into its place." And he healed the servant. (3) Jesus was abandoned by his disciples and dragged before Annas. Peter, who had followed from a distance, denied Jesus. Jesus was struck in the face.

Before Caiaphas: (1) Jesus, bound like a criminal, was taken before Caiaphas. Peter denied Jesus again. When Jesus, passing by, looked at Peter, the apostle rushed out and wept bitterly. (2) Jesus was condemned to die. (3) Those who held him prisoner blindfolded him and struck him and asked, "Prophesy, who is it that struck you?" And they continued to blaspheme him.

Before Pilate: (1) They brought him to the governor and said, "We have found this man perverting the nation, and forbidding payment of taxes to Caesar." (2) Pilate examined him several times and said, "I find no crime in him deserving of death." (3) Barabbas, the robber, was preferred to him. The mob cried out, "Away with this man, and release Barabbas to us."

Before Herod: (1) Pilate sent Jesus of Galilee to Herod, the Tetrach of Galilee. (2) Herod, because of his curiosity, asked Jesus many questions, but Jesus answered him nothing, even though the scribes and priests accused him unceasingly. (3) Herod and his entire court mocked Jesus and made fun of him.

St. Ignatius Loyola   *February 25*

St. Ignatius gives other examples for reflection: Jesus condemned: (1) Herod sent Jesus back to Pilate. Because of this, Herod and Pilate became friends, although before this they were enemies. (2) Pilate had Jesus scourged and the soldiers make a crown of thorns and placed it on his head. They put a purple cloak on him and came before him and said, "Hail, King of the Jews!" And they struck him. (3) Pilate brought him before the crowd. Pilate said, "Behold the man." They cried, "Crucify him, crucify him."

Carrying the Cross: (1) The people said, "We have no king but Caesar." Pilate delivered Jesus to be crucified. (2) Jesus carried the Cross on his shoulders, and as he could not carry it, Simon of Cyrene was forced to carry it with Jesus. (3) They crucified him between two thieves, placing over him: Jesus of Nazareth, King of the Jews.

Upon the Cross: (1) Jesus prayed for those who crucified him; he pardoned the thief; he entrusted his mother to St. John; he said in a loud voice, "I thirst", and they gave him gall and vinegar; he said that he was forsaken; he said, "It is consummated"; he said, "Father, into your hands I commend my spirit." (2) They blasphemed him and said, "Come down from the Cross and we will believe you." (3) The sun was darkened; rocks rent, graves opened; the veil of the temple was torn in two from top to bottom. His side was pierced with a lance and blood and water flowed out.

The Resurrection: (1) Jesus appeared to the Virgin Mary. (Although this is not mentioned specifically in the Scripture, it is considered as mentioned when the Scripture says that he appeared to many others.) (2) The women went to the tomb and they saw the stone rolled back and an angel said, "You are looking for Jesus of Nazareth. . . . he has risen, he is not here." (3) Jesus appeared to Mary Magdalen who remained near the tomb after the others had departed.

Before the disciples: (1) He appeared to them even though the door was locked for fear of the authorities. (2) Jesus stood in their midst and said, "Peace be to you." (3) He gave them the Holy Spirit saying, "Receive the Holy Spirit, whose sins you shall forgive, will be forgiven; whose sins you shall retain, they are retained."

St. Thérèse of Lisieux   *February 26*

St. Thérèse of Lisieux wrote that in periods of dryness in prayer, Jesus is still with us. She said, "It comes to this, Jesus dwells unseen in the depths of my miserable soul, and so works upon me by grace."

Before she took her vows she was tempted to leave. She wrote, "Darkness everywhere. I could see nothing and think of nothing. I was in agony of mind." Most fortunately, the novice mistress, with more wisdom and experience in the spiritual life, was able to set her mind at ease.

Thérèse prayed, "Jesus, heavenly Bridegroom, may I look for nothing but you. May my love have no eyes but for you, only for you."

An old nun told her, "Serve God with peace and joy; remember always that our God is a God of peace." Thérèse left the saintly old soul in tears of joy for all that day she had been ill at ease and on the verge of melancholy, experiencing such deep spiritual darkness that she almost doubted if God loved her. Now she was bathed in consolation, like the sun coming out after a cloudy day.

Thérèse wrote that after Communion she often had no special comfort. But she offered this up to her beloved Spouse. She only asked the Blessed Mother to clear her soul of its rubbish so she could welcome her Son with joy.

We must accept our failures and not fret, she stated. When we go through a bad time let us put even more confidence in Jesus. Sometimes we feel sad in spirit because in our hearts we are homesick for heaven, for we live here on earth in exile.

God helps us. He is more tender to us than any mother can be.

"Without love nothing we do can be worth anything, even if we dazzle the world by converting whole nations", she wrote.

St. John of the Cross   *February 27*

The mystic St. John of the Cross, the little Spanish Carmelite friar and close friend of St. Teresa of Avila, said, "By putting on the mind of Christ we are delivered from our natural, sin-engendered, darkened view and walk as children of the light. And Christ's outlook dominates our view of life. His attitude is ours. We have no desire but what he desires. We let his wishes penetrate our hearts." This is the sum and root of all virtues. Self-sacrifice helps us do this. Otherwise life is a wandering as though in a maze.

Prayer is vital to all this. He wrote, "In all our necessities, labors and difficulties there remains to us no better or surer means than prayer and hope that God will provide for us." Prayer enables us better to understand the things that concern our salvation. These are of the greatest importance. And God gives us what we need, even though we may not have prayed precisely for it.

God gives us first what we need for salvation. His primary concern is saving souls. In a psalm, David said, "The Lord is nigh unto them that call upon him in truth, that ask of him the things of highest truth, such as those of salvation." He goes on to say, "God will fulfill the desire of them that fear him, and will hear their cries, and will save them. For God is the guardian of those who truly love him."

God is ready to satisfy unselfish souls. He assists those who do for him what he desires. Our Father alone knows what is best for us. "It behoves us to pray and never falter", the Carmelite said. In the Our Father is contained the will of God and all that is good for us. St. John of the Cross said that it is our love for God that moves him to hear our prayers. When God is truly loved, he readily hears the prayers of his lovers. If at times in prayer we do not desire enough, then God gives us more than we ask for. If first we seek him, then all the other things will be given to us.

St. Augustine   *February 28*

"What is it to love God?" asks the great St. Augustine. It is more than a cringing fear, he stated. One considers, rather, how we may please him. "It is done with an inner beauty, with a charm concealed from the eyes of men, with a charm of the heart which stands exposed to the eyes of the Lord", Augustine wrote.

Beware of all lawless love. You must obey Christ who shed his blood for you. Love God. You will find nothing more worthy of your love. You love the light; Jesus is the Light of the World.

The blind man called out for light. He shouted, "Jesus, Son of David, have mercy on me." He cried out as Jesus passed by. He feared lest Christ go on and not heal him. Greatly did he cry out.

Not even the chiding multitude could silence him. He overcame those who would restrain him and continued to cling to his Savior. Even though the throng was shouting him down and trying to silence him, Jesus came to a halt and called and said, "What would you have me do?"

"Lord, that I may see."

"Receive your sight, your faith has saved you."

Augustine tells us to love Christ and long for the light that is Christ. If the blind man longed for light for his eyes, how much more should we long for light for our soul.

Let us call out to Christ, said St. Augustine, not with our voices, but with our virtues. Love of the earth knows only dust. The crowd thinks seeking spiritual things is foolish, but it is wisdom. And if we cry out to Christ he will also come to us as he did to the blind man. Cry out to Christ with all your strength. Pray fervently. Let him illumine you. Let him enlighten your mind and heart.

"If you long to be with Christ", Augustine wrote, "then fear to be without him." Do not abide with evil desires, abide with Christ. If you are not influenced by the light of heaven, fear the fire of hell.

St. Thérèse of Lisieux   *March 1*

The Little Flower, St. Thérèse, said she trusted God like an unconcerned child going to sleep in her father's arms. "Simple hearts draw near to me", God tells us in the Book of Proverbs. It is the insignificant who are treated with mercy. Isaiah says that God will "tend his flock like a shepherd, gather up the lambs and carry them in his bosom". God says, "I will console you, like a mother caressing her child." When God makes promises like that, wrote Thérèse, what is left for us except to keep silent before him with tears of gratitude and love? No one should be gloomy or despair. Our Lord doesn't ask for great achievement, only for self-surrender and gratitude. God is thirsty for our love. He has a deep longing for our love.

Thérèse said, "Jesus, my well-beloved, how considerate you are in your treatment of my worthless soul; storms all around me, and suddenly the sunshine of your grace comes out." She said she knew that great things were not for "unimportant souls like mine".

She had a dream that God would not leave her much longer on the earth. Soon he would come to take her home.

She felt certain that her problems, "Jesus, my Beloved, are only a prelude to greater graces still with which you have determined to enrich me."

Thérèse longed to do more for Jesus. In the convent she could be only a lowly Sister, but she could increase her love for Jesus. She loved him with all her heart. She knew that he loved a heart burning with love. This love enabled great souls to act greatly. It made the apostles preach boldly and the martyrs suffer greatly. She said, "Jesus, my Love, I have found my vocation and my vocation is love."

St. Thomas More   *March 2*

St. Thomas More, who gave his life to uphold the Church against the stubborn Henry VIII, wrote, "Unlearned men are not able, nor learned men neither, to discern and judge the true meaning of Scripture." We cannot each interpret the Bible the way we want to, as the reformers said. How foolish they are who are their own guides in religion, and make out the Scripture to mean anything they decide. In this, truth is the victim. It is destroyed. And religion is man-made and not God-made, and a man-made religion is useless.

We cannot learn higher mathematics without a teacher, and we cannot learn religion without a teacher. Jesus in his great goodness gave us the Church to show us the way to heaven. The Church sagely interprets the Bible.

Thomas More said that some texts of the Bible seem to speak to both sides. Only a very wise teacher can tell us the true meaning. We must not be so proud or so foolish as to think we can figure everything out on our own. God has provided for us because we are so unlearned. St. Thomas wrote, "God left some surety as may bring us out of all such perplexity." This is the Church, which leads us on the right road, as Christ promises, for all necessary truth.

Thomas wrote in a time of great confusion, during the reformation. Reformers of every kind were telling the people, in effect, that each individual was in religion his own pope.

Thomas More served the king well as his lord chancellor, which in those times was the prime minister. But the proud king, like a spoiled child, always wanted his own way. And when the Church would not give him what he wanted—a divorce—he broke with the Church and made himself the head of the Church in England and then gave himself what he wanted.

St. Bonaventure   *March 3*

St. Bonaventure, the outstanding Franciscan scholar, said that pride is the root of evil. Pride poisons the heart and blinds the mind, ruining a person. Jesus gives us the example of humility. He did not love riches. He became poor for our sake. He did not wish honors; he wished only to save souls. The Bible says, "God fills the poor with good things, the rich he sends empty away." It says in the psalms, "They that seek the Lord shall not be deprived of any good." Jesus told us not to be solicitous for the things of this world. God will take care of us. St. Peter said, "Cast all your cares on the Lord, and he will care for you."

St. Bonaventure wrote that our heavenly Father's love for us is so intense it cannot even be described in words. How confused we are when we are unduly concerned about worldly goods. Then we turn away our affections from God, who is our salvation. The fire of divine life grows dim in such souls. They no longer walk with the poverty-stricken Christ. Their hearts are cold to Christ. They are unwilling to give up the wretched world. Their hearts are not with Jesus.

He said to keep your heart free from the love of honors,

sions and riches. Possessions waste our energies. Fondness
:hes is different from the way of Christ.

Jesus said, "Blessed are the poor in spirit, for theirs is the
Kingdom of Heaven." Those with the spirit of poverty will
possess Christ. They do not have earthly possessions but they
have the greatest possession of all, Jesus. They do not have
spiritual things, but Christ is in their soul. And they will rejoice
both here and hereafter. Jesus with them gives them delight and
satiety.

St. Francis of Assisi   *March 4*

Everyone loves St. Francis of Assisi. He loved everyone.

He knew that humility is the key to all the virtues. To show
one of the gifted Little Brothers the need for humility, he assigned
him all the ordinary household tasks — cooking, cleaning, washing
and the rest. And all the other Brothers did nothing to take care
of the house. This talented Brother put down his hood, bowed
his head and went silently about the work. In time the other
Brothers thought it was unfair and told Francis this. Francis
called the Brother to him and said, "Your brothers wish to share
the charges I have given you." Humbly the Brother said, "Whatever
charge you put upon me, whether small or great, I accept and
obey you as I would obey Jesus."

Francis loved him dearly for his humility, as did Jesus.

On arriving one day at a certain town, Francis and a Brother
companion, being very hungry, began to beg for bread. Francis,
being a small person and not handsome, received little. The other
Brother, tall and good looking, was given a good deal of bread.

Francis said, "Brother, we are not worthy of this great treasure."
The Brother replied, "How can you talk of a treasure when we
are so poor and lack all things? We have no house, no table, dishes
or knives."

Francis said, "This indeed is why I call it a treasure, because no
man had a hand in it, but all has been given us by divine

Providence, as we clearly see in this bread of charity and this sturdy stone for a table and a clear fountain of water nearby."

Soon after they came to a church and, entering in to pray, Francis cast himself down on the floor before the altar. He begged the saints to teach them to be grateful and to gain humility for them so they could freely commune with God.

St. Francis of Assisi   *March 5*

St. Francis of Assisi said that humility is such a great virtue that with it the soul is able to converse with the angels. This is the virtue of Christ. It enables us to speak to him. It is the guardian of true charity.

The holy saints were lovers of this great pearl. If one is humble, Jesus gives him the graces, because of his great mercy, to become a true lover, a faithful disciple of the most precious beloved Jesus.

Francis prayed with great devotion and tears and was blessed by God. He was consoled and filled with joy. He said, "Let us thank God, who has deigned to reveal to the world, through his humble servants, the treasures of divine wisdom. For the Lord it is who opens the mouth of the dumb and makes the tongue of the simple to speak wisdom."

There was the time when Francis wondered whether he should spend his days in praying or in preaching. He was troubled in mind and perplexed by this. Because of his great humility he did not trust his own decision but begged God for an answer. He sent a Brother to St. Clare to ask that she and her Sisters pray also. And he had the holy Brother Sylvester pray as well.

Brother Sylvester told him, "The Lord says, he has not called Brother Francis to this state to save merely his own soul, but that he may produce fruit in others; and through him many should be saved." And Sister Clare gave the same answer.

When these messages were brought to Francis he received them with great charity, washing the feet of the Brothers and waiting on them at table. Since all agreed that Francis should go about the world and preach, with fervor he got up and started out, saying, "Let us go in the name of God."

St. Philip Neri

In his early days in Rome, St. Philip Neri prayed a good deal in the many churches of that city. People noticed this in time and would ask him questions about religion. Philip always showed the most exquisite tact. He charmed people. He spoke in such an engaging way people enjoyed listening to him. His affability made them not take offense when he advised them to pray more. And his humor made him especially popular. Philip had common sense, the most important thing for a spiritual director. He was a layman but more came to him than to most of the priests around. His advice was sound; he was no academic theorist spinning impractical dreams. And he practiced the charity that he preached. He went to the poor hospitals, where he swept the floors, made beds and did whatever was needed; he always encouraged the sick.

When in mid-life his confessor told him that he should be a priest, he obeyed. He was ordained when he was thirty-six years old. Attached to one of the churches of the city, he was soon sought out by people from all over the city. He heard many confessions; he gave spiritual conferences. Afterward there were discussions. Many of those who sought him out were young men.

With the youth he had a group who had simple devotions in his room. When the room became too small, they met in a hall. Gathering youth around him and having devotions with them became his first apostolate. The young men were inspired by his intense fervor.

One time a man who was dying told him that he was leaving his money to Philip. St. Philip answered, "I your heir? I do not want your money; leave it to someone else. To show you I don't want it, I am going to St. Peter's to pray for your recovery. If

God won't give it in any other way, I shall offer my life for yours."

By the time Philip came back from St. Peter's, the man was recovering.

St. Angela Merici   *March 7*

St. Angela Merici was born in Italy in the fifteenth century. She was deeply grieved by the ignorance and lack of religious instruction among the young, and so she gathered the children of the village around her and began to teach them of Jesus.

Angela was a girl of striking beauty. At the age of ten she was left an orphan and lived with an uncle. Not long after, her sister died. Seeking out poor children and telling them stories about Jesus, young Angela treasured every soul she taught. Time passed. Then one day she had a vision. She saw a ladder stretching up to heaven. There were angels and maidens on it singing, and a voice told her she would found a religious community that in years to come would be as numerous as the many maidens she saw in her vision.

The years passed and yet she was no nearer to fulfilling the promise in the vision than ever. But then a rich widow asked Angela to come to her town. Angela knew instinctively that this wealthy woman would help her found a company of ladies to educate the young.

Angela made a pilgrimage to the Holy Land. There she learned about St. Ursula, a holy woman of England who went to Germany to teach the faith and was martyred. In the Holy Land Angela prayed fervently for God to direct her. On reaching the place where Christ was crucified, "she knelt and covered with tears the ground that had been worthy to receive the precious blood he shed for sinners."

On the way back, in Rome, Pope Clement VII blessed her and encouraged her work of teaching religion to the young. She greatly impressed the Holy Father. After the audience the Pope told the priest who had introduced her to him that he did not agree with the priest's appraisal of her. The other said, "Perhaps my admiration for Sister Angela made me speak too well of her."

"Not well enough, not well enough", the Pope said.

St. Angela Merici   *March 8*

St. Angela returned to teaching poor children about the Savior. She worked at this for forty years and many of these years were times of discouragement and delay. But then suddenly the difficulties dissipated and she was able to found her first convent of Sisters. They called themselves Ursulines.

God rewarded Angela for her patience. Success came late for her. But once established, the community grew. In her lifetime she saw only the beginning, but she was able to see that her vision would be fulfilled. And the great glory of the order came long after her death.

Her Sisters not only taught the young but they went out into the streets to visit homes and help the sick and assist the poor. Stories were everywhere told of their works of charity.

St. Angela's spirituality was simple. She attributed all the good to God. She wrote her spiritual daughters, "In order to become an instrument in his hands we must be of no account in our own eyes." She told them they would do many things for Christ if they were faithful to solid, unostentatious devotion each day.

After Angela went to heaven, the Ursuline Sisters spread through many countries, praising Jesus and teaching his little ones in the spirit of Angela.

St. Angela emphasized prayer for her Sisters. Jesus was the example. He spent thirty years in prayer before he began to preach. He often prayed, sometimes spending the whole night in prayer. And because of prayer, though weary of limb, he was able to have time for people. His love was ever searching for souls. He pursued them constantly.

St. Angela said that her Sisters must do the same. And their special mission was to introduce souls to Jesus when they were young. As the tree is bent, so it grows, the proverb tells us. Teach children about Jesus and it will be with them all their days.

St. Vincent de Paul   *March 9*

St. Vincent de Paul said to his priests, "Follow the example of the Master, and you will overcome the devil. You will rejoice for all eternity in heaven and the good souls of earth who see and hear you will be inspired."

No task was too small for Vincent. He readily advised teachers of religion to have short catechism classes so the youngsters would not become restless. He said that sermons, too, should be brief and that the speaker should adapt himself to the moods, places and times of the people. This would win souls for God.

Vincent wrote, "Simplicity is the virtue I love the most." He said ordinary progress of soul comes about because of humility. "This is the way our Lord prepares those whom he wishes to use profitably." And how many times he himself was humiliated from the very outset of his mission. Those who labor in anguish and under pressure—their sadness will be turned into joy, Vincent stated. He added, "May not a person die of shame for claiming a reputation in the service he gives to God when he sees Jesus rewarded for his work by disgrace and the gibbet."

St. Vincent de Paul wrote, "Remember, we live in Jesus Christ, through the death of Jesus Christ, and we must die in Jesus Christ through the life of Jesus Christ, and our life must be hidden in Jesus Christ and filled with Jesus Christ." He told his associates to disclaim the applause people give. "Let us work humbly and respectfully, and with compassion, for otherwise God will not bless our work and we shall drive the poor away from us. They will judge that there was vanity in our behavior and will not believe us. We do not believe a man because he is very learned but because we consider him good and love him. The devil is very learned and yet we believe nothing that he says."

St. Anthony of Padua was one of the greatest preachers in Italy in his day. He was a Franciscan and very humble; once he was thrilled to see St. Francis himself.

When Anthony, the son of a prominent official in Lisbon, Portugal, told his father that he wanted to be a priest, the man flew into a rage. He had dreamed of his son taking his place. But the next day his father had changed completely. Anthony was amazed. Later he learned that his father had been told that the youth spent the whole night in prayer in the cathedral before making his decision. When the father learned this, he said it must be God's will.

Anthony had become a monk and a famous preacher in Portugal, when one day two Little Brothers of St. Francis came to the door begging for food. He had never heard of the Franciscans. He was ashamed that he in the monastery had food, clothing and shelter. He decided to join the followers of Francis. He learned that five Friars Minor had been martyred in Morocco and he volunteered to be one of those who replaced them. He made the sea voyage to Africa but became extremely ill when he arrived there. He said, "It is the Lord's way of showing me how ugly my pride is." He was too weak to be a missionary and was sent home with a heavy heart. But the ship ran into a furious storm and the wild winds drove it onto the island of Sicily. There, an unknown Franciscan, Anthony went to the nearest Franciscan house where he was assigned the humblest tasks. He enjoyed the kitchen work, which gave him more time to pray.

One day there was a special Mass and the superior had forgotten to appoint a preacher. Several famous orators were asked but all said they were unprepared and declined. The superior then told Anthony to preach, knowing he would obey. In the pulpit this kitchen worker electrified the large festive audience. From that time he was sent to preach, most often in Padua, where there was not a church large enough for the crowds who wanted to hear him.

St. Anthony, after becoming the most famous preacher in Italy, received a letter from St. Francis of Assisi. Francis complimented him on his unearthly wisdom. He added, "I am pleased that you also teach sacred theology to the Little Brothers, provided that with such study they shall not extinguish in themselves the spirit of holy prayer and devotion." To Francis, as with Anthony, study was always secondary to prayer.

It was said of Anthony, "His eloquence was magnificent; he preached not with human wisdom but with the wisdom of heaven. He spoke like an angel. The love of Jesus flowed from his burning heart."

People noted that he had a special love for the Christ Child. The statue of St. Anthony shows this noble Franciscan with the Child. People said, "When he speaks of the little Jesus his whole face lights up." His devotion to the Infant started when he was a child. He and his prominent family went to visit another wealthy family in their palace. They had a daughter who was crippled and walked with crutches. She could never walk without them. She had fallen under a carriage in the courtyard and was fortunate to be alive. The boy Anthony noticed that she was very cheerful and always pleasant. Later, she told him why. She said she wanted to show him something in the castle chapel. They passed by the beautiful, large main altar and went over to the side to a small altar. There was a statue of the Child Jesus. The girl told Anthony that after her serious injury she was bitter. But then she came often to pray to the Child, and he changed her and made her cheerful again. And she said she wanted Anthony to be devoted to the Child Jesus also. And he was all his life.

When he first went to Padua it made him sad. He said, "They are like lost children." After he preached there, the people changed. And they loved him especially when with great courage he faced up to the tyrants from the city's powerful families and forced them to stop mistreating the people.

St. Francis of Assisi entered one town and began to preach, after ordering the swallows to be silent until he finished. He preached with heartfelt zeal and the people were amazed. Many wanted to follow him at once, but they were people with families and with work to do. So he established the Third Order for those who could not leave their responsibilities. They could stay home and do their duties but still pray in the spirit of Francis. They were greatly consoled by this way of life.

At the end he blessed the swallows and according to the story, they began to sing again. Francis said to the little birds, "My little sisters, you owe much to God, your Creator, and when you sing you praise him for giving you the freedom to fly. He gives you good clothing and plentiful food. He has given you fountains and rivers to quench your thirst, mountains and valleys in which to take refuge, and many trees where you can build your nests. The Creator has been most good to you, so always praise God with your singing."

And the birds burst into song, sounding as sweet as a cathedral choir.

When Francis was given a blessing he would say, "Lord, I am unworthy of such a gift. But for it I rejoice with all my heart and thank you with all my soul."

While on a journey after having comforted many with holy words, he went into a church to pray. But the people followed him and gathered around the church and trampled down the grapevines there. This greatly grieved the priest to whom they belonged. Francis asked how many measures of wine the vines produced and was told twelve. Francis said, "Father, I pray you have patience and let the people stay a little longer; I promise you that hereafter they shall produce twenty measures." And so they did.

St. Bonaventure said that silence is necessary for prayer. He insisted on prayer. He wrote, "The practice of prayer is a virtue of such efficacy that it can subdue evil impulses." He quoted St. Isidore who said, "Prayer is the remedy for temptations." And Jesus said, "Watch and pray that you enter not into temptation."

Devout prayer brings many blessings. An hour of prayer is golden. In prayer you ask Jesus to lead you. And you thank him for all his help in the past. "Nothing makes a man more worthy of God's gifts than the constant offering of thanks", Bonaventure wrote. He pointed out the words of St. Augustine, "What better thoughts can we have in our minds, what better sentiments in our hearts than thanksgiving? What better words than 'Deo gratias'?"

Pray with a grateful heart, Bonaventure said. Thank God because he made you, because he has forgiven you, because he daily takes care of you. He keeps you from harm, comforts you and gives you all you need. Thank him for redeeming you and for giving you the Eucharist.

St. Bonaventure wrote, "All prayer is valueless without the element of thanksgiving." He told us that St. Bernard said, "Ingratitude is a parching wind which dries up the source of piety, the dew of mercy, the stream of grace."

Be thoughtful in prayer. A half-hearted prayer is hardly a prayer at all. "A heart divided obtains nothing", St. Augustine said.

Bonaventure said, in prayer you rush to the embrace of your Beloved. You will be transformed and be Christlike. Your fire of love will intensify beyond measure. Divine light floods the soul and it cries out, "I see you, Lord, as an angel of God; you are admirable; your Face is full of grace."

The disciple's heart is purified and washed by prayer, St. Bernard said. Bonaventure wrote that instead of praying many pamper their body in its many desires—and go nowhere.

St. Thérèse of Lisieux

St. Thérèse of Lisieux, the Little Flower, said she knew quite well that she was only a child with all the weaknesses of a child. But she knew, as well, that "Love has chosen me. I know that Jesus loves me and that love can only be repaid with love. I return love for love. I must make use of my small love to win heaven. And to help Jesus win souls for heaven."

Thérèse readily admitted her failings, but that was all the more reason to ask the Lord for love. She said she scattered her flowers before the Lord and sang his praises.

A smiling look, though small, is an act of love, as is a kind word. Suffering is a sign of love. Jesus receives these fragrant flowers and will give them to souls in need.

She wrote, "Jesus, if the mere desire to love you can yield such happiness, what must it be like to possess and to enjoy your love?"

Thérèse found her consolation amid storm clouds in doing her duty and directing her gaze to Jesus. She said that she called upon the angels and saints to help her. She knew they would protect her and defend her from evil.

"Divine Word," she prayed, "worthy of all admiration and all love, you draw me continually toward yourself. You came down into this world of exile ready to suffer and die so as to bring souls to you. Even today you still frequent this valley of tears, hidden under the appearance of the sacred Host.

"Jesus, my gratitude bids me thank you for fondly loving me. How can my heart fail to go out to you? I am too poor a creature to do anything wonderful, but please accept my love."

She prayed to the saints to win her the graces she needed.

St. Bernard of Clairvaux
March 15

St. Bernard of Clairvaux was the most popular personality and the most honored saint of his time in the Middle Ages. He was the abbot of a Cistercian (Trappist) monastery in France and a great reformer of the Church. He was a contemplative and yet, against his will, he often had to leave the cloister and go into the world and settle religious disputes and reform houses of religion. Bernard did not hesitate to rebuke kings and emperors, bishops and even the pope himself.

He had a burning zeal. But in his early years, before Christ became everything to him, he admitted that he was very ordinary. He wrote, "I am not ashamed to acknowledge that I was myself, very often, and especially during the early period of my conversion, experiencing a dryness and coldness of heart. My soul sought him whom I was one day to love, because I could not love him whom I had not yet found; or at least I could not love him as much as I desired, and I was in doubt as to what I should do in order to make myself love him more. However, I would not have gone in search of him, if I did not already love him to some extent. Therefore I sought him in whom my torpid soul could find shelter and warmth, but nowhere did I find one who could help me, who could melt the stiffening frost that numbed my faculties, and awaken in me the sweet springtime of spiritual joy. More and more my soul was filled with weariness, inertia and disgust. I was melancholy to the point of despair and I murmured within myself, 'Who shall stand before my cold face?' Then all of a sudden, at the sight perhaps of a man advanced in the spiritual life, or even at the sound of his voice, or again at the thought of some friend dead or absent, the spirit blew and the waters ran; my tears were my bread day and night." And things changed.

St. Vincent de Paul   *March 16*

"Our Lord has to predispose with his love those whom he wishes to have believe in him. Do what we will, people will never believe in us if we do not show love and compassion to them. Then our Lord can do great things through us", said St. Vincent de Paul. "And if you act in this manner, God will bless your labors. If not, you will produce noise and fanfare, but with little fruit. Labor constantly and humbly. Labor in a spirit of humility."

St. Vincent wrote to a woman, complimenting her on doing well her works of charity despite many difficulties. He said, "When I set up the works of charity here, everyone made fun of me and would point at me in the streets with laughter. But when the deed was accomplished, everyone wept for joy. The town magistrates paid me so much honor that I could not stand it."

To another person he wrote, "God does everything for the best. We must be resigned to his divine will in all things. You think about yourself too much. You must go along in a simple and ordinary way, helping others. In this work a spirit of gentleness is needed. I beg our Lord to strengthen you more and more. In order to honor the humility of our Lord, we must be humble. I beg God with all my heart that he perfect you and sanctify your soul."

Vincent advised a superior of a house of his Daughters of Charity to take in a young woman as a candidate because "she seems to have a fair amount of common sense and good will."

When one nun was disappointed that Father Vincent could not visit and comfort her after a good Sister in the house had died, he sent a letter saying, "Do not give way to grief. This is the good pleasure of God, whom you love so much. . . . What better motive is there than accepting his will? Realize that this good Sister is now enjoying the happiness of God's glory. Concentrate on this thought and do not depart from it, I beg you."

St. Patrick   *March 17*

"I am Patrick, a sinner, the most unlearned", wrote the patron saint of Ireland, "the least of all the faithful." He wrote this when he was sixteen and was taken into captivity to Ireland. As a slave, he said, "The Lord made me aware of my unbelief that I might at last remember my sins and be converted with all my heart to the Lord my God, who had regard for my abjection and mercy on my youth and ignorance, and watched over me. . . . I cannot be silent about the great benefits and the great grace which the Lord deigned to bestow upon me."

Patrick was able to escape his slavery in Ireland and return home. He then wanted to be a priest. He went to the seminary, but he kept feeling that the voices of the people of Ireland were calling to him to come back to them and teach them about Jesus.

And so he returned to Ireland as a youthful missionary bishop. It was most difficult at first, but in time he won over the kings, and all of Ireland believed in Christ.

He said that he was unworthy and the Lord was most gracious in granting his blessings to him. "Now, it would be tedious to give a detailed account of all my labors", he wrote. "Let me tell you how the merciful God was good to me." He said, "I am very much God's debtor, who gave me such great grace that many people were reborn in God through me, and that clerics were ordained for them everywhere."

He said, "So now I commend my soul to my faithful God, for whom I am an ambassador in all my wretchedness; God chose me for this office, to be, although among the least, one of his ministers.

"Wherefore may God never permit it to happen to me that I should lose his people which he won for himself at the end of the earth. I pray to God to give me perseverence and to deign that I be a faithful witness to him for his own sake until my passing from this life."

St. Thomas Aquinas   *March 18*

St. Thomas Aquinas said, "The daily Mass, the sacrifice that goes on being offered in churches, is not another sacrifice over and above the one Christ offered on the Cross, but its remembrance. Christ is the offering and Christ is the priest who offers it; he wills the sacrifice of the Church as her daily sacrament."

Christ humbly bore his sufferings as a devotion of love, he said. By dying, he prepared the way to heaven for us.

A man adopts a son when, in his goodness, he admits him to share his inheritance. God in his infinite goodness admits men to share his goods. He made thinking creatures, created to his image, capable of sharing happiness in himself because they can love. And so he made them rich in his inheritance.

When God admits men to his inheritance he is said to adopt them. He shares with men a likeness to his goodness when he creates them, and by adopting them he shares a likeness to his natural Son with them. Those whom he foreknew he made conformable to the image of his Son, St. Paul tells us. By adoption we become brothers of Christ, having the same Father as he does.

Christ, Thomas wrote, is our mediator. The function of a mediator is to bring together those between whom he mediates. Christ, having reconciled man to God through his death, is the mediator between heaven and earth. The power to take away sin belongs to Christ as God, but making amends for mankind's sin belongs to Christ as man.

We can reasonably suppose that the woman who gave birth to the "only Son of the Father" received greater privileges of grace than anyone else. The angel confirmed this by saying to Mary, "Hail, full of grace".

St. Joseph   *March 19*

This is the feast of St. Joseph, who was the man closest to Christ in this world. In the Gospels we never hear him speak but he always faithfully did his duty. He was called "a just man". This is one of the highest compliments. He was honest with God, honest with others and honest with himself.

Joseph suffered many trials but always he put his trust in God. When he found that Mary was with child, he was greatly disturbed, until in a dream he learned from an angel of God that this Child was conceived without a human father.

His heart went out to Mary as they made the difficult journey to Bethlehem. She was so brave and yet he knew she suffered, and her suffering was his suffering. And when they got to Bethlehem it was even worse. He was chosen by God to be the protector of Mary and the Child, but he could not even find a room where the Baby could be born. He went up every street and knocked on every door, but there was nothing. He was very discouraged and disheartened.

The Baby was born in a cave. Joseph did all that he could to make it warm, but his heart ached for Mary. Later, when the Child was born and Mary was so happy, her face aglow, and the Baby so beautiful, Joseph too smiled and rejoiced.

But next he had to take the Child and his Mother to Egypt. They left in the middle of the night. In a dream an angel had warned him that the malevolent King Herod was sending soldiers to murder the Baby Jesus. How terrible it must have been when they learned later of the many babies in Bethlehem that had been put to death. How difficult it must have been for Joseph to live in a foreign land.

When the Child Jesus was twelve Mary and Joseph could not find him after they had started home from celebrating the Passover in the great city of Jerusalem. They returned and searched for him. Joseph and Mary prayed as they had never prayed before, and at last they found him in the temple. Jesus' words then remained always a mystery to faithful St. Joseph.

St. Ignatius of Antioch   *March 20*

St. Ignatius of Antioch was appointed by St. Peter as the Bishop of Antioch. He was martyred in Rome in 107. He said, "I do not want to court the good pleasures of men, but to please God." He told the faithful, "You should form a choir of love and sing a song to the Father through Jesus Christ." He asked them to beg God that he might have "strength within and without, that I may be a man not merely of words, but also of resolution. In this way I shall not only be called a Christian, but also prove to be one. . . . Whenever Christianity is hated by the world, what counts is not power of persuasion, but greatness."

This early martyr wrote, "I die willingly for God. . . . God's wheat I am, and by the teeth of wild beasts I am to be ground that I may prove Christ's pure bread." He added, "I would rather and come to Jesus Christ than be king over the entire earth. Him I seek who died for us; him I love who rose again because of us." He said, "The prince of this world is resolved to abduct me, to corrupt my Godwards aspirations. . . . My Love has been crucified, and I am not on fire with the love of earthly things." He told them, "Do not have Jesus Christ on your lips, and the world in your hearts."

St. Ignatius said, "If I but make my way to God, then by his mercy I shall be someone."

He wrote to the people of Philadelphia in Asia, "A church which unwaveringly exults in the Passion of our Lord, and firmly believes in his Resurrection through sheer mercy, this church I salute in the Blood of Jesus Christ. She is a source of everlasting joy. . . . Being born then of the light of truth, shun division and bad doctrine. Where the shepherd is, there you, being sheep, must follow. For many wolves there are, apparently worthy of confidence, who with the bait of baneful pleasure seek to capture the runners in God's race; but you stand united and they will have no success."

St. Teresa of Avila   *March 21*

St. Teresa of Avila was, as she said, an ordinary nun for many years, but then she realized that it was more prayer and penance that she and the other Sisters needed the most. And she reformed herself and set out to reform her convent and other convents as well. And in the end she helped reform the Faith in Spain.

She said that we should let our hearts be faithful servants of him who purchased them with his blood. Otherwise we become entangled with the world and cannot get free. We are easily overcome by the foolish childishness that comes from loving possessions too much.

Our Lord and Master, Jesus Christ, urged this and emphatically insisted upon it. She said, "Of this I wish to talk to you a little, as well as my ignorance will allow." We will be able to help others if we are constant at prayer. Praying faithfully is the first step.

Our Lord teaches clearly anyone who is willing to be taught. In prayer he imprints his love deeply in our hearts. He makes us generous. One learns that possessions are shadows.

Be grateful to people who help you and commend them to God in prayer. Those help you the most who pray for you.

God loves us with such a great and warm love, all other love seems small. Because of this a soul should be much more willing to give than to receive. "This, I say, deserves the name love, all other base affections have usurped the name."

St. Teresa was very humble. She prayed that Jesus would always be with her. She said, "If at times I talk nonsense, that is because it is most natural for me not to do anything right." But she knew Jesus would help her.

St. Francis de Sales   *March 22*

"When we are filled with weariness, grace lifts us up", said the saintly bishop Francis de Sales. "Grace helps us bear our troubles patiently and assists us in overcoming temptations."

We need help, we need direction, he said. We are incapable of doing anything alone. Jesus assists us, but at times he teaches us by trials. Let it be enough for us to know that God wishes these things, and accept them and move on. We need not occupy ourselves with wondering why. We do not understand, as Mary did not understand, but, as Mary did, let us walk simply in the happy path of a tranquil humility, which is so pleasing to God. We do not have to know. But we do have to trust God. We need not keep all our cares in our heart; share them with Jesus.

We with Christ as our companion and our help need not be fearful. He will uphold us. He said, "It is I—do not be afraid."

Trying to figure everything out, the bishop said, makes us lose our tranquility and ruffles our emotions. To lament because we are unknowing is a waste of time. To be excessive in sorrow over our failings is not to be like the saints.

Sometimes we say, "I am dry in mind and cold in heart. Have

pity, Lord, have pity." We must then hold fast to the notion that Jesus loves us, and that this will pass.

The Father loved his only Son with infinite love — and yet he suffered. God loved Mary and Joseph with a tremendous love and yet they knew grief on many occasions. So let us not be complaining and disturbed about our trials. Mary and Joseph and, above all, Jesus, give us the example. They simply bore their troubles and prayed. They were calm in the midst of numerous trials and allowed God to look after them.

St. Augustine   *March 23*

"Let fear of punishment lead you to God. He is your master and guide", wrote St. Augustine.

We tremble, he said, when we hear the words of the psalm, "As smoke vanishes, so let them vanish away: as wax melts before the fire, so let the wicked perish." Our hearts are deeply moved, our minds are troubled. Time is short. What are we to do?

We look to Christ crucified. We beg his assistance. We must strive to make ourselves better.

Judgment is to come soon, that judgment which the impious now deride. Prepare yourselves. Alter your ways. Let tomorrow find you a changed person.

In our wrongful thinking we want God to be so merciful that he would no longer be just.

Let the sinner in man perish now. Live honestly, justly, kindly.

God created man, he wrote, and man created sin. The proud individual rises on high against God like smoke against the heavens, and he is scattered by God like smoke. He swells in inflated greatness, full of vanity. Like smoke there is nothing to him. He is a fool. You must submit to God, beat your breast and try to be better, St. Augustine said.

Let us not return God evil for good. He is so good to us. We cannot begin to express it in words. When Jesus bound fast the devil, he released us, the slaves of the devil, from his power; let us, rid of all evil through his grace, now seek to be filled with his abundant gifts. Let us not fear. Let us toil to summon virtues in place of vices, so that we may attain to the compassion of Christ.

St. Augustine   *March 24*

"Arise from squalid desires that you may abide in resplendent love. You do not see God. Love him and you shall possess him", said St. Augustine.

He wrote, "O brothers and daughters and children of the Catholic Church, O divine and heavenly progeny, O those reborn in Christ and born anew from on high, listen to and listen through me. 'Sing ye to the Lord a new canticle.' 'Behold, I am singing.' Indeed you are singing and I hear you. But do not let your life bear witness against your words. Sing with your voice, sing with your heart, sing with your deeds. You ask what you may sing of him whom you love. Sing his praises with your deeds."

If you live rightly, you are praising God, he said. "Not in the ravings of pagans, not in the fallacies of heretics, not in the applause of the theatre is the proper praise of God to be found. You ask where is the proper praise to be found. Look after your deeds and let them be his praise."

Seek to increase your love of God. Look after the treasures of your soul so that you may be rich within.

Love speaks with wisdom. God, who is Love, says, "My son, give me thy heart." When you were in charge of your love you did foolhardy things, wanton and ruinous. Take your heart from these attachments and give it to God. God says, "Let your heart be subject to me and your love will never die." Do not be grieved that nothing remains for you. For in this you will find joy. Then you will love yourself because you love God with your whole heart.

God is not diminished if you do not love him. You will be diminished. When you love God, you add unto yourself. "You will have attained a place where you cannot perish", Augustine wrote. When you do not love God, you do not love yourself. You in your selfishness thought you loved yourself, but actually you hated yourself. As the psalm says, "For he that loveth iniquity hateth his own soul."

Mary, Mother of God   *March 25*

On this Feast of the Annunciation we look to Mary. The angel came to her and asked her if she would be the Mother of the Messiah. She did not hesitate. She could never refuse God anything. She said, "Be it done unto me according to thy word." Whatever God wanted, she wanted.

Because she was a pious Jewish woman and had read the Scriptures, she knew that the Messiah would be a man of sorrows, and to be his Mother would mean that she would be a Mother of Sorrows. And yet this young woman immediately told the messenger from God that she would accept this difficult role. She knew that she was not learned by worldly standards. She did not begin to comprehend what saying Yes would mean. But, as she had always done, she put all of her trust in God. He would take care of her, as he had before. He would look after her as a mother looks after her small child.

Later, old Simeon said a sword would pierce her heart. She did not give a thought to self-pity. She remained calm. Inner peace reigned in her soul, for she put all her trust in God.

The Blessed Mother could have said "no" to the angel. But then she never once thought of this. How could she who loved God so much possibly refuse him anything? He had done everything for her. She was full of gratitude because she was "full of grace".

And how grateful we should be to Mary. God in the beginning had been exiled from his own world. Now through the angel he was asking if he might reenter the world. Mary made all this possible. If Christ had not been born, we would be lost. Jesus came to rescue us. He is our Savior who saved us from our sins. He is our Redeemer who reopened for us the gates of heaven.

Let us thank dear Mary, our sweet Blessed Mother, with all our hearts.

St. Augustine was walking along the beach one day, while pondering the great mystery of the Trinity. As this brilliant thinker walked he noticed a small boy. The lad had dug a little hole in the sand and with his small pail was going down to the sea and bringing back water and pouring it into the hole. St. Augustine was amused and stopped and asked, "What are you doing?" The boy replied, "I am putting the ocean in my hole." St. Augustine smiled and said, "But you can never do that." And the little lad said, "And you can never understand the Holy Trinity." And the boy disappeared, for, according to the story, he was an angel.

Confusion and violence marked the age in which St. Augustine lived in the fifth century. As a youth he was pagan in heart, like his father—his mother, Monica, was a Christian—and he lived wildly, doing whatever he wanted. He later wrote, "In the sixteenth year of the age of my flesh, the madness of lust ruled over me, and I resigned myself wholly to it." He said he "was ashamed not to be shameless" with his bad companions and so did what they did, fearing if he didn't they would laugh at him. And so he did wrong for the sheer excitement of it. Sex confusedly boiled over in him. Augustine wrote in his *Confessions,* "My God, my mercy, how much gall did you mingle into my lustfulness. I secretly entered the prison of pleasure and was sorrowfully bound with its chains."

One incident, he recalled, deeply affected him—the death of a young companion. It was a terrible shock. The youth had been Augustine's favorite friend. One day this friend had fallen ill with a serious sickness. He asked to be baptized a Christian. Augustine had then made fun of him. Augustine wrote that the sick boy "shrunk from me as from an enemy. He told me if I wanted to continue to be his friend I must not talk like that. I was dismayed but said nothing, wishing to wait until he had recovered to talk to him." But the friend did not recover. "A few days later the fever attacked again and he died." The loss cast the young Augustine into a "delirium of grief".

Though his best friend died and it was a great and painful loss for the young Augustine, he did not change his sinful ways. He was intelligent and quickly advanced in his studies.

But while his mind prospered, he continued to sin with his bad companions. Following graduation he set up a school in Carthage in North Africa where he lived, and he was very popular. So in his pride he decided to go to Rome and have a school and become even more famous.

This upset Monica, his mother, very much. She had prayed and prayed that he would change his lustful ways. In her grief she went weeping to the bishop. The old man told her, "It is not possible that the son of so many tears should be lost." But now he was going to Rome, "the cesspool of iniquity". And yet it was in Rome, where his school failed, that he began to be more humble. He then went to Milan to teach and there he came under the influence of St. Ambrose, one of the great orators of the time. In time Augustine became a Christian. He returned to North Africa and became a priest and later a bishop. His writings have saved many souls throughout the centuries.

He told his priests that in preaching it was the thought and not the eloquence that counted. "What is the use of a golden key if it will not open the door?" He wanted them to be spiritual. "He who ministers at the Lord's table has no right to defraud the guests."

He told the people that God said, "I am the Food for the strong." Christ said, "Grow and you shall feed on me; but in truth it is not I who will turn into you, but you will be changed into me."

In his day this great intellectual saved the Church from disintegration. There have been few minds in history as gifted as his.

St. Benedict left Rome where he had been a student and went into the hills to be alone and pray. He felt that much of his schooling was "learned ignorance" and he yearned for the "unlearned wisdom" of Christ.

He lived in a cave in a rocky place called Subiaco where he could listen to God. Others came and joined him. From this the first European monastery sprang up and, later, hundreds all over the continent and in England and Ireland. And during the Dark Ages, when the barbarians overran Europe, it was the monasteries that saved learning. In their libraries and scriptoria, where by hand the monks copied out the great books of the past, they preserved the tremendous thoughts of the ancient world. The monasteries were lighthouses in the darkness.

Benedict said, "You will be truly monks if you live by the labor of your hands." Work, he knew, was healthy, and it prepared one to pray. St. Benedict's Rule was known for its common sense and moderation. Benedictine hospitality is most beautiful.

Benedict knew that all depends on God. He wrote, "Whatever good work you begin, beg of him with most earnest prayer to perfect it."

Cardinal Newman wrote, "Benedict found the world, physical and social, in ruin, and his mission was to restore it." "The barbarians destroyed while the monks were silent builders." He said that sometimes all the monks built in an area was destroyed, but they built again. "They were", Newman wrote, "like the fruit trees they nurtured in their orchards. When ill-treated they did not take vengeance, or remember evil, but they gave forth fresh branches of even richer quality."

Benedict, above all, emphasized humility. It is the key to sanctity, he said.

St. Thomas More, the gifted thinker and able writer, was the most famous literary figure of his day in England. He served the king faithfully but Henry VIII turned against his good friend when he would not agree with the monarch who made himself the "Pope" in England.

Thomas was reasonable; Henry acted foolishly. During the turbulent times of Henry many people gave up the true faith and reasonable thinking. They followed their emotions, but our emotions in religion, as Thomas knew, are untrustworthy. An emotional religion lasts only as long as one is feeling good. True religion, based on reason, helps us in the bad times when we need it the most.

Thomas More said that some individuals are so proud that they are busy changing the religion that has been given us by God. They act as though they can make it better. They lack humility, which is so very necessary for sanctity. "A few men there are", he wrote, "who think, I am sure, that if they had been in God's council in the making of religion they could have done it better." So much for the reformers who in his day were changing the religion Christ gave us. So much for the changers in every age who try to improve on the sublime theology of Jesus.

In a true religion the "making things of another fashion" is the work of the fool, who should be using his time not in changing things but praying more fervently. Then they would follow the faith Christ established. The Christian faith need not be changed, but hearts must be changed to conform to Christ.

Thomas prayed, "Take from me, good Lord, this lukewarm fashion, this key-cold way I pray and my dullness in thinking of you."

St. Bernadette *March 30*

St. Bernadette of Lourdes is noted for her childlike humility. This is what made her a saint—humility is the secret of the saints—and the reason the Blessed Mother appeared to her. Mary, in all her apparitions, appears to the humble, most often children or people with childlike faith.

Bernadette was at first the only one who believed in her visions. It all began when she was out gathering fire wood for her family's poor little dwelling. Her sister and another girl were on the other side of the small stream. Bernadette was suddenly aware that something was different. She looked up at the nearby cavern. There was a beautiful lady standing in golden light. She was dressed in white and had yellow roses on her bare feet.

Although filled with fear, the girl then had suddenly felt washed with love as she looked at the face of the beautiful lady. Bernadette raised her eyes again and the lady smiled graciously. Then the girl knelt and made the Sign of the Cross, and the beautiful lady smiled and did the same. Bernadette took out her Rosary and the lady smiled even more and the lady held her Rosary which had white beads and a chain the same color as the roses. The lady looked like a queen. She slipped the Rosary beads through her fingers while Bernadette prayed the Rosary.

When the other girls returned with their branches from across the stream, they were frightened because Bernadette, kneeling in the rubble, looked so pale. She was staring in the direction of the cavern, but they saw no one. Bernadette had a rapt faraway look in her eyes. The girls spoke to her, wondering at her strange actions. Bernadette did not answer. But then she got up and helped them carry the wood. She asked, "Didn't you see anything?" They hadn't.

St. Bernadette   *March 31*

St. Bernadette did not have a gifted mind, but her example of humility spoke louder than words. She stuck to her story of the visions even when no one believed her.

That fateful day of the first vision the three girls walked home. Bernadette told them what she had seen. She asked them to promise to tell no one. But at home her sister immediately told her mother, who became angry. She told Bernadette that she had not seen a lovely lady, but rather maybe a white stone that from the distance could have looked like a lady. Then the youth's father joined in the ridicule. However, no matter what they said, Bernadette would not change her story. She fixed her soulful eyes on her father and said, "Oh, Papa, I really did see the lady."

Poor little Bernadette felt lonely and confused. Her father refused to let her go back to the grotto. But a neighbor lady, hearing the story, got him to relent. Bernadette returned. She looked up and said with delight, "Look! A bright light!" Then, "Look at her.... She has her Rosary slipped over her right arm.... She is looking at us!" The girls with her questioned one another. None of them saw anything. Bernadette stood up. She sprinkled the rock with holy water. The lady was pleased.

The girl knelt again, silent and motionless. She kept her eyes fixed intently on the rock. One of the girls remembers, "Her face was lit up."

After a time the girls became afraid. They ran to a nearby mill. Antoine, the miller's son, returned with them. He said that Bernadette "was on her knees, deathly pale, her eyes wide open and fixed on the niche. She had her hands joined and her beads between her fingers. Tears were streaming from her eyes. She was smiling and her face was lovely, lovelier than anything I have ever seen."

Because she was so pale he took her right arm, raised her up, and took her home.

St. Bernadette   *April 1*

Bernadette went back to the grotto a number of times and each time the beautiful lady appeared to her. Then on one visit the lady told the girl to go to the spring and wash. But there was no spring there. Bernadette looked around anxiously. She saw a damp spot and began to scratch the earth at that place. She dug in the mud and tried to drink it and wash with it. Many people thought she had lost her mind. But then this hole began to fill with water and trickle over and run down to the river.

In the village a baby was dying. In desperation the mother snatched up her child and ran to the grotto. She put her very sick baby into the spring. People shouted, "You're killing your baby— that water is ice cold." However, the next day the child was well. Many more now came to Lourdes, and, of course, today it has been visited by millions of pilgrims.

On one appearance someone asked Bernadette to inquire of the lady what her name was. Afterward, the girl was asked, "Did the lady tell you her name?" "Yes," she answered. She said, "I am the Immaculate Conception." This was a title Bernadette had never heard. The doctrine of the Immaculate Conception had only recently been defined by Pope Pius IX in faraway Rome.

The lady then told Bernadette to go to the parish priest and tell him to build a chapel there. When she arrived he was in the garden. Bernadette was frightened. He turned around and asked who she was. She said, "I am Bernadette." He scowled. Poor Bernadette could hardly speak but she was able to get the message out. The priest responded curtly saying she should tell the lady that if she wanted a chapel, she would have to supply the money. He thought the whole thing was nonsense. As the girl was leaving he said, "Bernadette, you are playing with fire." She ran away in tears.

St. Philip Neri   *April 2*

St. Philip Neri, the Apostle of Rome, was fond of jokes. And when proud youth came to him, he gave them as a penance something to humble them. One wealthy, splendid gentleman was obliged to carry Philip's dog through the streets like a lowly servant. Philip had another make his servant's bed and then sweep the church porch.

Philip's church was called the Oratory, a place of prayer. A part of the devotion in the church was beautiful music. The famous composer Palestrina directed the music and wrote Masses and wonderful madrigals and motets in honor of the Blessed Mother.

On the feast of the Purification, 1594, Palestrina was dying. Philip said, "My son, would it not gladden you to go and enjoy the feast which today is held in heaven in honor of the Queen of the angels and saints?"

The outstanding musician replied, "Yes, I do most eagerly desire it. May Mary obtain for me this grace from her Divine Son." And he died.

This was the post-reformation era, and there was a good deal of suspicion in Rome, especially of those who, like Philip, were doing new things. Some said he was seeking a high office. They did not know that he had already refused to be made a cardinal. Nobody wished ecclesiastical promotion less than he.

Even the Cardinal Vicar of Rome was suspicious of him. He said, "I am surprised that you are not ashamed of yourself, you who affect to despise the world, and yet go about enticing numbers of people to follow you, and all to win the favor of the multitude, and work your way, under the pretext of sanctity, to some prelacy or other!"

Philip was flabbergasted. He wished for nothing but to save souls. But often those who do the most good, like Jesus, are accused on false charges.

St. Gertrude   *April 3*

The Savior told St. Gertrude, "Fear nothing, my daughter, but rather be filled with holy confidence." She cried, "King of heaven and earth, withhold the torrent of thy mercies, for a fragment of dust and ashes such as I am is unworthy to receive great favors."

He answered, "Why be so amazed, my daughter, if I give you great graces, when I have so often communicated to you the secrets of my friendship.

"All those when overcome with sadness and, having their hearts oppressed with any affliction, when having humility and true sincerity, shall never be disappointed."

When our Lord said that she should commit her revelations to writing, her humility made her oppose this. But he said she must: "Be firm and immovable, my daughter, for I am with you." He told her that making known what he said would enkindle the zeal of those who read it and show them his love. The writing would "produce devotion in the hearts of those who, seeing the effusion of my grace and the excess of my mercy, shall try to improve".

Jesus said, "The majority of mankind are so weak and unspiritual" that they need this inspiration.

From this Gertrude realized her visions were to help others. Jesus does not want those who love him to compromise with the world or to timidly conceal his great message.

St. Gertrude prayed, "O my Beloved, how is it that thy mercy bears with my iniquity? I love you because of your perfection and adorable goodness."

Jesus said to her, "I instruct you that you might know and make known the designs of my will."

St. Vincent de Paul   *April 4*

St. Vincent de Paul founded the Congregation of the Mission, priests now most often called the Vincentian Fathers. He said to a priest who was troubled, "He who from all eternity has chosen you to assist the poor will preserve you as the apple of his eye insofar as his glory and your welfare require it. Mortify your conflicting feelings, realizing that our days are numbered and that we cannot add a moment of life to the one God has determined for us. That being so, let us abandon ourselves to Divine Providence.

"Speaking of Providence, are you not aware that God takes such care of you that he is concerned for you in a special way? If that were not the case, why would he have chosen you from among so many holy souls to do the work of giving glory to God for the good of the poor? God provides for all that you need. Let this, then, be a motive for entrusting yourself entirely to him."

Vincent said that our Lord took pity on his Little Company (his community of priests) through the intercession of the Blessed Virgin. "May his Holy Name be blessed! He is the Master and does everything for the best. Let us leave the care of everything to him."

To some individuals on retreat he gave this suggestion, "You can take your spiritual reading from the *Imitation of Christ,* stopping to reflect a short time after each sentence. Also read a Gospel in the same way. For the rest, do not drive yourself too hard during these exercises."

To another who wrote him he answered, "Our Lord will reward you for all you suffer and put up with. I am asking the Holy Virgin, to whom I am devoted in a special way, to obtain from her Son his blessings. I hope our Lord will make use of you."

St. Bernadette   *April 5*

Eventually St. Bernadette of Lourdes went to stay at a convent. There were so many pilgrims that wanted to see her that in her home she had been bothered night and day. It was very hard for her to leave her family but she knew it was for the best. And at the convent, when she saw a statue of Mary near the door of her room, she said that she was certain the Blessed Mother would take care of her.

By this time the pastor in Lourdes supported her. When she had told him that her beautiful lady said, "I am the Immaculate Conception", the pastor asked if she knew what that meant. She replied simply and directly, as she always did, "How could I know anything like that!" The priest replied, "How could you indeed, my child?"

At the convent the Sisters were very nice to her, except for one skeptical nun. She said to Bernadette, "What a little trickster you are. You have tricked the stupid mob, but not me. You whistle and everyone dances—except one person, myself."

Poor little Bernadette replied, "I never asked anyone to believe, Sister."

The proud Sister drew herself up and announced that she would pray for the girl's soul, that she would be saved.

The bishop visited her. She was so sincere in telling her story that the old man was moved to tears. In the meantime not a few cures that baffled the doctors were reported from the grotto.

After a time Bernadette asked to be a Sister. Mother Superior asked what she could do and she answered frankly, "Nothing much." She was content to wash and sweep and scrub floors and was very happy.

A great artist, the greatest in France, was commissioned to sculpt a statue of Mary for Lourdes. Bernadette was taken to see it. She said, "It is not nearly so beautiful as my lady."

The time passed and Bernadette's knee became very deformed by a large tumor. She was bedfast. One of the Sisters said she should go to Lourdes and bathe in the water, but the humble nun said, "O no, it is not for me."

And soon after she died.

St. Bernard of Clairvaux   *April 6*

St. Bernard of Clairvaux went to become a monk. The abbot asked him, "What do you seek?" He replied, "God's mercy and yours".

In time he became the abbot and he was called upon to reform the Church. He upbraided bishops and kings. To the king of England he wrote, "The King of kings has for long chastised your royal majesty, for he is more powerful than you."

He spent long hours in prayer and penance. When he preached, people listened. One observer described him in the pulpit, "His face was pale, emaciated by fatigue and fasting, so spiritual and impressive that the mere sight of him persuaded many to repent, even before he opened his mouth." Bernard preached with profound emotion, clear diction and eloquent gestures. He did not accept praise for himself, saying, "I am at the most the one who sows the seeds and waters them, but what would I have done without the One who makes them grow?"

St. Bernard prayed for a full heart, "My God, my Love, how you love me! Oh, incomparable Love, violent, burning, impetuous, that fills our souls with thoughts only of you."

He said of the Blessed Mother, "Do you want an advocate near Jesus? Then turn to Mary. I say unhesitatingly, Mary will be heard because of the consideration due her. The Son will listen to his Mother. And so this is the sinner's ladder. On this I found my hope."

He declared that a prelate who is proud of his high office is "no more worthy of respect than a long-tailed monkey perched on top of a tree".

Bernard was outspoken. He was often called upon to be a peacemaker because everyone knew he was fair and afraid of no man. He even told the pope of his wrongs when he did not measure up to his commitment. Because he had to journey often he said, I feel "like a featherless little bird, always exiled from his nest".

St. Bonaventure
April 7

St. Bonaventure, said Alexander of Hales, "was great in learning, but no less great in humility and holiness". Bonaventure said, "What made me love the life of blessed Francis so much was the fact that it resembled the beginning and growth of the early Church. In this way God shows that it was not founded by the prudence of men but by Christ." And so he became a Franciscan, and in time the superior of all the Franciscans.

Bonaventure wrote, "To grow in the things of the spirit, love must go hand in hand with learning. At a certain point one must leave study behind while the heart runs ahead with joy to the gift that is God himself. Speculation is not sufficient without devotion. To know Christ is to live."

Bonaventure encouraged students to be devoted to the Blessed Mother, so that "studying, praying, sleeping, you have her before your eyes, and she will in turn have her eyes of mercy on you."

It is said that when St. Thomas Aquinas, the learned Dominican, was visiting him, Thomas found Bonaventure writing a spiritual treatise. Thomas asked, "Where do you get your inspiration?" Bonaventure did not say a word but with his pen pointed to the crucifix and then finished his thought.

Bonaventure said, "There is no other path in the spiritual life but through a burning love of Christ crucified. God is close to every soul. All one need do is to reach out in prayer and Jesus touches you. Christ is the tree of life, and if we but partake of this tree Christ gives life to the soul."

Bonaventure was so humble he was like a little boy. He was devoted to the Baby Jesus. He praised the Child in Mary's arms. This great scholar and mystic bowed low before the Babe of Bethlehem.

The story is told that when they brought him the cardinal's red hat, he was doing the dishes in the kitchen garden. He motioned with his elbow that they should hang it on the nearby cherry tree and went back to washing dishes.

St. Francis de Sales   *April 8*

A famous spiritual writer, St. Francis de Sales wrote that God wishes us to be peaceful and calm and proceed faithfully along the road marked out for us by Jesus. We are to repose in the fatherly care of God with a restful heart.

Keep your soul calm, he said, like a peaceful lake, so that it reflects Christ. The soul, unstirred and untroubled, even amid troubles, with faith in God, makes us like our Lord. Let the winds of superfluous cares and uneven temper pass over us. For the tempest of passions keeps us unable to reflect Christ's image and our soul is not fit to serve him.

We must leave our cares to the mercy of Divine Providence, and work cheerfully without complaining, giving each day to the Lord. He will teach us and direct us.

St. Joseph did not question or debate about what he was told to do. His only concern was to do the task. Let us be like Joseph. Joseph did not delay; he knew God sends us forth. Joseph never made excuses; he knew that God will preserve us and help us advance along the way, the bishop said.

Let us cease talking so much that we have no time to pray. Be cheerful and courteous to one another. Francis de Sales quoted St. Bernard, who said, "The measure of loving God is to love him without measure." In our love for him there should be no limits. We should allow our love to branch and spread out as far as possible. That which is said of our love for God should also apply to our love for our neighbor, provided the love of God remains foremost.

He urged affability. It spreads a certain agreeableness in talking with others. Cheerfulness renders a person gracious and generous. And people are attracted to us, and we can attract them to Jesus.

St. Catherine Labouré   *April 9*

St. Catherine Labouré gave us the Miraculous Medal. She was practically the last person in the world anyone would think of in this regard. She was the kitchen Sister in a convent in Paris of the Sisters of Charity of St. Vincent de Paul. She did the laundry, washed the dishes and fed the chickens, and yet the Blessed Mother appeared to her. Not to the cardinal or the king or the Mother Superior, but to Catherine.

She had a dream and in it a priest told her that one day she would follow him. She had no idea who he was. She wanted to be a Sister but her father was set against it. They lived in a little village in France, and so her father sent her to Paris to visit her brother and his wife to get this silly notion out of her head. But the brother lived near a convent and one day Catherine visited there. When she was shown into the parlor, there on the wall was a picture of a priest, the very priest she had seen in her dream. She asked who it was. The nun said it was the founder of their Sisters, St. Vincent de Paul.

Catherine wrote her father again, asking if she could join this convent. Miraculously, he gave her permission.

One night an angel appeared to her in her room and took her to the chapel. The Blessed Mother was waiting there for her. Mary appeared to her more than once. One time the Virgin Mary told her she must see to it that a medal be made of her the way she appeared in the vision.

Catherine told her confessor. She asked many times. He would do nothing. Mary asked the Sister again; Catherine said her confessor would do nothing. But the next time she told him, he gave in. She drew the picture and gave it to him. He took it to the Archbishop, certain that he would laugh at him. To his surprise the prelate told him to have the medal made and that he wanted one of the first of them. It did so much good for so many people in Paris and France and around the world that it came to be known as the Miraculous Medal.

Few knew of Catherine Labouré's involvement until near the end of her life.

St. Catherine Labouré   *April 10*

One of St. Catherine Labouré's favorite ways of praying was to kneel in the chapel and say, "Lord, here I am. Give what you will."

In her first appearance to Catherine, Mary told her that she should open her heart to her Son in the Blessed Sacrament, and there at the altar she would receive all the consolation she would need. Then the Blessed Mother told her that she was to be entrusted with a special mission. She would be opposed; she would suffer because of it, but she would be given the graces she needed and her mission was for the glory of God.

The Blessed Virgin said, "Come to the foot of the altar. Here graces will be poured out on all who ask for them, rich or poor." Mary predicted that in the coming conflict in France religion would suffer. "The Cross will be despised and trodden under foot. The streets will run with blood; there will be sorrow everywhere. People must pray." All the things that Mary predicted soon happened during the horrifying French Revolution.

In another vision Mary said that God had entrusted her with many graces to give to people. They must pray. "Graces will be bestowed abundantly upon those who have confidence."

When Catherine first told her confessor that the Blessed Mother wanted a medal made, he scolded her and said her so-called visions were mere illusions. Yet later he wondered how this simple country girl could possibly make up all these things. She asked several more times and he was always cold and indifferent. The Blessed Mother told Sister Catherine she should keep trying. After a time, however, though it was very embarrassing for Catherine to continue asking, the confessor gave in. He told her to write down everything. Catherine seemed to be writing so much that another nun inquired what she was doing. She replied with a smile that lit up her blue eyes, "I keep busy writing about all the exciting things that happen around here."

Eventually the medal was made and its popularity was instantaneous.

St. Catherine Labouré   *April 11*

The devotion of the Miraculous Medal spread throughout Paris and the rest of France and Europe, and then it spread to the New World. In Italy the king gave silver medals to each member of his family. The Holy Father in Rome placed it at the foot of his crucifix. St. Catherine Labouré rejoiced.

She continued to work at her humble tasks in the convent. Sometimes she worked in the nearby hospital, busy every day sorting and folding sheets and towels in the linen room and scrubbing pots and pans in the kitchen. When she had some spare time, she helped clean and prepare the food. They had many poor people to feed. She also visited patients, praying with them and cheering them.

Although there was a rumor that spread about that a Sister at the convent had had the visions for the Miraculous Medal, there were many Sisters, and the last one anyone would suspect was Catherine.

All her days she remained a faithful, obedient Daughter of Charity of St. Vincent de Paul. She practiced beautifully what the Mother Superior told the new Sisters when they entered, "A Daughter of Charity should be a resting place where all may come to lay down her burdens. Let us have the heart of a child of God and of a mother for our neighbors."

Catherine was humble. It is noticed that the Blessed Mother always appeared to the humble—to children or to those with childlike hearts. Jesus could not preach to the proud Pharisees for they did not listen. They were too self-centered to hear his beautiful message. The Pharisees, pompous and egotistical, were not invited to honor the Christ child in the cave at Bethlehem, for they would never have come. The invitation went out to the simple, pious shepherds on the hillside. And Mary also gave her message of love to the humble as well, for she knew they would listen.

Thus, she gave the Miraculous Medal to Catherine. Toward the end of Catherine's life this saintly soul felt she must tell her superior of her visions before she died. She did so and the astonished Superior said if she had known that, she would have treated her better.

St. Teresa of Avila   *April 12*

St. Teresa of Avila, mystic and Carmelite, has been declared a Doctor of the Church because her thoughts were so profound. Despite her mysticism she was a very practical Spanish woman.

Her thoughts were beautiful because she was so close to Christ. She said the true follower of Christ must be generous in soul. Because of Christ, his disciples must love others more than most people do; their love is more true, more ardent, more helpful.

Unless the soul is virtuous and loves Jesus ardently, one cannot truly help others in the best way, assisting them in saving their souls. The soul that prays is given true wisdom by God. Otherwise, a person does not really know what to do for others. And, in fact, he might do something harmful in the long run. Only a soul rich in goodness can show Christ to others and introduce him to them. And without this, little is done for souls. Jesus is the captain of love, our highest good, she wrote. Sinful souls must come to know this.

How many prayers and penances are needed to gain a great love for Jesus. And even more are needed so that others will love him. Most of all Jesus desires to save souls, and so must we. "This love for the other is wholly without self-interest", Teresa wrote. "It has only one desire; to see that the other soul it loves is laden with heavenly riches." Here is true friendship. This is truly being Christlike, for Christ on the Cross cried that he thirsted, and his thirst was for souls. More than anything our prayers and penance help other souls please Jesus. "This, in short, is love like to that which Christ bore us by dying for us", she said.

In helping others, we are distressed by their difficulties, but often we see that trials cause an increase in virtue, so this is a reason for rejoicing.

St. Teresa of Avila   *April 13*

"We cannot imagine the love Jesus, the Good Lover, bears for us", said St. Teresa of Avila. "And we know he wants us very much to pray for others. We do as St. Monica, who prayed for her son St. Augustine for many, many years and then at last gained the graces for his conversion." Happy the soul who has friends to pray for him, she said. "Indeed, I would far rather have this than be loved by all the kings and lords on earth."

To be with God's friends is a good way to keep close to him. You will always benefit greatly from being with them, Teresa wrote. Reading the lives of the saints is very helpful also. "After God himself, it is due to such persons that I am not involved in evil", she observed. And she begged her readers to read the lives of the saints.

Love for others will not be perfect at first, but Jesus will gradually perfect it. If God has given us greater spiritual strength than others, let us share it, helping others in their trials. And to stay strong "we must continually watch and pray." Jesus said, "Watch and pray that you enter not into temptation."

St. Teresa wrote, "Try to be happy with others." This is a great blessing for you and for them.

Have compassion for others in their needs. "This is love: to bear with the faults of others." This shows greater friendship than all our endearing words. Besides, others put up with our many faults without complaint.

God helps us to love one another. "What could be easier for God, when he made us out of nothing", she wrote, perhaps with a smile.

We should realize how small created things are compared to the Creator. And when we are humble, virtue grows.

God generously and graciously gives us graces. He is the source of all our blessings. Our Lord defends us. Let us offer our thanks to him.

St. Cyprian   *April 14*

St. Cyprian was an early Christian, the Bishop of Carthage, in North Africa. He was martyred for the Faith. He wrote, "Our Lord solemnly warns us: You are the salt of the earth, and bids us in our love of good to be not only simple but prudent as well. Accordingly what else ought we to do but be on guard and watch vigilantly, in order to know the snares of our crafty foe and to avoid them? Otherwise, after putting on Christ who is the Wisdom of God the Father, we may be found to have failed in wisdom for the care of souls."

He points out that it is not persecution alone that we should fear for then the Enemy shows his true colors. There is more need for fear when the Enemy creeps up on us secretly and tempts us, like a serpent, beguiling us little by little to turn away from Christ. "Such is ever his craft: lurking in the dark, he ensnares men by trickery." In this disguise Satan tried to tempt our Lord himself, telling him of all the good things that he would do for him. The devil constantly seeks to deceive us. We must then constantly pray and do penance, as Jesus said. Let us follow in the steps of Christ to victory, for he beat back Satan. Let us observe the Commandments and gain strength from prayer. Jesus said, "If you will attain to life, keep the Commandments. . . . If you do what I command you, I call you no longer servants but friends."

Those who pray can be strong and firm in time of temptation. They are close to Christ and he protects them.

How can a person say that he believes in Christ if he does not do what Christ commands him? How can a person who, when under command, will not keep faith, hope to receive the reward of faith?

St. Vincent de Paul   *April 15*

St. Vincent de Paul wrote, "I recommend to your prayers our Little Company and the most frail and miserable of all, myself."

To the Mother Superior of a convent he wrote, "Blessed be the work of your hands. It has pleased God to grant you grace for it. I hope, dear Mother, that you will obtain some graces for us so that we may serve him according his plan. O dear Mother, how many precious, beautiful stones you are adding to the crown our Lord is continually fashioning for you. Their number will certainly be as great as the souls who will be saved by this means. But so that the sins and wretchedness of this poor, worthless Little Company, and especially my own, may not hinder our Lord's work, I entreat you, dear Mother, to ask him either to take us out of his world or to make us such that we may render him the services his Divine Goodness expects of us. I am not going to thank you for all this; God alone is worthy of doing so."

St. Vincent told his Little Company to teach the faith gently and humbly and in a simple language, showing that what they say comes from deep compassion and love and patience. If so, God will bless their work abundantly. To God be the glory.

He prayed that material matters would not distract them from the spiritual. If one continually gives his full attention to the things of the world, he neglects the spiritual, which is all-important.

God knows, he said, that I have a great desire to render you an agreeable service. May he be pleased to make me worthy of doing so.

He wrote this in regard to foolish rumors about the work of his priests: "What shall we do about it? We must put up with such rumors patiently. Our Lord will bring about their disappearance since they have no foundation."

St. Catherine of Siena   *April 16*

When St. Catherine of Siena was born, she was so small and frail that her chances of survival seemed impossible. Yet she grew up to be one of the most influential persons in Europe.

As a young woman she was attractive, with long and beautiful hair. Her family wanted her to marry, but she wanted to dedicate her life to God. Catherine loved to work in the garden where she grew roses, lilies, violets and vegetables. Very often she sang hymns as she worked. When her little nieces and nephews came, she would play with them in the garden. She also helped at Mater Misericordiae Hospital. And people, knowing how much she prayed, came to talk to her about their problems. Despite her youth, they asked her advice.

When a woman became jealous of Catherine and spoke viciously about her, she only prayed for the woman. However, Catherine was summoned by the superior of her religious society to answer these charges. It is one of the tragedies of saints that they are like eagles in a hen house. The main charge of the hypocritical woman was that Catherine was a hypocrite. Catherine defended herself admirably; everyone who heard her admired her. Far from being an unbalanced, hysterical, self-willed woman, as charged, they found her most humble and full of common sense. Cleared of the foolish charges, she went back to helping the poor patients in the hospital, continuing her work of comforting the sick.

When Catherine was troubled she always prayed. Sometimes

Christ came to her. On one occasion she said to Jesus, "Where were you, while my soul was being sorely tormented?" He replied, "I was in your heart, Catherine, for I will never leave anyone who does not first leave me."

St. Gertrude   *April 17*

Even when St. Gertrude did not receive a reply to her prayers, she felt consoled. When people sought spiritual advice of her, she at once felt her soul filled with the necessary light and was inspired about what to say, with assurance and certainty, as if she had known it all her life.

St. Gertrude governed her monastery for over forty years. All recognized her devotion and wisdom. She was a great help to the many who came to her to solve their problems. She was ever sweet and prudent, charitable and loving. It was said, "Like a mystic rose she emitted a sweet odor of sanctity."

Soon after becoming Abbess she was attacked with a serious illness. She accepted this as coming from the hand of God. The Sisters were exceedingly sad but she looked upon it as a favor. She comforted the apprehensive nuns, and, in time, God delivered her from her sickness. Jesus told her that by her illness he purified her soul.

Gertrude praised God, Uncreated Wisdom, Omnipotent Power, for his amazing charity and infinite mercy. "O most sweet God of my life and only love of my soul, lead me through the desert."

When Jesus appeared to her he "surpassed in beauty the children of men", she said. He was young and amiable and his words were full of tenderness and sweetness. Her first vision came when she was twenty-six, on the Vigil of the Feast of the Purification. Jesus said, "Your salvation is at hand. Why are you consumed with grief?" She had been sad because she felt her prayers were so tepid. Jesus said, "I will save you, I will deliver you; fear not." And he placed his hand in hers.

St. Thomas Aquinas   *April 18*

The great St. Thomas Aquinas said of the Blessed Mother that she would not have been worthy to be the Mother of God if she had ever been a sinner, so she was without sin. Others have been sanctified by the Lord but Mary's purity of soul was the greatest after Christ.

Thomas wrote, "Since Mary was closest to Christ, she rightly received from him fullness of grace; grace in such abundance as to bring her closest in grace to its Author. She gave birth to him who, full of every grace, brought graces to all men." We should pray to the Blessed Mother frequently.

Thomas said that the baptism of John the Baptist prefigured the baptism of Christ that admits people to the Kingdom of God. Christ's Passion and death opened heaven. By baptism we are born again as God's adopted children.

Christ preached to the people, St. Thomas wrote, telling them the good news. He came to save sinners. And by the victory of the Cross Christ would win our salvation.

The Pharisees maliciously opposed Christ out of envy. Undeterred Jesus continued to preach the truth, and he would have done so even if no one had listened to him. Christ taught the people that they must love God in their neighbor. And he so impressed many of them, he imprinted his truths in their hearts.

In the end he gave his life for the people, the sinless one a victim for sinners. He accepted his cruel death willingly. He suffered for the sake of all sinners. He endured the agony to set men free, so great was his mercy. This showed us how much God loves us. "You were bought at a great price", St. Paul said. Man had been enslaved by sin. Now he was set free.

St. Catherine of Siena   *April 19*

A plague struck Siena and St. Catherine worked tirelessly to care for the suffering. More than a third of the population perished. It was a tremendous tragedy. Work at the hospital was overwhelming.

Nor was her family spared. Her sister died and then a brother and another brother and numerous other relatives. Catherine was crushed, but kept on working day and night. And when the horrible ordeal was over, she herself collapsed and was gravely ill for several weeks.

Catherine never wasted her time. When ill she wrote frequently to public officials reminding them of their Christian duties.

Then Catherine was asked by Pope Gregory XI to go as his legate to Florence and be a peacemaker. She was successful. And when Florence sent a delegation to Avignon in France where the Pope was in exile, she was asked to be a member of the mission.

In Avignon at the papal palace this slight woman rose to face the Pope. She was dressed in her Third Order Dominican habit. With complete composure she spoke and the Pope listened. She said the "stench of sin" in Avignon smelled all the way to Siena. She condemned the sinful clergy, not a few of whom served at the papal court. She was fearless and Pope Gregory was impressed.

The Pope called her several times to visit him privately. She never failed to urge him to return to Rome where he belonged. As a cardinal he had resolved that this was the very thing that he would do if elected pope. Catherine reminded him of this resolution. He was amazed, for he had never spoken of this promise to anyone. She awakened his conscience. Yet he procrastinated, for all his advisers told him the people of Rome were too dangerous for him to return. The French cardinals did all in their power to get him to stay in France and to get rid of this meddlesome woman. But she persisted.

St. Catherine of Siena   *April 20*

Finally with strong and continual encouragement from St. Catherine, Pope Gregory said he would return to Rome. It was a most courageous act, and he was not strong, but he turned his back on his learned advisers and followed the advice of this "ignorant nun".

The Pope started for Rome by sea. Catherine left to go back home by land. She got as far as Genoa on her journey. There she lingered, she knew not why. Late one night, there was a knock at the door of the place where she was staying. It alarmed her. She was further disturbed when the night attendant knocked on her room's door and said that a priest was below who said he had known her in Avignon and must speak to her. The attendant had tried to close the door, but the priest exclaimed, "My need is great. Admit me in the name of Jesus Christ."

Catherine dressed and went down to the parlor. She fell to her knees. This man in the simple black cassock was the Pope. He had come out of desperation. A sudden storm on the sea forced their ship into the harbor here. Everything was going wrong for his return to Rome. Every day he had to argue with those who were travelling with him. All told him to return to France; Rome would be unsafe. They said the city was in a state of revolt and he would be taken prisoner there and worse. He was almost ready to agree with them. Amid all his worries and indecision that very night he had been informed that Catherine was in the city. And so he had come to her.

The Pope said he would do whatever she said. She said he must go on. He left inspired, determined that despite all he would go on to the Eternal City, for he was the Bishop of Rome.

Rome indeed was in a foul mood. For the Pope to remain in Rome took courage. Yet he stayed.

St. Cyprian   *April 21*

St. Cyprian warned his people of the wiles of the devil. We must be on our guard, he said; we must not only be beware of all that is obvious and unmistakably wrong but also of all that is cunning and deceitful. One of the Enemy's deceits is to mislead unwary Christians. "He invented heresies and schisms so as to undermine the Faith, to corrupt the truth, to sunder our unity", he said. "He leads people on a new road of illusion. He snatches away people from within the Church herself. He plunges them into darkness.

They still call themselves Christians even after abandoning the Gospel of Christ and the observance of his law."

The Enemy cajoles and deceives people, he said. They now call the day night and damnation salvation and teach recklessness under the pretext of hope. Disbelief is now belief; the Antichrist goes under the name of Christ. By lies that have all the appearance of truth, they undermine the truth with trickery.

St. Cyprian continued, saying that in prayer we learn the truth. The truth is plain, simple and convincing. The Church teaches us the way to heaven. The Lord said to Peter, "I say to thee, that thou art Peter [rock] and upon this rock I will build my Church, and the gates of hell shall not overcome it. I will give to thee the keys of the kingdom of heaven, and what thou shalt bind upon earth shall be bound also in heaven, and whatsoever thou shalt loose on earth shall be loosed in heaven."

This early Bishop reminded people that Jesus said to Peter after the Resurrection: "Feed my sheep." It is on him that Christ builds his Church, and to him he entrusts the feeding of the sheep.

St. Philip Neri   *April 22*

St. Philip Neri was in Rome, and to attract the young to Christ he developed new devotions, new ways to get them to say old prayers and sing old hymns. This happened after the reformation and at that time anyone saying anything new was suspect. His devotions caused consternation, and he was investigated by the Cardinal Vicar. He was suspended for two weeks. But instead of shouting out against this injustice, he humbly accepted it and spent the time in prayer. Philip, who had heard so many, many confessions, was now told not to do so. Nor could he lead the youth in going to visit churches and having a picnic along the way. The whole action was foolish, but the saint, of course, obeyed.

The sour and suspicious prelate in his investigation could not find that Philip's devotions were superstitious and so his suspension was lifted. Actually, the investigation found that the preaching at Philip's church, the Oratory, was full of fervor and soundness. Fortunately, the gatherings now went on, with even greater crowds.

In visiting churches to pray, the group would sing hymns on the way, or they would engage in animated discussions. This displeased some puritanical people. Religion wasn't supposed to be fun; it seemed to want to make you miserable, they thought. But Philip had other ideas. The youth would play games along the way and tell jokes. The long-faced, sour-looking were shocked. They could not get it into their small minds and hard hearts that religion was healthy and wholesome for souls.

In the beginning, sometimes the gatherings in Philip's room disturbed the other Fathers in the house. Philip said to the youth, "Pay no attention to what they are saying, go on with your play." He told one visitor, "They may chop wood on my back, so long as they commit no sin." He knew that keeping the young busy kept them out of trouble.

St. Thomas More   April 23

St. Thomas More prayed, "Give me, Lord, a warmth and delight and eagerness in thinking of you. Give me the grace to long for your holy sacraments, and especially to rejoice in the presence of your very blessed Body, sweet Saviour Christ, in the Holy Sacrament of the altar, and duly to thank you for your gracious presence in the tabernacle.

"At Holy Mass, the high memorial of your dying, Lord, may I with tender compassion remember your most bitter Passion. Make us all, good Jesus, every day lively members, sweet Saviour Christ, of your holy, mystical body, the Catholic Church."

Thomas said, "We are so wont to set so much by our body which we see and feel, and in the feeding and fostering thereof, we set our delight and our wealth upon it; and also so little and so seldom we think of our soul, because we cannot see that but by spiritual understanding, and most especially by the eyes of faith; the loss of our body we take for a sorer thing and for a greater tribulation than we do for the loss of our soul." Thomas More attributed this to our lack of faith because we seem to have so little time for prayer.

He said that we sometimes feel the withdrawal of God's hand with his high goodness and unsearchable wisdom. We feel this in particular because we are not wise and turn away from him.

We are often too timid to do many good deeds, which, if a person put his trust in God's help, he would do and could do. The devil makes us cowards and so we leave good things undone, when God offers us opportunities and occasions. Such people have the need "to lift up their hearts and call upon God, and by the counsel of spiritual individuals cast away the cowardice of their own conduct, and look in the Gospel upon him who laid up his talent and left it unoccupied, and therefore utterly lost it, with a great reproach".

St. Catherine of Siena *April 24*

In Rome amid all the turmoil of the city, the Pope summoned St. Catherine to come to him. He had followed her strong advice to return to Rome, but here the Church was besieged by schism and hostile soldiers kept him from the Vatican.

Catherine at the time was in Florence where another civil war was going on. The rebels were burning down many houses. When they reached the house where she was, she went out to meet them, and falling to her knees said, "I am Catherine—if you have been appointed to kill me, do so."

The leader of the wild mob had his great sword out and lifted it high in the air—but then lowered it and turned and left her, leaving the saint kneeling in prayer. And in time she was able to bring peace to the city.

Then, returning to Rome, she addressed the Pope and his frightened cardinals. She spoke serenely of the never-failing providence of God. When she finished, the Pope explained, "This little woman puts us all to shame by her calmness and strength. In the face of these, how can the Vicar of Christ show fear and fail his Church, even if the whole world seems against him?"

The Pope continued to live in Rome even though he was in a state of siege. Several cardinals deserted him but his perseverance paid off. The following spring he was able to take up residence at the Vatican. He went in procession there, barefooted at the urging of Catherine. An enormous crowd joyfully welcomed him back.

Catherine became very ill. It was soon apparent that she would never leave Rome. She said, "Beloved, you call me and I come. . . . Father, into your hands I commit my spirit." St. Catherine made the Sign of the Cross and died. After her death her face was so radiant that those who were standing nearby said she looked like an angel.

St. Francis of Assisi   *April 25*

In the family of the Little Brothers of St. Francis of Assisi there was one of noble birth and delicate habits. He entered the community with great fervor but then came to hate this life and the poor, course habit that he wore. He determined to leave. Now it was his custom that when he passed before the altar of the Blessed Sacrament he would kneel down with great respect, and, covering his head with his hood and crossing his arms on his chest, he would prostrate himself.

It happened that on the night he decided to leave he passed the Blessed Sacrament and did as was his custom. And he was ravished in spirit and had a vision. He saw a great multitude of saints in a long procession. Their faces shown like the sun and they sang beautifully a great celestial hymn. The youth was struck with wonder. He was amazed and speechless. At the end of the procession he asked who these people were. They answered, "Know, my son, we are Little Brothers who are in paradise." The youth saw now how their poor, coarse habits were shining with splendor. From this vision he gained new strength and put away the notion of leaving. Ever after he loved the poor Franciscan habit. He at the end of his life was known for his great sanctity.

In prayer one day St. Francis saw, by the revelation of God, that a Little Brother, being offended by another, was thinking in his heart how he could do him harm. An ever vigilant shepherd watching over his flock, Francis called the Brother and told him what he had seen. The Brother was much alarmed that Francis was able to see his secret thoughts and humbly asked pardon. Francis then beheld the devil fleeing from the Brother's heart, and he thanked God.

St. Clare of Assisi   *April 26*

St. Clare of Assisi was inspired by St. Francis to give up the wealth and comfort of her home and give herself to God as a nun. She founded a community of Sisters following the rule of St. Francis.

Clare was a beautiful young woman, but even more beautiful in soul. She heard Francis speak of the only love worth seeking, the love of God, and she secretly left her home and went to talk with him. The family was horrified that she would converse with this vagabond, and especially one so "demented" as to voluntarily give up wealth for poverty.

In a grove near the small church where Francis and his companions prayed, Clare met with him. She was very impressed. She determined despite all obstacles that she would follow him. Later, she ran away from home and became a nun following Francis' rule. Her family was enraged.

Clare knelt before Francis. He cut off her beautiful, long golden hair and received her vows. She put on a veil and a rough, plain habit. Her family was certain she had gone crazy. What was this insanity that infected Assisi? They demanded she leave the convent and come home at once. Her father threatened; her mother pleaded. But Clare had found what she wanted: she was in love with Jesus. She would not budge. And a new order of women religious was born. They gave all their possessions to the poor and devoted their days to prayer. Each day some of the Sisters went out into the streets to beg for bread. And when they returned to the convent, Clare herself removed their sandals and washed their feet and kissed them.

They became a thriving community. Their greatest joy was when Francis came and spoke to them. When Francis was near death and brought down from his mountain retreat to Assisi, the first place he stopped was at Clare's convent. On the mountain a mystical experience had come to him and he had received the stigmata, the wounds of Christ, in his body. His dear Sisters cared for him and listened to his beautiful words.

St. Columban   *April 27*

After the invasion of the barbarians St. Columban had a tremendous influence on the continent of Europe. He was an Irish missionary, and he founded a number of monasteries in France, one which came to be called the nursery of bishops. As a contemporary wrote, he "hurled the fire of Christ everywhere he went". He and his monks brought back the faith and learning to Europe. Everywhere he went he raised the standard of Christian living and fostered scholarship. Pope Pius XI in our century said, "The renaissance of Christian learning in France, Germany and Italy is due to the work and zeal of St. Columban."

In Columban's day Ireland was "at the edge of the world", but the Faith burned brightly there and the zeal of its missionaries was tremendous. From this fire, the torch of faith and learning came back to the continent.

Columban was a handsome, healthy youth with a good mind. His attractive personality and keen intelligence and spirituality made him a well-known preacher of the word of God. In time his longing to be a missionary grew.

Columban and his companions went to France. The noted Church historian Daniel-Rops wrote, "From 511 until 613, the land of the Franks was really nothing more than places where brothers and cousins slaughtered one another." Violence prevailed, and vice, lust, jealousy, war and murder. These wild uncivilized people did respect sanctity, however, and they saw this in Columban and his holy monks.

His sermons and letters were masterful. Columban said, "Understand created things, if you want to know the Creator." About penance he said, "If abstinence is pushed beyond right measure, it becomes a vice, not a virtue."

In Europe Columban established nearly a hundred monasteries and convents.

St. Columban   *April 28*

St. Columban, the great Irish missionary, said, "Let us concern ourselves with heavenly things, not human things, and like pilgrims always sigh for our homeland of heaven. Let us not become entangled with earthly desires, but let our concern be, 'When shall I come and appear before the face of my God?'"

At the first monastery in France his frank speech, not unlike John the Baptist's, disturbed the local monarch. He openly said that the king was living in sin. His honesty cost him his monastery; he was sent into exile. He and his companions went into the wilderness, where they were frequently hungry and always cold. Yet he said, "How wonderful are God's ways, letting us be in want, so that he can show us his love in coming to our aid; allowing us to be tempted so that we will draw closer to him." He said, "The true disciple of Christ crucified should follow him with the cross. That man is blessed who shares in his Passion and shame." He added, "If we suffer with him, we shall also reign with him."

Columban said that the mysteries in religion are not to be argued over. Rather we must dedicate ourselves to live for Christ and in Christ, "for we have been bought at a great price, an immense ransom, when the Lord gave himself for the slave, the King for the servant, God for man."

Columban reminded his monks that human life is fragile, quickly passing, and deceptive. The fleeting nature of earthly things is most evident; life here is ephemeral and superficial. We must seek eternal life. He said, "Let us pray that God will wound our hearts with his love, that the Lord will light the flame of his goodness in us." He said to the monks, "Be strong in trial, useless at quarreling, slow to lose your temper, quick to learn; slow to speak, quick to listen. Be gentle to the weak and poor, always generous; stay unmoved in turmoil, bold in the cause of truth, joyful always. Be grateful, unweary in kindness, and forgetful of past injuries. Be moderate in all things, do not envy, and be ever faithful in prayer."

St. Dominic   *April 29*

St. Dominic was trying to convert the heretics in southern France. He tried to get them to return to the Faith, but he failed. Then one day the Blessed Mother appeared to him. He said, "I have failed in the work your Son has given to me." He was very discouraged. It was then that, according to pious legend, she gave him the Rosary. After that, things began to turn around.

Others joined him, it was the start of the Dominican order, called officially the Order of Preachers. They started a house of prayer. In each Brother's room he put a crucifix and a statue of the Blessed Mother "to remind you that you belong to her in a special way. Turn to her in every need. She will never fail you."

His Brothers wore a black and white habit. He exorted them, "Serve the Lord with gladness." When they went out to preach to heretics he said, "Go without fear. Pray constantly. Never forget that you belong to our Lady. Pray that you will always remain pure in heart and humble. Live always in poverty."

At this time the Pope offered to make him a bishop but he refused.

Dominic knew that we must follow Jesus. Even when Jesus was weary of limb, he had time for sinners. His love was ever searching for souls. He pursued sinners constantly as must we who love him.

On the Cross, Jesus' blood, his lips, his throat were parched and he suffered intensely, but Jesus refused the wine. He showed that his great and burning thirst was for souls. He endured all the intolerable pain and suffering on the Cross to gain graces for souls. Christ will give us the victory, if we but follow him.

When Dominic was dying, the brothers around his bed sang, "Hail, Holy Queen", the hymn he dearly loved, and which he frequently sang as he walked along the lonely, dusty roads preaching to the heretics in France.

At his death he was so poor that clothes had to be borrowed for him to be buried in.

St. Bonaventure   *April 30*

St. Bonaventure tells us to picture Christ dying on the Cross. Draw near to Jesus wounded for you, he said. "Burn with love for Christ crucified, fastened to the Cross, bleeding and suffering so. Christ endured most bitter pain for you. Condemned to death like a murderer, he was judged to be unfit to live on the earth and was hanged between heaven and earth. The world rejected the Lord of the world. He was ridiculed, insulted, defiled and shamefully and outrageously treated. He died on the vile hill of Calvary.

"The wicked soldiers made game and mockery of our dear Jesus. They forced the Cross upon his bleeding shoulders. He was scourged until his back was nearly broken. All this for a crime he never committed."

Bonaventure said that Jesus chose a death more humiliating and agonizing than any other. Harassed, weary, in unbearable pain he hung for three terrible hours in anguish and torture. He suffered in every part of his body. "O all you who pass by the way, look and see if there is any sorrow like unto my sorrow." Grief overwhelmed his soul and his body was bathed in blood. Rivers of blood flowed down his body.

St. Bonaventure prayed, "O good Jesus, O sweetest Jesus, it was all simply to show us how much you love us. You spent yourself on our behalf. The grief, the tears, the spittle, the sneers, the cruelty and insults, the blows, the nails, the blood, all you suffered for us. And I weep."

The saint said that Christ suffered, not for his sins, for he was sinless, "but for mine; to save a slave he became a slave. Out of his kindness of his heart, despite our unworthiness he died."

When you are sad, look at the crucifix and see how much you are loved. When you enumerate your hardships, Bonaventure said, think of Christ on the Cross.

Mary, Mother of God   *May 1*

May is the month of Mary, our Mother. God has been so gracious to us. Not only has he given us mothers on this earth to care for us, but he has generously given us a wonderful mother in heaven, his Mother. Christ on the Cross, even though in terrible agony, thought of us. The one who had been most wonderful to him was Mary, and so he shared her with us so she could help us. His Mother is our Mother. Can we ever thank him enough?

Mary was the light of his life. She loved with deepest love the Baby born to her in Bethlehem. She endured any sacrifice to show her love for him. Joseph was upset in the beginning because she was with child. His worry was her worry, and she perhaps wondered why God did not tell him—finally, he did. She would have loved to have her child at home among relatives and friends. It was not to be. Though with child, she had to make the long and arduous journey to Bethlehem. Mary and Joseph could not find a room so Jesus was born in a stable. And yet she was so joyful to have him in her arms. She cared about nothing, the cold, the dark, the cave, only this Child.

For his safety she and Joseph fled into Egypt. Then there was the great trial when the Boy was lost in the temple. Mary's love is greater than that of any other creature.

This is the love that she brings to us, for we too are her children. Let us thank her every day for her love to her Son and her love for us. Let us pray to our heavenly Mother for help. Shouldn't mothers always be there when you call to them? Shouldn't they always help when you ask them? All we need do is pray to our Blessed Mother. She will come to our assistance. Why? Because she *is* our Mother.

Mary, the Mother of God   *May 2*

The Second Vatican Council saw Mary as "the sign of sure hope and solace for God's people in pilgrimage". How helpless we are, how hopeless when alone. Mary, our heavenly Mother, comes to our assistance. We are her children. She gives us warmth and comfort and strength.

We in life are a people on pilgrimage making our way through the dust and toil of the world to eternal happiness in the life to come. By her obedience to God, she gave us hope by bringing the Savior into the world. What darkness of heart life would be without Jesus. And by her *fiat* Mary made possible his coming to us. We pray to her as a virgin, a mother, a queen. We pray to her in sorrow and in joy.

The Fathers at the Council thought of devoting a separate document to the Blessed Mother, but then decided to give over the final chapter in the Constitution on the Church to her, showing that she is a vital part in the work of the Church. As the Council says of her, "Taught by the Holy Spirit, the Catholic Church honors her with filial affection and piety as a most beloved mother." The document states further, "The union of the Mother with the Son in the work of salvation was manifested from the time of Christ's virginal conception up to his death." It "exhorts theologians and preachers of the divine word that in treating of the unique dignity of the Mother of God, they carefully and equally avoid the falsity of exaggeration on the one hand, and the excess of narrow-mindedness on the other."

The Council document ends with the prayer, "that she who aided the beginnings of the Church by her prayers, may now, exalted as she is in heaven above all the saints and angels, intercede with her Son in the fellowship of all the saints". Her intercession is implored by her loving children everywhere.

Mary, the Mother of God

We never think of Mary in isolation but always close to her Son. He had done everything for her and she was grateful with all her heart. She said, "My soul magnifies the Lord . . . for he who is mighty has done great things for me." She knows her smallness. God took her and clothed her with immaculate grace and gave her a share in his glory. And then he brought her to the splendor of Paradise. St. John in the Book of Revelation writes, "A great sign appeared in Heaven; a woman clothed with the sun and the moon under her feet, and on her head a crown of twelve stars." There she is, Queen of Heaven, amid the saints and angels, close to her Son, interceding for us and winning graces for her children.

The Fathers of the Second Vatican Council remind us that Mary is vital in winning over many souls to the love of God. She gave us the One who brought us out of darkness into the light.

Mary is foreshadowed in the very beginning of the Bible. In Genesis, after the fall, God tells Satan, "I will put enmity between you and the woman, and between your seed and her seed; he shall bruise your head, and you shall bruise his heel." God is telling us that mankind will eventually gain the victory over the powers of evil. This victory was won by the Messiah who is the seed of the woman, of Mary his mother.

The Second Vatican Council states: "In the public life of Jesus, Mary made significant appearances. This was so even at the very beginning, when she was moved by pity at the marriage feast of Cana, and her intercession brought about the beginning of miracles by Jesus the Messiah."

Mary, our Mother, wishes us with all her heart to turn to her Son. He will show us the way to live and to die. He said, "I am the Way." He will guide us home to heaven.

St. Thérèse of Lisieux

The Little Flower, St. Thérèse, wrote, "As long as you will it, my Beloved, I am ready to remain without any power to fly, as long as I may keep my eyes fixed on you, fascinated by your gracious regard, the prey of your love."

She said she wished she could explain to all souls conscious of their littleness how much Jesus loves them and will help them. He gives everyone great graces, if they but trust him. She implored infinite mercy to teach others of his love, as he taught her. "I implore you to look down in mercy on a whole multitude of souls that share my littleness. The little are worthy of your love."

She told of her gratitude to God for the many graces he gave to her, a "little flower" in his garden.

She was grateful too for her superiors for their firm, motherly discipline, which made her grow in soul. She was glad they had not pampered or spoiled her. "I thank God from the bottom of my heart for you not having treated me too gently", she said to the prioress. She was well aware that one treated too well can easily be spoiled. She continued, "Jesus knew well enough that the little flower he had planted was in need of watering; only the waters of humbling could revive it—it was too weak a plant to take root without being helped in this. And it was through you, Mother, that this blessing was bestowed."

St. Thérèse said that Jesus used others to help her grow in soul. He knew his little flower needed sunshine, so she got "nothing but smiles from him". The gentle sunshine made the flower grow well, instead of withering up. But at the bottom of the cup there were still drops of that precious dew of hardship to remind her how insignificant and how frail a thing she was.

St. Bernard of Clairvaux   *May 5*

St. Bernard of Clairvaux, the outstanding reformer of the Middle Ages, had such a charm and personality that it was said it was sufficient to see him to want to follow him. He had lost his mother as a youth and so turned to the Blessed Mother to replace her in his life. He developed a beautiful devotion to Mary. Of her he said in prayer (the Memorare), "Remember, O most gracious Virgin Mary, that never was it known that anyone who fled to thy protection . . . was left unaided." He confided in the Blessed Mother; she was his advocate, his beloved. He wished to become a loving singer of praise to Mary.

After he became fully dedicated to Jesus he knew that "to praise Mary is to praise her Son". As a young monk he rejoiced in the favors he received, but at the same time was overcome by humiliation because he made so little progress in soul. He delighted in the saints but was far off from them. He looked to them with eagerness but was deeply grieved that he was unworthy. He was ashamed that he fell so far short of what he wished to be.

But as time went on he grew in grace. He wrote, "Since, in loving God, we love the Infinite and the Eternal, what bounds, then, I ask you, can we set on our love?" He said, "My God, my love, how you love me! How you love me!" He wrote, "It is not surprising that I who am but a leaf in the wind, a piece of straw, should be myself in the hands of God." The love of God gave him, he said, great devotion for the Son of Man. "He who is filled with the love of God is moved by every aspect of the Word made flesh."

St. Francis Xavier   *May 6*

St. Francis Xavier was an amazing man, one of the most generous individuals who ever lived. He brought the Faith to thousands in Asia. He gave himself heart and soul to save souls. He thought that he was a failure and many around him thought the same, but he is now the patron saint of missionaries.

This great missionary as a youth loved learning and at eighteen went from his native Spain to the great University of Paris to study philosophy. After graduation he taught this subject brilliantly at the university. Being a missionary to Asia was the furthest thing from his mind. His lectures on Aristotle were highly praised. He was destined for a high academic career as a priest—until he met St. Ignatius Loyola.

At first Francis Xavier disliked Ignatius; later he was puzzled by him. The last thing he would have thought of would be to join Ignatius and his little band of followers. He looked down on Ignatius, a grave, mature ex-soldier and now a student-beggar.

In Spain where Francis was born to a wealthy family, his father was an important government official. As a child he had charm and intelligence, and he had a happy, sunny childhood. But then when he was nine the family fortunes reversed. An invading king seized their land. When he was sent to school in Paris he was poor, but he studied hard and was very successful. All went well for him, and he had splendid prospects. Then Ignatius came on the scene, reminding him constantly that the glory of this world was nothing compared to the glory of serving God.

Francis more or less ignored him. After all, he was a busy, popular professor who loved his teaching, aware of his power and his future in academia. Ignatius, he thought, was some kind of eccentric, a religious fanatic. But over the weeks and months what Ignatius said sunk in. And at length he gave in and joined Ignatius.

St. Francis Xavier   *May 7*

St. Francis Xavier was reminded by Ignatius Loyola, the older beggar-student, of the words of Christ, "What does it profit a man to gain the whole world and lose his own immortal soul?" At first Francis brushed off the words. However, in time he began secretly to pray over them. And then he shocked the whole university by joining St. Ignatius and his rag-tag little group which was later to be called the Society of Jesus.

He, when first meeting Ignatius, treated him with disdain and even ridiculed him. For the head of Francis was full of glorious academic ambition. He fiercely resisted the other man's influence. But Ignatius had a bulldog tenacity and in the end he won out. He continued to talk with Francis despite the insults. He kept telling Francis that a mind so noble should be used in the service of Jesus. And drop by drop the words of Ignatius entered Francis' soul. Little by little he began to see the emptiness of earthly success. As he came close to his goals of fame and fortune, the less glow they seemed to have.

The grace of Christ triumphed. Later, Ignatius commented that "the stiffest clay I ever had to handle was Francis Xavier." But now this aristocrat, this athlete as hard as nails, with great personal magnetism, was a follower of Ignatius.

Many at the university were very disappointed. Some thought he had lost his mind. His family was upset, friends were unhappy, the faculty was distraught. If he had to be a priest, then surely he could be one with a little respect. To put in with this new, motley unknown group was an embarrassment to everyone. But Jesus must have smiled.

St. Bernard of Clairvaux   *May 8*

"At prayer, the sacred image of the Man-God must be constantly before our eyes: see him at his birth, see him grow to manhood, see him teach, see him die, rise from the dead and ascend into heaven", said St. Bernard of Clairvaux, the Trappist abbot who did so much to renew the Church in the Middle Ages. He went on, "My entire philosophy consists in the knowledge that Jesus is and that he was crucified." He knew that following Christ is not always joy. He wrote, "He who wishes to enter the Kingdom of Christ must first drink of his chalice." Bernard in his own life suffered physical ills, humiliation, and often he was cruelly calumniated. He was accused of being fanatical, vain, foolhardy. He was denounced more than once for being proud, unstable, arrogant and vainglorious. But at times he won over his enemies. One man, whom he had often rebuked, wrote to Bernard, "When shall I have the opportunity again to look upon your angelic countenance?"

Bernard was criticized because when his dear brother and fellow monk, Gerard, Bernard's secretary, died, Bernard was so brokenhearted that he made a public display of his grief. But surely Bernard was justified, for, as he said to the other monks, Gerard "my brother by blood was even closer to me than a brother, since we were members of the same monastic family. You know how understandable is my sorrow, how deep my grief. You know the worth of the companion who has been taken from me. I was weak in body and he sustained me, cast down in spirit and he consoled me, indolent and negligent and he spurred me on, improvident and heedless and he admonished me. Oh, cruel separation which only death can effect. Where can I find consolation now that I have lost my mainstay?"

And yet he battled on, fighting for the truths of Christ.

St. Edmund Campion   *May 9*

St. Edmund Campion would give his life for the faith in England under the persecution of Queen Elizabeth.

Earlier, when he was a young student at Oxford he had made a speech to welcome the Queen, and she had been very impressed. His future seemed assured. He was referred to as "one of the diamonds of England". He seemed surely destined to be a bishop. But in time he left Oxford and, leaving England and all the things that he had dearly loved, he went to the Catholic University at Douay in Belgium. His study had convinced him that he could no longer in conscience give his spiritual allegiance to Elizabeth's Church. Campion, as a Catholic, studied to be a Jesuit priest.

Then he was assigned to return to England. He had to go in disguise, for priests were then being persecuted. Still, the English Catholics so loved the Mass and the sacraments that they begged for priests. Campion responded to their call. He moved around in the Catholic underground for many months. He was hidden in attics, barns and basements. In various disguises he went from village to village. And in secret offered Mass and the sacraments to the Catholics of the area. He wrote to Rome, "The harvest is wonderful and great." He might have gone on for years. His undoing, however, was that he wrote and distributed widely a pamphlet proving that Elizabeth's Church was illegitimate. Beautifully written, wonderfully logical, the Queen's court could not refute Campion's contention, and this made them furious and even more determined to capture him.

If Campion had less courage, after publishing the widely read and praised pamphlet, he could have hidden out for a few months. But his zeal made him continue on. He did not have the heart to refuse the Mass to the Catholics. He kept going his rounds, and each new contact was very dangerous.

St. Edmund Campion   *May 10*

The Queen's government gave a great reward for Campion. They spread every kind of false tale — no story too extravagant — against Edmund.

Then this happened. After offering Mass at a Catholic estate, Campion was having dinner with seven or eight Catholics who remained behind to eat with him. They were still at table when the alarm was given. The house was surrounded by a squadron of soldiers, who had been tipped off by two spies. The traitors knew the cook and had pretended to be Catholics. In this way they learned about the Mass. They made an excuse and left and went at once to the sheriff.

With the soldiers all around, Campion wanted to surrender, but the Catholics insisted that he hide. Two other priests were present and the three of them were hastily led to a secret room where there was just enough space for them to lie side by side. Some provisions were given them and the panel slid back in place.

The woman of the house let the officials in. She demanded to know the meaning of this search. The people denied everything that the spies had said. The traitors, however, insisted that the house be searched. They were looking for the big reward. They found nothing. The local magistrate, not liking the business and having done his duty, was about to apologize and withdraw. The spies protested. They went outside and argued, and the household rejoiced that it was over. But then the soldiers demanded readmission. They went through the whole house again but again found nothing.

The next morning the search was renewed. They decided that Campion had escaped. Just then, though, one of them noticed a little chink of light in the well over the stairs. He seized a crowbar and ripped the panel open and discovered the priests.

Campion, the noble priest, was hanged at Tyburn. Earlier, he had prayed whenever he had passed this place where martyrs gave their lives, and it was here that he gave his for the sake of Jesus.

St. Francis of Assisi   *May 11*

After a grave illness Francis was confused. He had been a playboy, but that no longer appealed to him. At Mass one day Francis heard the words of the Gospel, the last command of Christ to the apostles, telling them they should go out and tell everyone about him. They were not to take gold or silver, or wallets, or two tunics, no shoes or a staff. Francis was filled with indescribable joy. He said, "This is what God wants—this is what I long to do in my heart."

He gave away his wallet and expensive clothes and went about telling anyone who would listen about Jesus. From village to village, he walked as Jesus did, and he would talk to the children along the way. They were so delighted they ran home and told their parents. Here was a man of religion who was very happy. So often in their pulpits the people heard only gloom and doom. Out of curiosity the parents came and found Francis to be just as the children had said. They thought him wonderful.

Francis thought of all nature as the mirror of God; he felt a closeness to all creatures. As St. Bonaventure said of him, "Francis called creatures, no matter how small, by the name of brother or sister because he knew they came from the same Source as himself." Francis used to beg pardon of "Brother Ass", the name he called his body, "for his having to tame it through penance".

Most of all Francis loved people. He said, "A man can consider himself no friend of Christ if he does not cherish those for whom Christ died." To help people he fell in love with "Lady Poverty".

Francis said that the more one gives love away, the more it comes back to you. No one can know love until he gives it to others.

St. Thérèse of Lisieux   *May 12*

St. Thérèse of Lisieux said that Jesus used various ways to help her grow in soul. This young Carmelite nun was very wise in spiritual things. Her great satisfaction came from realizing she was helpless without Jesus and from knowing that daily he would assist her.

She said that she would not trade her humbling experience at any price "for such brackish waters as are the world's compliments". So now praise did not make her proud. She gave all credit for everything to Jesus. Like Mary she knew that all came from God and she offered everything to God. She attributed all to "God's mercy for whatever there is good in me, because it is he who put my virtues there". She said, "If he wants to make me appear better than I am, it doesn't worry me; he is free to do what he likes. He loves souls in different ways."

All is well, Thérèse wrote, as long as we want only the will of Jesus. "And here am I, in my small way, obeying the will of Jesus by trying to do what my superior asks of me."

She noted, "Whenever I compare myself to the saints there is always an unfortunate difference. They were like great mountains hiding their heads in the clouds, and I am only an insignificant grain of sand, trodden down by all who pass by." But she was not discouraged. She hoped for sanctity by her little way, which she looked at as a shortcut to heaven. Many climb the stairs to heaven, she hoped she could use an elevator, by the kindness of God, because she was small and weak.

She was but a child in the spiritual life; the Book of Wisdom says, "Is anyone simple as a little child? Then let him come to me." This greatly encouraged her. "I will console you like a mother caressing her child; you shall be like children carried at the breast, caressed on a mother's lap." How joyful reading these words made her.

St. Francis Xavier   *May 13*

St. Francis Xavier left his post as a popular and talented professor at the great University of Paris, and joined St. Ignatius and his followers, then a small, poor band that seemed doomed to failure. The whole university thought he had lost his mind. Even the few companions in Ignatius Loyola's little company thought him peculiar. To them his penances were too severe, his enthusiasm too zealous and his prayers too intense. He would quickly burn out, they said. What they did not realize was that with Francis there were no half-way measures. All his heart and soul now belonged to Christ.

Francis was sent to Bologna, Italy. There he preached often and was greatly loved. The people with their peasant wisdom saw his sincerity, his great love for Jesus and for them. It often happens in the Church that saints are misunderstood and "no one loves them but the people". They instinctively prove wiser than the learned, so the learned turn against them, as the Pharisees turned against Christ. So often the saints are persecuted, while the ordinary people take them to their hearts.

Then, Francis returned to Rome, where he became the secretary of Ignatius Loyola. Exchanging a thriving preaching apostolate for a desk must have been very difficult for Francis, but he said nothing. It may have appeared that he was taken from being useful and now was almost useless. However, in retrospect the change seems providential, for just then the companions were working on the first constitution for the Society of Jesus, and it was fortunate that this remarkable man was at the elbow of Ignatius.

St. Francis Xavier, serving as the secretary of St. Ignatius Loyola in Rome, was suddenly sent to the missions. The man Ignatius had intended to send to India with Father Simon Rodrigues was ill. Ignatius, in bed and greatly suffering at the time, hardly knew what to do. One priest he might have sent was asked for by the Pope for a special assignment. Only Francis was left, Francis who was the half of his soul. Ignatius said to him, "Francis, you know that by order of his Holiness two of us have to go to India." He pointed out that the second priest who had been assigned was now ill and that the expedition could not wait. "This is your enterprise", he said. Francis replied with great joy, saying, "Good enough! I am ready."

He went to Portugal and there awaited the ship for India. As always he did not waste time; his stay in Lisbon was very apostolic. He labored in the jail, comforting the wretched prisoners, many of whom were bitter because they were there unjustly. He preached often and officials in high office were impressed by his sermons. When at last he was about to depart they wished to detain him, saying, "Here is a good man being utterly thrown away on the missions." That was not how Francis felt. When appointed to go to India, he, with tears in his eyes, was astonished that Ignatius chose one so weak. He had offered himself with the whole power of his soul to do and to suffer all things for the salvation of souls.

The journey East was very long. They endured numerous severe storms at sea, excessive heat, pestilence and many other difficulties. Then at last they landed at Goa, the Portuguese colony in India.

Francis discovered that in this city the Europeans vied with the Asians in performing acts of vice. Many hated religion because it reminded them they were doing evil. Even the priests there were lax in morals. Into this cesspool of sin and corruption Francis plunged. He visited the poor and needy. The officials and men of the higher class seemed too corrupt to deal with, but the poor welcomed him. They said, "He always looks happy, no matter what his sufferings and burdens."

St. Cyprian wrote of the Church, "The spouse of Christ cannot be defiled, she is inviolate and chaste. It is she who rescues us for God, she who seals for the Kingdom the sons and daughters whom she has borne. Whoever breaks with the Church cuts himself off from the promises made to the Church. He who turns his back on the Church of Christ shall not come to the rewards of Christ; he is an alien, a worldling. You cannot have God for your Father if you have not the Church for your mother."

Cyprian continued, "Our Lord warns us, 'He who is not with me is against me, and he who gathers not with me, scatters.' Whoever breaks the peace and harmony of Christ acts against Christ; whoever gathers elsewhere than in the Church, scatters the Church of Christ. Our Lord said, 'I and the Father are one.'" Cyprian points out that there must be unity in the Church. "This holy mystery of oneness, the unbreakable bond of close-knit harmony is portrayed in the Gospel." He said that the seamless garment of Christ symbolized unity.

Discord and ambition, he said, lead to schism. Beware of false prophets. He wrote, "Heresies have often arisen and still arise because of this, that disgruntled minds will quarrel, or disloyal troublemakers will not keep the unity. But these things the Lord allows and endures, leaving man's freedom unimpaired, so that when our minds and hearts are tested by the touchstone of truth, the unswerving faith of those who are approved may appear in the clearest light."

He said, "Thus are the faithful proved, thus the faithless discovered; thus too even before the day of judgment, already here below, the souls of the just and unjust are distinguished, and the wheat is separated from the chaff."

St. Cyprian *May 16*

St. Cyprian said, "Let us do our utmost, dearest brethren, to rouse ourselves and, breaking off the sleep of our past inertia, give our minds to the observance and fulfillment of our Lord's commands. Our loins must be girt, so that when the day comes for the campaign it finds us unencumbered with trappings. Let our light shine brightly in good works, so that it may lead us from the darkness of this world into the splendor of eternal light. Let us await the sudden coming of our Lord, ever attentive and on the alert, so that when he shall knock, our faith may be watching." In this he sounds not unlike St. Paul.

St. Cyprian continued, "Let us be ready to receive from our Lord the reward of its vigil. Were but these commands obeyed, were but these precepts and warnings observed — it is impossible that we should be tricked and overcome by the devil; from being watchful servants we shall, under Christ's lordship, come to reign ourselves."

He warns that when unity weakens then the generosity of charity crumbles away. The people must lay up for themselves treasures in heaven. This is what the disciples did when they gave their money to the apostles to distribute to the poor. Christians must continue to do this and not seek money just for themselves. Then an active faith withers to such an extent that people lose their old steadfastness in belief. Our Lord said that we must be prepared so that when he comes he will find us faithful to his teachings. Faith must inspire us. We must reflect on the torments appointed for those who betray the faith. And the reward that will come to the faithful. The faithful heed the words of Jesus, those lacking faith are thoughtless. They do not think and they do not fear.

St. Thomas More   *May 17*

St. Thomas More, martyred for the faith in England by King Henry VIII, wrote that we must call upon God for divine assistance and cast away our cowardice and conceit. He stood up for the truth when practically all the bishops submitted to the monarch. Pusillanimity characterized so many; they excused themselves with feeble reasons and no reasons at all. The faith, Thomas said, must be uppermost; one must not fear to be steadfast.

Worldly prosperity, he mentioned, so often makes men foolish. A man rejoices in his wealth and the devil makes him proud. Life at most is "but a very short winter day". Surely we should turn our thoughts not to earthly honors and riches but to Christ. Those who rise high in this world so often fall back down. For a short while they are going up, for a long time they are going down. In going up they are pompous and proud, busy like a bee in activity flying about in the summer, foolishly unaware that winter is soon coming, and that soon we will die. "So fare many people. May God help us." For in the short day of worldly wealth and prosperity, when our spirits are high and our pride swelling, we think we can reach the clouds and sit on the rainbow, Thomas More said. We live in glory, but suddenly it is all over. May God grant us to see how foolish we have been before the end.

Thomas More had the common sense of the saints. He saw how soon life ends, and he lived accordingly. Some people never do. He was aware that he was a child of God and that God in his goodness will guide us. With the help of God the thoughtful individual does good while he is on earth. The fruit of his faith is kind deeds. He listens to the teachings of the Church that Christ gave us. Faith is the first gate into heaven; good works are the second.

St. Cyril of Jerusalem   *May 18*

St. Cyril was the bishop of Jerusalem in the fourth century. He was banished several times for defending the Church. He wrote one of the first catechisms.

St. Cyril said, "Vice mimics virtue and cockle works into the wheat." Thus, he said, the devil disguises himself as an angel of light, and strives to deceive us in this way. He tries to blind us. Many wolves go about in sheep's clothing, their fleece is that of sheep, not so their claws and fangs. Clad in gentle wool they beguile the innocent by their appearance. They pour forth from their fangs the deadly poison of impiety.

He said, "We have need therefore of divine grace and a sober mind and eyes that see clearly, lest, taking the cockle for the wheat, we are deceived." Mistaking the wolf for a sheep, we become his prey.

True religion, he wrote, consists of pious doctrine and virtuous actions. Neither does God accept doctrines apart from good works, "nor are works, when divorced from godly doctrine, accepted by God. What does it profit a man to be an expert theologian if he is a shameless fornicator; or to be nobly temperate, but an impious blasphemer?" He went on to state that the knowledge of doctrines is a precious possession; there is need of a vigilant soul, since many there are who would deceive us by philosophy and vain deceit. The pagan scholars by their smooth tongue lead men astray, for honey drops from their lips, but they are false in what they say. They speak in most beautiful terms but they twist the truth by false interpretations.

We must pray and sit at the feet of Jesus so that we will always be faithful.

St. Bonaventure   *May 19*

St. Bonaventure wrote, "Look at Christ on the Cross, look at him, his head bent down as though he longed to stoop to kiss you. Look at him, his arms extended to take you in his loving embrace. Look at his hands deeply pierced, pouring out rich blessings. Look at his sacred side opened wide to let the love of his Sacred Heart reach us. Look at him, his whole body extended to give himself entirely to us."

Jesus says, "Look what I suffer for you. What grief there is in such as I suffer. In the act of dying for you I appeal to you. Look at the suffering heaped upon me. Look at the nails which pierce my flesh. You can see my suffering, and, within, my grief of heart is even greater when I realize, in spite of all this, many will be ungrateful and ignore me."

Bonaventure wrote, "Charity is the life of virtue and the

death of vice." Charity makes us lovable in God's sight. A charitable soul is spiritual wealth and happiness. St. Augustine said, "Possess charity and you have all else."

First we must love God. Love Jesus most lovingly. Conform your will to his. One must persevere to gain glory. The crown is for the one who finishes the race. Grow in good works as you grow older, said this outstanding Franciscan saint.

He added, everything is prepared for you. The whole court of heaven awaits you. Whatever one can think, heaven will be greater. Christ desires you to come to him with his whole heart.

Take courage, Bonaventure said, and continue the journey. Then in heaven you will love the Good in which all other good is contained. In heaven you, with the saints and angels, will love God more than yourself.

St. Francis of Assisi   *May 20*

St. Francis of Assisi on one occasion healed a person in body and soul. The man was a leper. Francis and his Little Brothers always served the lepers.

This person was very impatient and insolent and severely ill-treated the Little Brothers who served him. He even struck them. He was violent and blasphemed so terribly that the Little Brothers gave up and decided to serve him no longer.

Francis learned of this and he himself visited the perverse leper. He said, "May God give you peace, my beloved brother." But the leper sneered and said, "What peace can I look for from God, who has taken from me my peace and every other blessing and made me a putrid and disgusting thing?"

Francis answered, "Be patient, my son; for the infirmities of the body are given by God in this world for the salvation of the soul in the next; there is wonderful merit in them when they are patiently endured."

The depressed leper replied, "How can I bear patiently this great affliction day and night?"

Francis began to pray. Then he said, "I myself will serve you", for the man who complained about everything was also complaining about the Brothers who served him so faithfully. Francis said, "Whatever you wish I will do for you." The leper asked Francis to bathe him all over, for, he said, "I am so disgusting I cannot bear myself."

Francis washed him and it so occurred that everywhere he touched him the leprosy disappeared and his rotten flesh was healed. And as the man's body was healed so was his soul. The leper's soul was purified with his tears and repentance. For two weeks he wept bitterly for his sins.

Francis returned thanks to God, the Author of these miracles. As always he gave all glory to God. Soon after, the leper died a holy death. His soul on the way to heaven appeared to Francis.

St. Francis of Assisi   *May 21*

When the leper whom he had cured died, he appeared to Francis and he said, "Do you know me?" Francis asked, "Who are you?" "I am the leper whom our Blessed Lord healed by your hands and today I will be in paradise. I give glad thanks to God and to you. Blessed be your holy works and words, for through you many souls are saved; and know that there is not a single day in which the angels and saints do not return thanks to God for the holy fruits of your preaching and of the other Franciscans in other parts of the world. Be comforted and thank the Lord, and may his blessings rest upon you."

Francis was much consoled and thanked God from his heart that he used him and his Little Brothers for good in the world.

Francis went to Bologna and began to preach. The Holy Spirit put into his mind what to say. He seemed like an angel. His words were like sharp arrows that pierced the hearts of his hearers.

Two students told him they wanted to be Little Brothers. He received them joyfully and they became fervent friars. Though learned, they were very humble. Then a devil tempted one of them. With prayer and penance and tears he fought back. But later he almost believed that God had abandoned him. At last, near despair, as a final remedy, he went to Francis.

Francis was very ill, yet he received him. Indeed he sent out two Brothers to greet him on the road. And then Francis embraced him with such sweetness that the distraught Brother was filled with joy. Francis made the Sign of the Cross on his forehead and before the other spoke he said, "My beloved son, the Lord has permitted this temptation that you may grow in merit." The temptation then left him and the Brother was comforted.

St. Cyril of Jerusalem   *May 22*

St. Cyril of Jerusalem said that God is One alone, without beginning, immutable, unchangeable, neither begotten by another, nor having any successor to his life; who neither began to live in time, nor shall ever have an end. He is both good and just, and so if ever you hear a heretic saying that the just God is one and the good God another, you may at once be warned and recognize the poisoned shaft of heresy, he said. For some have dared to divide the One God in their teaching; and some have said that the Creator and Master of the soul was one, and that of the body another—a notion at once absurd and unholy. For how can the same man be a servant of two masters? God is One, the Maker of souls and bodies, the Creator of heaven and earth, the Maker of all the angels and humans and all things. He is the One before all ages and his only-begotten Son is our Lord Jesus Christ.

St. Cyril reminded people that God is not in one place but is everywhere. He is above all. He fashioned the sun and the earth and the universe, all things visible and invisible.

He is mightier than all things, surpassing, greater and brighter than all things. He is not subject to change; he neither increases nor decreases, but is ever and always the same. He it is who rewards the good.

Some men in ignorance have worshipped creatures, but the true Faith worships the Creator, God, the Maker of all creatures.

God is most worthy of our worship. Honor and praise and glory be to him.

There is but One God and the thoughtful individual cuts himself away from worshipping things and the errors of heretics and puts his faith in the true God, Creator of all things that have been created.

St. Francis Xavier *May 23*

St. Francis Xavier was one of the greatest missionaries of all times. In Asia he was first in Goa in India, the colony of the Portuguese. With limitless charity he drove himself day and night. He sought out and comforted the prisoners in their subhuman conditions. These were locked up in fearsome and frightful places. The jails were called "the filthiest, foulest dens on this earth". The prisoners loved him; he consoled them and they poured out their hearts to him.

Then in a small church in the center of the poor district he started to give simple religious instructions to the native Indians. Most of the Portuguese were wealthy and wicked and would not listen to him. Many of the Indians came to hear him and learned about Jesus.

Going through the streets, up and down, he had a bell that he rang, crying out for the children to come. They did, and so did the adults in large numbers. Xavier taught by singing the catechism answers. The children learned these little songs and loved them, and they taught them to their parents. He would then explain these little musical poems.

This method was later adopted by missionaries in all parts of Asia. In this way Christian truths remained in the minds of the people. They were easy to memorize. The children in his classes delighted as well in his dramatization of the Gospel story. He would act out each part.

On Sunday he offered Mass for the neglected lepers outside the city. They became his close friends.

Of course, many of the Portuguese, especially those who kept harems of Indian girls, did not like all this religion going on, especially the natives being made Christians. They, however, did not mind becoming pagans.

Francis continued almost alone, striving with all his strength to save souls.

St. Francis Xavier   *May 24*

St. Francis Xavier was disgusted with most of the Europeans in Goa. They were Christian in name and pagan in heart. Many of the natives were pagan in name and Christian in heart. The teachings of Jesus greatly appealed to them. Francis found the natives a graceful, gentle, mannerly people, shamelessly exploited by the greedy "civilized" colonists from Europe. Francis tried to protect the Indians, whom the Portuguese had abused outrageously. He was embarrassed for his own. Most of the Europeans there, even many of the clergy, were complete hypocrites.

In Goa Francis all but gave up on the shockingly worldly ruling class. He worked mostly with the natives. He who was from an aristocratic family was seen shabby and dusty, walking through the streets and byways, telling the people of Jesus. They loved his stories from the Gospel. He brought love, consideration and comfort to these people who were overworked and oppressed. The natives could see that here was someone who lived like Jesus. They were impressed.

Working with the poor meant privation, danger and even threats to his life from all sides. Some of the Christians did not like what Francis was doing, nor did the Hindus like it. He was isolated. In his loneliness he more and more began to look like the Galilean whom he preached and served.

He said that his gifts were no longer his—they were God's. He took very seriously the Jesuit motto, "Ad Majorem Dei Gloriam", "For the Greater Glory of God". His gentleness and generosity were amazing.

He was constantly at odds with the Portuguese who ran the city over their continual injustices to the Indian people. They disliked him because he did not promote the flag of Portugal, only Christ. Christ was everything to him. His heart was filled with him. Everything was for Jesus.

St. Francis of Assisi   *May 25*

St. Francis of Assisi was praying in the old, ruined church of San Damiano before the crucifix when he heard a voice say, "Build up my Church." Francis could only think that this old church on the edge of the town was falling down. He started to clean it up and repair the building. While he was working, Francis often looked at Christ on the Cross and prayed. And it came to him that from the Cross Jesus said, "I thirst." Jesus thirsted for souls, and when he said, "Build up my Church", he did not mean just to repair a building, but to build up souls in the Church. And so Francis went out and began to preach Christ.

Francis was a true reformer. There was nothing wrong with the Church; it was founded by Christ. What was wrong were the people in the Church. They did not live up to the ideals of the faith. One does not reform a divine institution; he reforms people. And Francis knew the first person the real reformer must reform is himself. Francis prayed very much. All real reform comes from prayer.

In preaching Christ he did not rail at, abuse or excoriate those in authority or engage in controversy or make fun of the clergy or propose elaborate programs. He simply spoke about Jesus from a heart filled with Jesus. What a difference that makes in a sermon! Francis, unpretentiously, told of the love of Jesus. He knew this from personal experience. It was because he spoke from a heart burning with love that people listened to him. Probably no other saint has ever affected so many.

Francis said of Jesus, "Being rich, for our sake he made himself poor."

St. Cyril of Jerusalem wrote about Christ. He said of him, he was "begotten God of God, Life of Life, begotten Light of Light, like in all things to him who begot him; who received not his being in time, but before all ages was eternally and incomprehensibly begotten of the Father, who is the Wisdom and Power of God and co-essential Justice; who before all ages sits at the right hand of the Father. For it was not, as some have held, after his Passion, as though crowned by God for his patient suffering, that he received the throne on God's right hand, but for as long as he has existed—and he is begotten eternally—he has the kingly dignity, sitting together with the Father, since he is God, and Wisdom and Power, as has been said; reigning together with the Father, and Creator of all things through the Father; lacking nothing for the dignity of Godhead, and knowing him who begot him, as he is known by him."

He quoted the Scripture, "No one knows the Son except the Father; nor does anyone know the Father except the Son."

St. Cyril said the Son must not be separated from the Father. There is only One God. There is only one only-begotten Son, who is before all the ages, God the Word—the Son, the Maker of intelligible beings, the Word who listens to the Father and who speaks himself.

Know that this only-begotten Son of God came from heaven to earth to save us from our sins. He was born of the Virgin Mary through the power of the Holy Spirit. He was truly made flesh from her and truly nourished with her milk. Christ was twofold in nature: man in what was seen, but God in what was not seen.

The early bishop-saint said that as man Jesus ate truly as we do—for he had like feelings of the flesh with us—but as God, he fed the five thousand from five loaves. As man he truly died, but as God he raised himself from the dead.

St. Thomas Aquinas, one of the most greatly gifted theologians of the Middle Ages, wrote about the last days of Jesus. He was, he said, deserted by his friends, his good name was blasphemed, his soul stricken with sorrow. He suffered from every side. On the Cross, dying a most painful death, the nails pierced his sacred hands and feet. There was inner suffering at the thought of all the sins he was atoning for and yet many sinners would ignore him. He was sad also that his disciples failed him. And then it seemed as if the Father had abandoned him as well.

Jesus died willingly. He accepted his suffering. He allowed himself to be nailed to the tree. Christ, filled with love, gave his life for us, giving himself over to his persecutors.

The Father, to make up for sin, gave Christ up and Christ gave himself up out of love, Thomas wrote. Judas gave up Jesus out of avarice, the Pharisees out of envy and Pilate out of fear of Caesar. The Pharisees in particular are to blame, for they saw his miracles and refused to believe in them.

Christ received grace not only as an individual but as head of the Church, and grace would flow through the Church out to her members. He earned salvation and blessings for all. The obedience of Christ, after the disobedience of man, pleased the Father. But Jesus, because of the greatness of his love, offered God more than was required to be a recompense for the sins of men. He did this to show his great love for us. He died showing us that he would do anything for us; he loves us so much. He gave his life. What more could he give? He gave it in great agony. What more could he do?

Thomas wrote that the amends made by Christ belong to all the faithful. Christ offered himself up for us through his sufferings and the voluntary endurance of them, motivated by the greatest love. No one loves us as he does.

When St. Philip Neri had his faculties suspended, he said simply, "I am a son of obedience." He merely accepted this as a penance and continued to pray with all his heart. (He was being investigated because after the reformation anyone who did something new was suspect.) Soon he was cleared and the Holy Father sent him a gift of friendship.

Then a new Pope came to the See of St. Peter. He was even more suspicious of new notions. He sent two Dominicans to investigate Philip. Again the Oratory, Philip's church, was said to be sound.

Through the years accusations were brought against this saint of Rome. These pained him because they were untrue. Some stiff-necked people seemed to think it better that youth did not go to church than for it to be made enjoyable for them. They did not like Philip's unconventional ways.

Amid his trials his cordiality remained. And his work went on. One person described it, saying, "For some time I have been going to the Oratory where they deliver every day a beautiful discourse on the Gospel, the saints, virtues and vices. Bishops and prelates attend. At the end there is a little music to console and recreate the mind." He continued, "Their superior is a certain Father Philip, an old man of sixty, but wonderful in many respects, and especially for holiness of life and for his astounding prudence and skill in inventing and promoting spiritual exercises."

When Philip's congregation, the Oratorian Fathers, was founded, one Father said that since they had no vows and few rules other than those for all priests, "Charity was to be the sole bond that united the congregation; it alone compelled its members to obey."

St. Charles Borromeo once asked St. Philip how it was that he was always obeyed promptly. Philip replied with a smile, "Because I give few commands."

St. Gertrude was a Benedictine abbess and mystic in the Middle Ages. Jesus spoke to her. Jesus acted so lovingly toward her, she could say, "[Thou didst] not cease to draw my soul from vanity to thyself."

Jesus said, "Come to me—I will receive you and inebriate you with the torrent of my celestial delights." With these words her soul melted within her. She said to him, "Thou only consolation of my soul". She wept over her faults. "With ardor of desire I desire you", she said. She was consoled by knowing that Jesus loved the poor. She saw in his precious hands his radiant wounds.

One day, wrote Gertrude, "after I had received the Sacrament of Life, and had retired to the place where I pray, it seemed to me that I saw a ray of light like an arrow coming forth from the wound of the right side of the crucifix in the chapel, attracting my cold affections." She felt a wound in her heart and Jesus said to her, "May the full tide of your affections flow hither, so that all your pleasures, hope, joy, grief, fear and every other feeling be sustained by my love."

Gertrude devoutly reflected upon the love of Christ's heart when hanging on the Cross, a love which was a remedy for all adversity and an ointment for all spiritual wounds.

Jesus said, "With blessings I will bless you." She knew he had such boundless love that he poured out blessings upon blessings in great and generous abundance. Words could not express his tremendous love for us. No one is more gracious than he. Because of this, Gertrude said, "I have hope for all Christians."

Jesus told her, "I am with you in all tribulations." He said that sickness sanctifies the soul. He instructed that none should apply himself to action if it means omitting one's prayers.

St. Bernard of Clairvaux *May 30*

During the Middle Ages, St. Bernard was the abbot of the Trappist monastery at Clairvaux in France. He was wonderfully devoted to the Blessed Mother. He knew she was our Mother in heaven and that she would take care of us as mothers always take care of their children. She has a special love for us because Jesus told her, as she stood at the foot of the Cross, to be our Mother.

Mary loved Jesus with all her heart. She looked to him for strength. Because he was always with her, at least in her heart, she was not disturbed by the tribulations of life, and she had many.

Mary, with saintly vision, saw beyond the horizon and discovered the wonderous things of God. She knew that God holds his protective hand over us. Even as she stood broken-hearted at the foot of the Cross, she had faith that God would come to her assistance.

People who pray grow wiser. They have the light of Jesus. He warms their hearts.

No one was more kind than the Blessed Mother. We cannot think of anyone knocking on her door in Nazareth whom she did not welcome in to eat with the Holy Family and, if he had no shelter, to stay the night.

We cannot think that any neighbor was sick or in trouble whom she did not help or to whom she did not bring food and good cheer or for whom she did not do the housework or care for the children. Mary is our guide to practical spirituality— helping our neighbor in need. She did not struggle to express with great theological thoughts. She left this to others. She was busy doing what her Son said rather than talking about it. She did not debate, argue, discuss; she rolled up her sleeves and swept the house of her sick neighbor.

Mary, the Mother of God   *May 31*

This is the feast of the visitation of Mary to her cousin Elizabeth. It was the first time she brought Jesus to another person. It is here that in response to the greeting of Elizabeth, Mary breaks forth into the beautiful song we call the Magnificat:

My soul magnifies the Lord,
and my spirit rejoices in God my Savior;

because he has regarded the lowliness of his handmaid;
for, behold, henceforth all generations shall call
   me blessed;
because he who is mighty has done great things
   for me, and holy is his name;
and for generation upon generation is his mercy,
to those who fear him.
He has shown might with his arm;
he has scattered the proud in the conceit of their heart.
He has put down the mighty from their thrones,
and has exalted the lowly.
He has filled the hungry with good things,
and the rich he has sent away empty.
He has given help to Israel, his servant,
mindful of his mercy —
even as he spoke to our fathers —
to Abraham and to his posterity forever.

Mary's words to Elizabeth show her great humility. All things are God's work. The two women embrace. They are joyful. We can hear the words in the background, "He comes! He comes!" The long-awaited Holy One has come to earth to save us from our sins. Hans Urs von Balthasar wrote, "In Mary, the Son is already with us, already he has begun to go about in the world." What joy! The old dispensation of strict justice and inhibiting fear has come to an end, St. Augustine tells us. Now we can begin to live the new life of freedom and grace.

The great consolation of the Incarnation is that God loves us and comes to us to help us, not because we are good, but because he is.

St. Vincent de Paul   *June 1*

St. Vincent de Paul founded the Daughters of Charity. Concerning one Sister who was a troublemaker he said to her superior that she had committed many faults and must be changed. He asked for a nun "of a more gentle and more accommodating disposition, and do this by tomorrow, so that she will not have time to put together an intrigue like the others; it is inconceivable how apt she is at it."

To another person, who was going to visit a difficult individual, he advised, "Please be very cheerful with her, even though you should have to lessen a bit that serious disposition that nature has bestowed on you and which grace is tempering by the mercy of God."

Vincent indeed was very diplomatic always in dealing with everyone. He would begin by pointing out their good points before he mentioned things that could be improved upon.

To the superior of a convent he wrote, "Most willingly do I pray our Lord to give his holy blessings to you and our dear Sisters there, and to grant them to share in the spirit he gave the holy women who accompanied Jesus and cooperated with him in assisting the sick poor and instructing children. *Bon Dieu,* what happiness for those good Sisters to continue the charity our Lord exercised on earth. It is a work so admirable in the eyes of God and the angels that Jesus found it worthy of himself as did his holy Mother. Oh, how heaven rejoices at seeing this and how admirable will be the praises they will receive in the next world. They will go to judgment day with their heads held high. Surely it seems to me that crowns and empires are as mud in comparison with the diadems with which they shall be crowned." Vincent continued, "Let them comport themselves in the spirit of the Blessed Virgin. Let them often see her as though before their eyes, in front of or beside them, and act as they imagine the Blessed Mother would have acted. Let them contemplate her charity and humility and be very humble before God, cordial among themselves and charitable to everyone."

St. Vincent de Paul   *June 2*

To the sisters of another convent, St. Vincent wrote these words, "Be the first to go greet the Blessed Sacrament, do good to the souls of the poor while taking care of their bodies, and loving your holy occupation. God will judge that you have led holy lives, and from being poor young Sisters you shall be great queens in heaven."

St. Vincent wrote to a mother worried about her son, "Allow God to lead him; he is more his Father than you are his mother and loves him more than you do. Allow God to guide him. God is quite capable of giving him the occupation which is proper for his salvation."

He said to another that he was angry with a man who was miserly with his money.

St. Vincent wrote one of his priests, "The priestly spirit is one of humility and simplicity; take hold of it. The spirit of meekness, simplicity and humility is the spirit of our Lord: that of pride will not last long on the missions.

"No one is able to serve two masters. Our Lord is diffusing humility and simplicity among our seminarians and how shocking is anything contrary to that spirit to them."

He confided to a fellow priest, "I rebuke my miserable feelings which are revolting against the acceptance I wish to give God's adorable Will."

The saint pointed out about the Little Company, "Our humble way of life is to go from village to village, preaching, catechizing and hearing confessions. We try to settle the disagreements we find among the people and we do all we can to see that the sick poor are assisted corporally and spiritually."

St. Vincent de Paul   *June 3*

St. Vincent de Paul wrote a priest, "Those who would truly know Jesus Christ crucified should be very glad to pass, as Jesus did, for the least of men. What good will it do to possess humility with regard to our person if we take pride in our state as priests? May Jesus grant us the grace to put ourselves in the last place among men. Pride makes men fall into such confusion that we shall be a subject of contempt both for them and for everyone. I believe this truth just as I believe that I shall have to die."

Of his Little Company he said, "We live in the spirit of the servants of the Gospel. We go where we are sent." He said that he who has the happiness of possessing this life is destined to live "in a little paradise in this world and to possess eternal glory in the next", if he but walk with Jesus.

St. Vincent de Paul, the apostle of charity, wrote to one young man, "Be aware of the need of the Master of the harvest for workers so that the harvest will be brought in." Jesus is in need. Let us help him so that our work will succeed for the glory of God. Let us pray to him for that intention.

He spoke of how fortunate are those who are not like the proud with their hardness of heart. This sort of sin captivates hearts in a tyrannical way and fortunate are those who are delivered from it. The humble before God will have their reward. They engage in good works and the charity that accompanies them.

He continued, "How fortunate we are to honor the poor family of our Lord by the poverty and lowliness of our own. I tell in my sermons that I am the son of a poor farmer and that I have looked after pigs."

St. Augustine   *June 4*

St. Augustine wrote: "What, therefore, is my God? What, I ask, but the Lord God? 'For who is Lord, but the Lord himself, or who is God besides our God?' Most high, most excellent, most potent, most omnipotent; most merciful, and most just; most secret and most truly present; most beautiful and most strong; stable, yet not supported; unchangeable, yet changing all things; never new, never old; making all things new, yet bringing old age upon the proud, and they know it not; always working, ever at rest; gathering, yet needing nothing; sustaining, pervading and protecting; creating, nourishing and developing; seeking and yet possessing all things."

The great Father of the Church said of God, "Thou dost love, but without passion; art jealous, yet free from care; dost repent without remorse; art angry, yet remainest serene." He added, "Thou changest thy ways, leaving thy plans unchanged; thou recoverest what thou has never really lost. Thou art never in need but still thou dost rejoice at thy gains, art never greedy, yet demand dividends. Men pay more than is required so that thou dost become a debtor; yet who can possess anything at all which is not already thine? Thou owest nothing, yet payest out to them as if in debt to thy creature, and when thou dost cancel debts thou losest nothing thereby.

"Yet, O my God, my life, my holy joy, what is this that I have said? What can any man say when he speaks of thee? But woe to them that keep silence—since even those who say most are dumb."

Augustine asked, "Who shall bring me to rest in thee? Who will send thee into my heart so to overwhelm it that my sins shall be blotted out and I may embrace thee, my only good? What art thou to me? Have mercy that I may speak."

St. Augustine   *June 5*

Few in history have surpassed St. Augustine in intelligence and wisdom and literary excellence. Some great writers appeal to the mind, some great writers appeal to the heart. The great Augustine appeals both to the mind and to the heart. Few are the writers in religion who are outstanding. Augustine numbers among these, perhaps at the top after St. Paul. He is head and shoulders above most spiritual writers.

He asks God, "What am I to thee that thou shouldst command me to love thee, and if I do it not, art angry and threatenest vast misery? Is it then a trifling sorrow not to love thee? Is it not so to me? Tell me, by thy mercy, O Lord, my God, what thou art to me. 'Say to my soul, I am thy salvation.' So speak that I may hear. Behold the ears of my heart are before thee, O Lord; open them and say to my soul, 'I am thy salvation.' I will hasten after that voice, and I will lay hold upon thee. Hide not thy face from me. Even if I die, let me see thy face lest I die."

He wrote, addressing God, "The house of my soul is too

narrow for thee to come in to me; let it be enlarged by thee. It is in ruins; do thou restore it. There is much about it which must offend thy eyes; I confess and know it. Who will cleanse it? Or, to whom shall I cry but to thee?" He said, " 'Cleanse thou my secret faults, O Lord, and keep back thy servant from strange sins.' 'I believe and therefore do I speak.' But thou, O Lord, thou knowest. Have I not confessed my transgressions unto thee, O my God; and hast thou not put away the iniquity of my heart? I do not contend in judgment with thee, who art truth itself; and I would not deceive myself, lest my iniquity lie even to itself. I do not, therefore, contend in judgment with thee, for 'if thou, Lord, shouldst mark iniquities, O Lord, who shall stand?' "

St. Thomas More   *June 6*

St. Thomas More, Lord Chancellor of England under King Henry VIII, lost his life because, although he loved the king, as he said, he loved God more. He wrote, "Whole kingdoms and mighty empires have collapsed. So the poor individual cannot put his trust in this world. His days on earth are quickly over." We cannot do the great things that we dream of, for death soon overtakes us. Possessions, heaps of silver and gold, cannot save our souls.

Thomas was gifted with a keen mind, certainly one of the greatest of his time. He wrote, "It is but a feigned faith" for man to tell God in prayer that he believes in him, trusts in him and loves him, and then openly where he should honour God, not to do good works. And if he flatters God's enemies, and honours them, he is a hypocrite. One who shamefully forsakes God's faith before the world is faithless in his heart.

He said, "When we feel ourselves too bold, remember our feebleness. When we feel too faint, remember the strength of Christ. In our fear let us remember Christ's painful agony that he suffered for our comfort."

He went on, saying that when we recall what Jesus endured in the Garden of Gethsemane we will never despair, but will look to

Christ in pain for divine assistance. He endured all for us and wishes mightily to assist us. We have no doubt that Christ will send us help and take care of us always.

If we but believe the Church, we believe Christ, said St. Thomas More. And we should believe as they believed who have gone before us.

The holy Church, as Christ promised, cannot fail to lead us to heaven. Men who in their obstinacy change the Church's teachings, saying the Church is in error, are betraying Christ. We cannot forsake Christ and his promise that the Church will be always faithful.

St. Thomas Aquinas *June 7*

St. Thomas Aquinas said that sin binds and enslaves men. It is slavery. Christ's suffering is the ransom by which we are freed from slavery. Christ purchased our freedom, not with money but with the greatest gift of all, himself.

By sin man ceased to belong to God in the sense that he ceased to be united with him in love. Jesus restored that union. By sin men left God's service. Christ on Good Friday offered his blood as a ransom to God. His death, which he accepted, earned freedom for us. We were delivered from sin.

We look at the crucifix and it stirs us to love. Our hearts are moved to pity and gratitude, and our souls are vivified. In Christ's Passion man has a remedy for sin. He knows that Christ protects him from the assaults of the devil. We are joined by love to Christ on the Cross, and we are freed by his suffering.

By rising from the dead Christ shows his power over death and gives us hope for eternal life, Thomas tells us. The women were the first to see the Risen Lord in glory because they loved him the most.

"We will rise again by Christ's burial", wrote St. Jerome. Christ's Resurrection causes ours. It sets a pattern for us. The good who have conformed their lives to his will find joy. His suffering and death set the pattern for forgiveness by which we die to sin, and his Resurrection is the pattern for newness of life by grace.

He ascended into heaven, where he is enthroned. He prepares a road to heaven for us. He said, "I am going to prepare a place for you."

In heaven Christ intercedes for us. He showers down graces upon us. By his suffering he removed sin, which is the obstacle to our entry into heaven.

St. Augustine *June 8*

St. Augustine wrote, "Dust and ashes as I am, allow me to speak before thy mercy, O Lord. Allow me to speak, for, behold, it is to thy mercy that I speak and not a man who scorns me. Yet perhaps even thou might scorn me; but when thou dost turn and attend to me, thou wilt have mercy upon me. For what do I wish to say, O Lord my God, but that I know not whence I came hither into this life-in-death. Or should I call it death-in-life? I do not know. And yet the consolations of thy mercy have sustained me from the very beginning, as I have heard from my fleshly parents, from whom and in whom thou didst form me in time—for I cannot myself remember."

The great saint continued, "Thus even though they sustained me by the consolation of woman's milk, neither my mother nor my nurses filled their own breasts but thou, through them, didst give me the food of infancy according to thy ordinance and thy bounty which underlies all things. For it was thou who caused me to want more than thou gavest and it was thou who gave to those who nourished me the will to give me what thou didst give them."

St. Augustine wrote that his infancy died long ago but he is still living. "But, thou, O Lord, whose life is forever and in whom nothing dies—since before the world was, indeed, before all that can be called 'before', thou wast, and thou art the God and Lord of all creatures; and with thee abide all the stable causes of all unstable things, the unchanging sources of all changeable things, and the eternal reasons of all nonrational and temporal things. O God, O merciful One," he said, "have pity on me."

"I give thanks", Augustine said, "O Lord of heaven and earth, giving praise to thee for that first being and my infancy of which I have no memory." He gave thanks to God for the great gift of life and for all other great gifts from him.

St. Thomas Aquinas   *June 9*

St. Thomas Aquinas, the great thinker of the Middle Ages, said Christ left behind his Church to help us gain eternal life. The sacraments of the Church are a means of dispensing God's grace to us. Through them we receive God's gifts and blessings; without grace man fails spiritually.

"A sacrament is a sacred sign", said St. Augustine. It is something with a hidden holiness. The sacraments bring holiness; they are used by Christ for the sanctification of men.

The sacraments suit man's nature, St. Thomas wrote. He comes to know the spiritual world that only the mind can grasp by way of the physical world one perceives with one's senses. The sacraments, an external action, cause something spiritual. It is the suffering of Christ that gives the sacraments their efficacy.

St. Thomas said that no one can be made holy, after Adam's sin, except through Christ.

The sacraments signify what has already taken place in Christ; they give grace merited by our Savior. Through them we are incorporated into Christ. As St. Paul said, "As many of you as have been baptized in Christ have put on Christ." We are members of Christ through grace. St. Augustine said of sacramental action, "All things come and go, but the power of God working through them remains."

Grace itself is a kind of a share in God's existence by likeness to him. It is a gift that disposes a person to act well. Baptism, as an example, achieves a spiritual rebirth in which a person dies to sin and becomes Christlike, a member of Christ.

Because of his freedom from material things, St. Francis of Assisi was unworried. In prayer he learned that it is illusion and degradation to devote one's time to money. The really rich person is he who does not set his heart on worldly possessions.

Francis lived a life of joyous poverty. And in time he and his companions invigorated Europe, kindling it with a new poetry, a new music, the music of heaven, a new art and a renewal of religious spirit.

At the end of his life this little poor man suffered because his followers had become so numerous they could no longer live as he wished, as beggars and vagabonds. Nor could many of the Little Brothers burn with his pure flame. It hurt him to see this, and he tried to understand it. No one was more understanding of the frailty of human nature than the humble Francis.

When the little poor man was dying, he said, "Praise ye and bless our Lord and give him thanks, and be subject to him with great humility." These words seem to summarize his whole life.

Prayer leads to the presence of Jesus, he knew. Nothing could be more wonderful. No one enjoys more happiness, even here on earth, than those who pray, because they are with Jesus. Few people could pray like Francis. Without Jesus we lack understanding and kindness and guidance; we pursue trivial projects and what we do are bad jobs badly done. Without prayer and Jesus we lose our way. With prayer and penance the soul is purified and the way is prepared for Jesus, who comes and gives us light and greater faith and greater love. What great love Francis had.

When Francis died a myriad of larks sang a happy hymn in the golden evening sky.

St. Francis de Sales was the greatest orator in Europe in his day. He became the Bishop of Geneva and was a spiritual guide for many souls.

"When we are troubled let us turn to God in prayer and not just sit and worry", he wrote. Anxieties should not discourage us, but, rather, make us raise our hearts to God. We do not trust ourselves; we trust him. We change but he never changes. He is always good and merciful, even when we are weak and sinful.

St. Francis said that we must abandon ourselves into the arms of God as a baby finds joy in the arms of his mother. We give ourselves over to God's providence.

Our lower nature and our natural inclinations tend to love honors, popularity, riches, glory. But Christ did not seek these things, and neither should his followers. Jesus sought the Father's will. So should we seek the pleasure of God. If we are not consoled when we pray, we accept this as God's will. As we pray for his help we know that trials purify the soul and make us more Christlike. All the saints were closely united to the will of God, he stated. We cannot be so perfect as Jesus, but we must try to imitate him.

In time of temptation, dryness, dullness and aversion let us turn to Jesus and beg his assistance. We show him our love. And we continue to pray with patience and perseverance, for we know we are beloved of Jesus.

Christ loves us with a most tender love, the saint said. We are happy when we rest in his arms. We find peace. In his arms we know nothing can harm us. His loving Sacred Heart protects us.

Prayer is the perfume of heaven bringing Jesus to us. Our Savior supports us and shows us the way to travel. Remain close to Christ. He is our guide. He leads, we follow. Often he carries us. He gives us repose and tranquility.

Ponder Christ. That is prayer. Especially, we must pray so that the merits of Christ's Passion and death are given us in time of trial. In prayer we see that difficulties can help us. We come to know the folly of a life without difficulties, St. Francis de Sales said. In this life trials make us grow in soul and become more like Christ. This is our great goal in life. We are unstable and changeable. We must turn to Jesus for assistance. He said we should not concern ourselves with what we feel or do not feel. We know the truth of Christ's teachings.

God said, "Let us make man to our likeness." He thereby bestowed on him the gift of reason in order for us to see the good even when we do not feel it. Reason makes us superior to all other earthly creatures. We must not be carried away by our feelings and passions. We cannot be unreasonable; we must follow reason.

When we are languid and dejected, reason tells us Christ is with us. He is always the same loving Friend, our gentle companion, no matter how we feel.

Reason must rule over our affections and inclinations. They should be subject to reason. This is why God gave us reason. Without reason in control we are in a continual state of vicissitude, anxiety, inconstancy and inconsistency. These states are fickle. Sometimes they make us fervent and sometimes slothful, sometimes pleasant and sometimes careless, idle and melancholy, sometimes calm and sometimes uneasy and restless. Following feelings, a person passes his life in confusion.

At times success both in temporal and in spiritual things is not good for us, because it can make us proud, and we suffer ourselves to be carried away by a feeling of importance.

Let us be humble. Let us have a holy evenness of mind and be steadfast amid change.

"One must persevere to gain glory", St. Bonaventure said. "The crown is for the one who finishes the race. Grow in good works as you grow older."

We must persevere in the struggle. We must pray for the strength and courage only God can give us. We are helpless, alone. We must turn to Jesus and beg his aid. In their pride some in the world feel that they can do all things by themselves, but they soon fail and despair. It is the humble who are wise and know that prayer is essential. In prayer we ask for divine assistance. In prayer Christ comes to us with his blessings. He gives us the light to see the way and the strength to walk with him.

God will love you intensely and intensely you will rejoice.

Sigh for Jesus until you fall into his loving embrace.

St. Bonaventure wrote that the true disciple of Jesus wants to conform to the Savior of all, who was crucified for our sake. St. Paul said, "With Christ I am nailed to the Cross." The follower of the Lord should pray until he can feel in himself the truth of St. Paul's words. No one will have the intimate and lively experience of such a feeling unless he contemplates, with vivid representation, penetrating intelligence and loving will, the labors, sufferings and love of the Crucified. As the Old Testament tells us, "A bundle of myrrh is my Beloved to me: he shall abide between my breasts."

The soul devoted to Christ knows that he is begotten of God. Christ is our Eternal Light. In the fullness of time, he was sent down from heaven after the consent of Mary. The Holy Spirit inflamed her soul with a divine fire and sanctified her body in perfect purity. The power of the Most High overshadowed her to enable her to bear such a fire. A child was given to her. His splendor and magnitude are more than we can conceive.

St. Bonaventure, the brilliant Franciscan scholar, said that at the Annunciation a flame came down from heaven. This fire of the Holy Spirit and the refreshing breeze that came down with it, and the consolation it poured forth, elevated Mary, glory of humanity, to the greatest of all creatures. And she sang, "My soul magnifies the Lord." Let us join with her in joyfully and jubilantly adoring the marvel of the virginal conception of the Savior.

And thus it was that in the quiet silence of a winter evening a Baby was born in Bethlehem, in the disposition of Divine Providence. He was the King of Peace.

"He who is great and rich became for us small and wanting", wrote St. Bonaventure. He added that the Child was "wrapped in swaddling clothes, fed with virginal milk and laid in a manger between an ass and an ox". It was then that, as the old breviary put it, "there shone upon us a day of redemption in the present, reparation for the past, and happiness forever; it was then that over the whole world the heavens were honeyed."

Bonaventure said, "And now, my soul, embrace the sacred manger; press your lips upon the Child's feet in a devout kiss; follow in your mind the shepherds' adoration; contemplate with wonder the assisting host of angels; join the heavenly hymn, and sing with all your heart and soul, 'Glory to God in the highest, and on earth peace among men of good will.'"

This innocent Lamb did not avoid the wound of circumcision, while we who are sinners, pretending to be just, flee from suffering, the very remedy which leads to eternal salvation. But this you cannot reach unless you follow the humble Savior.

The Magi came from the East because of the star. Do not yourself turn from the brightness of this star that shows us the way, "but, rather, joining the holy kings pay homage to the Child.... In company with the first fruits of the gentiles to be called to the faith, confess and praise this humble God who lies in a crib."

St. Bonaventure said, "It was not enough for the Master of perfect humility, who is equal to the Father in all things, to submit himself to the Virgin. Also he was obedient to the Law so that he enabled men to be delivered from its slavery to corruption into the glory of the sons of God", as St. Paul said.

Jesus then was presented to the Father in the temple. Simeon rejoiced to hold this Child. Bonaventure wrote, "Do you also receive the Child into your arms and say with the bride of the Canticle, 'I took hold of him and would not let him go!' Let your love overcome all timidity and your tenderness remove all fear. With the holy old man dance for joy and sing with him." Then the Holy Family fled into exile. They showed great patience, humility and obedience and lived in poverty.

In time the Child was brought back to his homeland. In Nazareth he grew in age and wisdom and grace. When he was twelve, he stayed behind in the temple, much to his Mother's sorrow. As Mary and Joseph sought him in tears, they feared the worst. They went to the temple to pray, and there they found him. "Like the beloved Mother searching for her beloved Son, never give up the search until you have found him", advises the saint.

Then when Jesus was thirty, he wished to be baptized by John, so as to give an example, "and so as to impart to water, through the touch of his most pure flesh, the power of regeneration.

"It is for you to remain faithfully by his side once you are regenerated (by your baptism) and delve into his secrets, so that, as the breviary states, 'on the banks of the River Jordan you may know the Father in the voice from heaven and see the Son in the flesh and the Holy Spirit in the dove; and, the heaven of the Trinity being open to you' ", you may be carried up to God.

St. Bernard of Clairvaux *June 16*

St. Bernard of Clairvaux was a great fighter for truth in the Middle Ages, during very difficult times. He battled on and never abandoned a just cause just because it seemed hopeless. For this reason he was called foolhardy, but he did not care.

Bernard would have been happy to remain in his cell in the monastery at Clairvaux, where his prayers, especially to the Blessed Mother, were so inspiring. But in obedience he went out, away from his beloved cloister, on long journeys to set things right. He wrote back, "My soul is sorrowful and will not be comforted until I return among you. Are you not my consolation amid the many trials I must endure in this land where I am sojourning? Are you not one with me in the Lord? But as, wherever I go, the dear memory of you all never leaves me for a moment, my separation from you is all the harder to bear. Alas, my time of exile will be even longer than I had anticipated, and my difficulties seem to increase."

God assigned to Bernard "the task of peacemaker" in many places. His great love for God made him an ideal judge in disputes for he had no ambitions and prejudices, unlike ordinary men. All he desired was what was best in the eyes of the Lord.

Bernard's greatest happiness was to be with the monks of Clairvaux. He told them of the value of silence and solitude. He said, "Remain alone, oh, holy soul. Keep yourself apart in spirit. It is good for you to isolate yourself from the company of men, when you have the opportunity; it is especially important for prayer."

He spoke with fervor of humility. "The humble man is close to Christ. Humility is the sign of Christ's presence in the monk's heart and of the purifying action of his grace. When you experience this virtue which transforms you, Christ's love consumes you and the Lord is present in your heart."

St. Francis de Sales was known throughout much of Europe for his love for Christ. He was sought after often as a spiritual director.

With humility we see clearly what the good God has done for us. We must not glorify ourselves but him, Francis said.

The things of this world fade, riches can be lost, popularity depends on the fickle masses which change, beauty goes. So why should we feel proud of these?

Humility must produce generosity. Put your confidence in God and you can do many things. Buoyed up by this trust, courageously undertake to do what Christ asks of you.

The humble soul sets itself with simplicity of heart; relying on God's strength it does his work. "If God calls me, I can attain it", the grace-filled soul says with generosity of spirit. The Blessed Virgin, our Lady, gives us the example. She referred to herself at the Annunciation as the handmaid of the Lord—a great act of humility after being told of the wonderful honor God was giving her. Her child, the angel said, would be called "the Son of the Most High", and yet she said she was but a maidservant. She spoke of her own lowliness and unworthiness despite all this praise and recognition of her greatness. She knew she was not in any respect worthy of this grace. She said, in effect, whatever was good in her was of God, and since this was God's will, she believed that it could and would be done. She said, "Be it done to me according to your word."

St. Francis de Sales said that putting all our confidence in God revives our courage and generosity. The good God, we are assured, will give the grace to follow his path of love. We should say, "Since I am fully assured that the grace of God will never fail me, I will also believe that he will not permit me to fail in corresponding with this grace."

St. Francis de Sales was remarkably open and available, unlike most prelates in that time. When chastised for being too kind toward backsliders and heretics, he replied, "God is the Father of mercy. Are you wiser than God?" A Protestant minister said of him, "If we honor any man as a saint, I know no one since the days of the apostles more worthy than this man."

Francis said frequently that whoever preaches with love preaches effectively.

Francis wrote, "The generous soul continues to labor to do the work of God without feeling it cannot be done. Even though we have many imperfections, we must not be discouraged. Do not be dismayed. We are called by God to spread his kindness in the world. We will do the best we can, and not worry about the results here and now."

We remember that he who sends consolations also sends us afflictions, moved in both instances by the same tender love, which is so very great. We should not grieve when we are troubled. Trust God. Let us run to him as a little child runs to tell his mother that he has been stung by a bee, so that she may kiss it and heal it.

God will provide, the saint-bishop said. In him we hope. We trust wholly in his providence. We are grateful God makes use of us to spread goodness and truth in the world. Jesus said, "As my Father has sent me, so I send you; go and give life to men." Give others a good example. You may not have success in this life; you are asked only to strive faithfully. You are asked only to cultivate the dry and barren soil. You are not asked to reap an abundant harvest but only to sow the seed.

St. Francis de Sales worked with St. Jane Frances de Chantel in founding the Sisters of the Visitation. In the beginning this order accepted many widows, a number of them in poor health. He described them as "strong souls with weak bodies". The Visitation Sisters did wonderful work.

St. Francis continued to write about the spiritual life. "We have the vocation to introduce people to Jesus so they can live a better, happier life. It is by means of you that grace comes to others. As our Lord came upon earth to bring blessings to people, so also do we as his disciples today. With ardor Jesus desires the fire of his love to be burning in hearts. We are his messengers. He makes us apostles, missionaries for his message", he said.

Be full of courage and do whatever you can do. If you have fears, say to your soul, "The Lord will provide for me." Cast yourself upon God. The apostles were for the most part ignorant fishermen, and look at the wonders they did. God worked through them. Lean upon the Lord and fear nothing.

St. Francis de Sales wrote, "Have no distress of heart. Christ will care for you. He will give you whatever is necessary for your well-being.

"When you spread kindness you are doing something very important for Jesus. So we bow our heads meekly in prayer and go forward.

"Keep Christ in your heart. Leave all your affairs to him, exactly as a child lets his parents provide for him. For God is like a good mother who knows what is best for us. Bravely, lovingly, calmly go about each day desiring to please God. And do all with cheerfulness.

"Let our Lord reign in you. Pray to the Lord, 'O Jesus, I give myself to you. I entreat you to give me prudence so that I may live well. Thank you for your countless favors.'"

St. Thomas Aquinas *June 20*

St. Thomas Aquinas had a gifted mind, but when he prayed he was like a little child. He was very humble, as are all *true* scholars. When in his spiritual writing he did not know how to continue, he would put down his pen and go to the chapel and pray before the Blessed Sacrament. He said that he learned more in five minutes on his knees in the presence of the Blessed Sacrament than from all the great books he had ever read.

Once when he was on a journey from Paris to Rome to advise the pope, he stayed, along the way, at a monastery where he was not known. He was in the garden early the next morning, meditating and contemplating great theological thoughts. The kitchen Brother came out with a basket and said to him, "As long as you're not doing anything take the basket and come with me to the market to get the food for today." Without a word this greatest thinker in Europe took up the basket, went with the Brother and carried back the groceries.

Thomas' thoughts were always direct and beautiful. He loved dearly the sacraments. He quoted Hugh of St. Victor, who spoke of the sacraments as "consecrated vessels of invisible grace".

Christ, who saved us from sin chiefly through his suffering, also because of his sufferings inaugurated the rite of the Christian religion. The sacraments of his Church then derive their power from his sufferings.

God alone gives grace. He alone has access to the soul.

The Eucharist is the great sacrament, the Blessed Sacrament. It is Christ with us. It is the spiritual food which gives us spiritual nourishment. The Church, the ark of salvation, gives us this food, as a mother feeds her children.

Notice that bodily food nourishes by being changed into the substance of the one eating, and it is needed to preserve life. But spiritual food changes us into itself: we are changed into Christ.

St. Francis Xavier   *June 21*

St. Francis Xavier, when in India, worked mostly with the Indians who were willing to listen to him. Most of the Europeans there would not. In his efforts he was often disappointed. Companions were sent out to work with him but only a few persevered. And when others were sent some of them too were poor in mind and in spirit. He begged for good helpers but got only these.

One activity he especially loved. Since he could not hope to have good help from Europe, he founded the College of St. Paul. This school was for the training of native priests and catechists not contaminated by European materialism.

Unfortunately, the superior sent out from Europe for the school did not understand the native people and made one blunder after another. He was a young Jesuit, more soldier than priest, and he tried to make these Asians like himself. It was a disaster. He ruled with an iron hand. The Indian students had to conform to the culture of Europe, so foreign to their thinking. He was inflexible, and many of the students left. Francis had to stand by—there was no talking to the little Napoleon—and see his greatest hope being destroyed. The young school superior replaced the Indians with European students, thus defeating the whole purpose of the college. And the Europeans were taught not to be missionaries but upper-class gentlemen.

The youthful head of the college always thought his own ideas superior to Francis, the veteran, and so always did things his way, which constantly made things worse.

Many of the Jesuits in India looked upon Francis as a failure. Francis found comfort in prayer. Talking to Christ gave him the strength to carry on with missionary work.

St. Francis Xavier   June 22

St. Francis Xavier in his great zeal wished to expand his missionary work. He went down the Indian coast six hundred miles to the native pearl-fishers. Their lowly villages had long been exploited by the Hindus and Moslems and then the Christians. They were never permitted to keep the pearls they retrieved, even though they dove deep down into the ocean at the risk of their lives to find them. Eight years before many had been quickly baptized but barely instructed. He began to teach them about the faith.

When he arrived he found this non-Aryan tribe lowly and indigenous. In the India caste system they were very low, only the pariahs were below them. The Portuguese, it would seem, gave this area the name of Fishery Coast. It is hot and barren consisting mostly of sand, about a fifty mile stretch. The villagers eked out a modest existence but were a pleasant people. They loved to sing and dance. Their cheerfulness never failed them despite years of being exploited and the great hazards of their work.

Francis admired these brave men who dove into the water with only a net for the oysters and a knife for the sharks. They had to hold their breath for a minute or more on the ocean floor. It was a very risky business and most of their profits were taken from them by the crafty Europeans.

Pearl diving was their only means of survival. Francis went from village to village and taught and baptized the babies. He instructed the children in their catechism and prayers. He said, "They were very bright." He said, "I began to understand that in very truth of such is the Kingdom of heaven."

He hoped very much to help these people but there were so many of them and he was so alone.

St. Augustine   *June 23*

"Hear me, O God! Woe to the sins of men!" St. Augustine wrote. He said that when a man cries thus, God shows him mercy, for he created man but not the sin in him. Thinking of his own youth, he wrote, "O my God! What miseries and mockeries did I then experience when it was impressed on me that obedience to my teachers was proper to my boyhood estate if I was to flourish in this world and distinguish myself."

But young Augustine was not obedient. He rebelled against all authority. He had a good mind and memory but he studied only what he had to. "My mind was absorbed in play, and I was punished by peers for not sinning as they did." Soon he was trying to outdo them.

He wrote, "I sinned, O Lord, my God, thou ruler and Creator of all natural things. I sinned, O Lord, my God, in acting against the precepts of my parents and teachers."

As he grew he went from bad to worse. He was vain and wanted to excel even in sin, so his companions would admire him. His teen years were years of idleness, lust and adolescent wrongdoing. He said, "By what passion, then, was I animated? It was undoubtedly depraved and a great misfortune for me."

Then Augustine went to Carthage, a much larger city than his hometown, and a greater opportunity for evil. "I came to Carthage," he wrote, "where a caldron of unholy loves was seething and bubbling all around me." Soon he was in the midst of all of it. He said, "Thus I polluted the spring of friendship with the filth of concupiscence and I dimmed its luster with the slime of lust. Yet, foul and unclean as I was, I still craved, in excessive vanity, to be thought elegant and urbane."

St. Monica, his mother, a good Christian, all but gave up on him. Yet she never lost hope.

St. Gregory of Nyssa   *June 24*

St. Gregory of Nyssa was a scholar in the early Church. He was the Bishop of Nyssa and was known for his learning and spirituality. He said that the foundation for the spiritual life is to walk in the footsteps of Christ. If we imitate him, we shall become like him.

What is Christianity? He asks this question first of all. It is Christ and the imitation of him. Christ did all things for the Father. So should we. We are united to him by faith, and we are with him in prayer. We must put on Christ. We must show his life in our life; we must be Christlike. Our Lord is our guiding light.

Life here on earth is difficult. We live, he said, "in the midst of moral filth". Many act more like animals than like men. We do evil deeds, and evil corrodes and destroys us. "The treasure of the heart is shut off through pleasure. The receptacle of the soul is rendered empty by virtue of evil." Many are distracted by desires for possessions. But we must seek the treasure that is above. We with our nature accomplish little. We must pray for divine assistance and guidance. God will recompense our smallest effort with great blessings. And after this life there will be our heavenly reward. He quoted St. Paul, who said of heaven, "Eye has not seen, ear has not heard, nor has it entered into the heart of man, what things God has prepared for those who love him." If we but try to do our best, the reward will be greater than we here can even imagine.

He wrote to a correspondent, "May you fare well in the Lord and may what is pleasing to God be always in your mind and heart."

On this earth we live in difficult times, so we must pray all the more, turning to Jesus as the source of sanctity and as the source, even here, of happiness.

St. Ignatius Loyola   *June 25*

St. Ignatius Loyola wrote the masterpiece *The Spiritual Exercises.* Just as a person must do physical exercise to be healthy in body, so he must do spiritual exercises to be healthy in soul. We are to imitate Christ, who is our exemplar. He wrote that there are four steps in the spiritual life: (1) purifying the soul, (2) having a greater knowledge of and love for Jesus, (3) making a generous decision to follow Christ, and (4) purifying the heart. These lead to joyous service for the Savior.

Devotion to Christ is the key. A soul journeys from spiritual childhood to spiritual adulthood. To imitate Christ means to be unselfish as was the Master. Self-denial is needed.

Jesuit spiritual life is based on the Spiritual Exercises. It helps create the wonderful Jesuit spirit. Each Jesuit bears the stamp of the Exercises, as St. Ignatius intended. The long and rigorous training of these men of God has helped them do magnificent work all over the world. They labor without any personal fame and they prefer it so. As Theodore Maynard wrote, "The attainments of the group have been really stupendous, nor have their members been able to hide their intellectual light under a bushel, try as they might."

One cannot think of any religious group that has had so prodigious an effect upon the world. Their great universities are everywhere. They have had tremendous achievements also outside the academic world. The Jesuits are in the forefront of the never-ceasing crusade of the Church against the powers of darkness. They go forward bearing the flame bequeathed to them by St. Ignatius Loyola.

Ignatius made it clear that while a member of the company should be concerned about his personal sanctification, he must also be concerned for others as was Jesus.

St. Thérèse of Lisieux   *June 26*

The Little Flower, St. Thérèse, when feeling gloomy was inspired to think of herself with God as a child sitting on his mother's lap. Like the child, she was not to worry. She was greatly encouraged. She said, "Never were words so touching: never was there such music to rejoice the heart—I could be lifted up to heaven, after all, in the arms of Jesus!"

She prayed, "It is you, O God, who have inspired me ever since the days of my youth, as the psalm says. I want nothing except to do what Jesus wants."

The Little Flower read the Gospels and was comforted. People stood in awe at the wondrous words that fell from Christ's lips. His heart was a treasure house of compassion and mercy, giving us a glimpse of the ocean of God's great love.

She wondered if she would die early, if Jesus was beckoning her to the glory of his Kingdom. She wrote, "As far as doing good here on earth is concerned, I have long realized that God has no need of any human agent; of me least of all."

We all do what we can here to "feed my lambs", as Jesus asked of us. We tell them which pasture is the richest and most nourishing, pointing out to the wayward the paths where they should not go. We all try to do this work because it is the best we can do and because God sometimes in his goodness sees fit to bestow wisdom on the least of us. The Father keeps things secret from the wise of this world and reveals his wisdom to his faithful little children. The wise of the world are short-sighted. They have no vision.

They measure everything with the wrong yardstick. Thérèse realized that if she in her youth had such light as might have come from many years of spiritual experience, it was a gift of God. She felt no vanity. It was God's doing, not something special on her part.

Thérèse concluded, "I prefer simply to recognize, like a true daughter of his Blessed Mother, that Almighty God has done great things for me, and the greatest of all is to make me conscious of my own littleness, my own incapacity."

St. Thomas Aquinas   *June 27*

St. Thomas Aquinas, the outstanding scholar, had a great devotion to Christ and his holy Mother. He was also humble. Toward the end of his life, though he had written masterpieces, he said he would write no more. He had been given a vision of heaven and, he said, "all my writing seemed like straw" in comparison.

It is said that one day he was praying before a life-sized crucifix and Christ came alive. Jesus said, "Thomas, Thomas, you have done so much for me, what can I give to you?"

"Only yourself, dear Jesus", he replied.

St. Thomas had a wonderful love for the Eucharist. He wrote that the Mass re-presents the past suffering of Jesus, and as such is called a sacrifice. It also expresses the present unity of the Church into which it gathers men together. Moreover, it prefigures the future enjoyment of God in heaven.

The Eucharist is food for the road. Christ left himself with his disciples. At the Last Supper, just as his sufferings were about to begin, he instituted this Blessed Sacrament. Things last said, especially by departing friends, are best remembered, and it was at such a moment that Jesus instituted this sacrament whose excellence our Savior wished most strongly to recommend to us. The Passover lamb prefigured this sacrament.

Bread and wine are appropriate for the Blessed Sacrament. They are among the most common foods of mankind; by separately signifying Christ's body and blood they commemorate Christ's

Passion in which his blood was separated from his body. And since bread is made of many grains of wheat and wine from many grapes they signify the Church being gathered together from many believers.

St. Thomas Aquinas $\qquad$ *June 28*

St. Thomas Aquinas wrote beautifully of the Eucharist.

"The bread which I shall give is my flesh for the life of the world", Jesus said. Thomas wrote that Christ is present here. He brings with him the life of grace and gives these blessings to men. Everything that physical food does for our bodily life—sustaining, building up, restoring and gladdening the heart—this sacrament does for our life of the spirit, Thomas wrote.

Thomas said that receiving this sacrament increases and perfects our spiritual life. We are made one with God. We are made Christlike. It gives us a love of Love, arousing our charity to activity. "The love of Christ presses us forward", St. Paul wrote. We are nourished in the spirit; the sacrament gladdens the soul and as it were inebriates it with the sweetness of God's goodness.

The Eucharist is health for the soul, God's grace flowing over the soul.

The suffering of Christ, which is the power at work in this sacrament, is quite powerful enough to win glory for us. The sacrament does not give immediate glory but it gives the strength to attain it.

Thomas loved the Eucharist because the Eucharist is Christ with us. Our faith is Christ. He must ever be before us, leading us on.

Jesus, as we know, was vitally concerned with human misery, having a special love for sinners. So must we have also. Christ's kindness and meekness were manifested daily in all that he did. In particular he was touched by infirmity, suffering and weakness. In this we can be consoled. We who are weak are in very great need of his help. Jesus welcomed all with gentleness and graciousness; he never wearied of helping others. We are to be like Christ.

In Italy St. John Bosco cared for boys, hundreds of them. The religious community he founded cares for thousands upon thousands of them all over the world today.

When St. John died one hundred thousand people came to his funeral. He had been born into a poor family in a tiny, remote village in Italy. His father died when he was small, leaving his mother to care for their three sons. The oldest boy was a bully and made life miserable for his mother, John and his little brother.

As a boy, John had a dream that led him to believe that he would be a priest and care for homeless youngsters. And that was what he did do so wonderfully. But at that time the family was so poor, it seemed impossible. John had to discontinue school and go to work. However, just when it seemed he could never be a priest, things fell into place—God has his ways—and he entered the seminary.

After ordination he was in a parish in the slums of Turin. The terrible conditions there appalled him. His heart went out especially to the street urchins, boys who lived night and day in the streets. They were fearful of adults because adults most of the time took advantage of them. In time, though, Father John Bosco was able, by his kindness, to attract some of them to come to the parish. He put on magic tricks to entertain them, and afterward was able to teach a little religion. The street boys would tolerate that. Most of all, the young priest wished to find them someplace to live. They were in abject poverty, sleeping in the streets and eating out of garbage pails.

He was able to get a building, almost miraculously. Everything St. John Bosco did seemed to have a touch of the miraculous about it. He was able to take over an old warehouse so that these street orphans could sleep inside out of the cold and the wind.

St. John Bosco, called Don Bosco, started a boys' club and then a night school for the poor youngsters of Turin who had slept in the streets. The boys came to his warehouse to sleep. This way he could teach them so that they could get work.

His faithful mother came to be the housekeeper. The number of boys grew from the first handful to more than four hundred.

Naturally he met with misunderstanding and opposition, as does anyone who tries to do anything worthwhile. The devil is always at work to turn people against good deeds. Indeed, as frequently happens, he was hindered by those who should have supported him the most.

Since he did things differently, he was suspect. A committee of busybody priests in Turin, who did nothing for the poor boys, set themselves up to inspect his efforts. He accomplished so much they could not believe it. They were so jealous they concluded he must be out of his mind—a malady often attributed to saints who practice real Christianity instead of just talking about it as most Christians do.

Don Bosco knew these were small-minded men. So many Christians, and even so many of the clergy, lack the vision of Christ. They came in a carriage to take Don Bosco to a mental institution to be examined. He was aware of their plan. So after their visit he walked with them out to the carriage and opened the door for them, as they thought proper, but instead of getting in, he slammed the door and shouted to the driver, "Off to the mental hospital." And off they went while he stood in the drive smiling. The committee of priests had a hard time explaining to the doctors at the mental institution that they were not the ones to be tested for their sanity.

St. John Bosco had many close brushes with danger. More than once when he was out collecting money for his orphanages for poor boys, robbers would come out of dark alleys to steal from him. But then, always mysteriously, a neighborhood dog would appear, at just the right time to protect him.

One day a man took a shot at him through the window while he was teaching the boys. The bullet passed through his cassock under his arm, ripping the cloth. All he said was, "A pity—it was my best cassock." And he went on teaching the lesson.

Don Bosco was a gentle man, but without softness. He shared in the sports with the boys, and they loved this, for he was always cheerful.

In time he organized an order of men to carry on his work with youth. Today they are found around the world, numbering in the thousands, training poor boys and teaching them a trade so that they will know how to make a living, but, even more importantly, teaching them about Jesus so that they will know how to live.

Loving Christ, St. John taught the youth, is the most important thing of all. Life should be a pilgrimage of prayer. By being faithful to prayer we stay close to Jesus. Prayer makes a person Christ-centered; it gives him peace of soul. Christ is daily present to us if we pray. The saints, who were always faithful to prayer, felt Jesus was more real to them than the sky above. Christ is with us in our trials and struggles, and he assists us with our problems in life.

Being too busy to pray is a great mistake. For prayer is the most important thing we do. It keeps our compass pointed due north. It puts life into perspective so we do not wander off, down paths that take us nowhere.

St. John of the Cross

St. John of the Cross met St. Teresa of Avila, who was reforming the Carmelite nuns in Spain, and he joined her work, striving to reform the Carmelite monasteries.

However, reform always brings controversy. Lazy people do not want to change, and they make a thousand excuses not to. So jealous Carmelite priests turned against John. They were able to get superiors to order him to leave the monastery of strict observance that he had established and return to one of relaxed rule. He refused and so the Carmelites locked him up in a small, dark room until he would obey and repudiate his reform. His little room was ideal for meditation and he grew in soul. In solitude, with just one small window, he had to stand on a stool to read his Divine Office. And yet there he wrote some of his most beautiful essays and mystical poems.

He was able to escape after some months in his prison cell. He tied sheets together and climbed down to the ground. A nearby Carmelite convent of nuns hid him until the search for him was over. And then in time the reform was recognized and he established several other reform monasteries. Again, however, the opponents got the upper hand. They persecuted John and threatened to expel him from the Carmelites.

John was small, hardly five feet tall, but his soul was that of a giant. In prison, for love of Jesus, he had suffered from the piercing cold and damp of winter and the stifling heat of summer. His bed had been a board laid on the floor. He had been imprisoned there for nine months and given no change of clothes and his food had been scraps. He had sometimes been beaten in attempts to get him to change. Throughout this ordeal he offered all his suffering up to Christ on the Cross. His body had been incarcerated by his own Carmelite order, but they could not imprison his great soul. Drawn into the mystery of God's love, he became a mystic.

St. Basil the Great July 3

St. Basil the Great was Bishop of Caesarea in Cappadocia in the fourth century. He was a gifted thinker, and his influence led to a victory for Christian orthodoxy over the heresy of Arianism, which held that Christ was merely man and not divine.

He wrote that those who believe in the Lord must do penance, as did Christ and St. John the Baptist. Penance helps atone for our sins. Those who believe in the Lord must obey the Gospel and not get too mixed up in worldly activity. By penance, the spirit becomes acceptable to God, the soul is purged of defilement and the spirit soars. A person must not allow anything to draw him away from God.

St. Basil said that if anyone does not keep the Commandments it shows that he does not love God, no matter what he may say. We must strive daily to obey the rules that God has given us for life. We must do God's will to give him honor and glory. Those who transgress God's laws dishonor him.

We must strive to be free of all enmity toward others. The mark of the disciples of Christ, as St. John tells us in the Scripture, is their love for one another. The Christian must serve others insofar as he is able.

The early Christian Bishop said that he who has the charity of Christ sometimes causes pain, even to one whom he loves, for his good. We cannot tolerate sin.

The Bishop also wrote that in religion we are not to rely on our own minds but on the words of the Lord. They are more worthy of credence than any human words. We must listen attentively to the Lord and strive to understand his words and do his will. It is the duty of those who are zealous for God's good pleasure to know what is right for them to do.

St. Thomas More July 4

The great English thinker, Sir Thomas More, saint and martyr, tells us to trust in Jesus and love him. We must not let our minds be deceived by men. We cannot believe men and lose Christ.

Thomas prayed, "Give me your grace, good Lord, to set my mind fast upon you, and not look to the ways of men. Gladly let me think of God, and call upon him for help. Let me know my unworthiness and humble myself and be meek before God."

Thomas wrote, "Yea, verily, good readers, to believe well is no little work; it is so great a work that no man can do it by his own strength without the special help of God." This is why we must pray faithfully. We cannot do it alone. Only pride makes a person think he can.

Sometimes we must suffer but we can make this a prayer. No servant is greater than his master, and Jesus suffered so very much. But his suffering helped us. By our suffering we help our souls and others.

"Jesus came into his Kingdom not without travail and pain", so his servant should not expect to sit and do nothing and be at his ease and then at the end be carried up to heaven. Jesus said to follow him, and he took up his Cross and carried it on his back and on Calvary he died for us.

We must keep our eyes on our goal, which is heaven, the jewel of great price. We must not listen to fools, even learned fools, or be distracted by the counterfeit riches of this world. False ideas may be craftily polished to look attractive, but only the things of God are important.

Thomas More said, "What thing is there that better tames the flesh than the grace of God?" We must leave the devil's deceitful service and pray for God's great blessings.

St. Bernard of Clairvaux   *July 5*

When St. Bernard of Clairvaux, Trappist reformer, was praised, he replied, "I am sure that the reason I am loved and venerated is not for what I myself am, but for what people believe me to be, and what people love in me is something—I know not what—which has nothing to do with my true self." Every saint knew that God was responsible for all the good that he did and all the truth that he spoke.

St. Bernard continued to reform though it cost him a great deal. One is amazed at Bernard's indomitable courage and unflagging energy, for he was often ill, yet he went on. He was strict and always demanded that justice prevail in temporal affairs, but he himself was kindly. He said, "If mercy were a sin, I could not help showing mercy." He added, "If your neighbor does something of which you disapprove, do not judge him; find an excuse for him. At least excuse his motives."

Bernard was compassionate by nature. He would weep at a funeral. And he had a keen sense of humor, especially when the humor was directed at him. Bernard accomplished great good work. He said, "We were two against one; with an assistant like myself, it would have been surprising if God succeeded in banishing the devil." In Rome he said to the people, "I address you, great and illustrious people, although I am an insignificant nobody, a child of no standing, I say a child, not because I am young in years, but because I am young in virtue."

He did penance daily, but he learned from experience the danger of excessive asceticism. He told his monks, "I warn you that the severity of the rule must be modified in the case of certain brothers for reasons of health." He applied the rule with moderation and was ever "gracious and kindly".

St. Bernard of Clairvaux   *July 6*

St. Bernard, abbot of the Trappist monastery at Clairvaux in the Middle Ages, wanted the monastery to be the school of Christ, a place of self-denial and gracious charity. The monks were to put their trust in Christ and attribute to him all meritorious action, because "in any wisdom other than the virtue of humility one is not only a fool but a madman." He said, "He is not truly wise who is not wise with regard to himself. There is nothing here below that remains the same: one must go either up or down. To begin to lose interest in improving oneself is to cease to be virtuous."

To novices the Abbot said, "Do not let yourself be discouraged by the difficulty of the rule because of your youth. If you remember that riches may be as hurtful as thorns, the coarseness of your garments will become easier to bear. The moment you feel the goad of the tempter, raise your eyes to Christ on the Cross, kiss the feet of the Crucified, or, better still, meditate upon his life. He will be like a mother to you and will cherish you as his son; I like to think that the nails, which held him to the Cross, will pierce your hands and feet, as they pierced his."

Bernard helped to reform the ecclesiastical morality of his time and to combat the lax behavior of the clergy. He had a Franciscan love of poverty and he rebuked those who were too interested in material things. He spoke out against grand churches while "the poor are starving and half-clad." Even prelates felt the sting of his words. He said, "If I dare to raise my voice against these abuses, they try to silence me, on the pretext that as a mere monk, I have no right to judge the bishops. Well, then, let them close my eyes, so that I cannot see what I am forbidden to denounce."

St. Augustine   *July 7*

St. Augustine relates that even though as a youth he was leading a life of sin, God was still close by. He wrote, "And still thy faithful mercy hovered over me. In what unseemly iniquities did I wear myself out, following a sacrilegious curiosity, which, having deserted thee, then began to drag me down into the treacherous abyss, into the beguiling obedience of the devils, to whom I made offerings of my wicked deeds. And still in all this thou didst not fail to scourge me." I was chastised with grievous punishment, he said, but nothing in comparison with my faults. "O thou, my greatest mercy, my God, my refuge from those terrible dangers in which I wandered with stiff neck, receding farther from thee, loving my own ways and not thine — loving a vagrant liberty!" he wrote.

Augustine said that this was a very unstable period in his

unstable life. He was doing well in his studies but not in the eyes of God. Still deep in his heart there was a longing to fly to God. But he ignored it and went on with his lustful ways. And he sought out companions like himself. He wrote, "I fell among men, delirious in their pride, carnal and voluble, whose mouths were the snares of the devil"—a trap made out of a mixture of evil ways.

He said, "But among all these vices and crimes and manifold iniquities, there are also the sins that are committed by men who are, on the whole, making progress toward the good." He was not one of these, for he had given himself over to sin. Still somewhere in his heart there was a thirst for God. Not only was he sinful but he mocked holy servants of God and ridiculed them. In his folly he made fun of them. This in many ways was the low point of his life.

St. Teresa of Avila   *July 8*

St. Teresa of Avila said that all creatures praise God. She hoped that she might do so too. She prayed, "I have so little deserved your blessings, Lord. Please watch over me. I have great need of thy forgiveness and mercy."

St. Teresa reminds us of how passing are the things of this world. She states that we should turn our hearts to everlasting things. Jesus will help us. He has already shown such great mercy for us. The great part of our efforts has been done by him. This is where true humility comes in, when we see this.

Humility is the sovereign virtue. That which makes us least is the greatest. Humility delivers us from pride and all of its pitfalls. "So dear are you to our Master, Jesus Christ, that he died for you." She prayed, "Whoever possesses you, O Jesus, can go forth boldly and battle the enemy. He need fear no one, for his is the Kingdom of heaven. He has indeed nothing to fear." Let us beg God to establish humility firmly in our hearts. Let us beg him so that we may never lose it.

Jesus showed us the merits of penance by his own suffering.

Penance purifies our souls and makes all things good so that Jesus will enter our hearts. She urges us not to pamper ourselves. "In my opinion, the more we look after ourselves, the less well the Lord lets us be."

She said, "Such complaining is among us". She asked that we stop complaining and pray for God to give us the light to do our tasks successfully.

Constant complaining is unhealthy. It turns us sour. Rather, we should wear ourselves out helping others. Let prayer and kindness be the rule. Care for one another. Get out of the habit of complaining.

The more you pamper your body, she said, the more it wants to be pampered. It becomes soft and flabby. Many people suffer from heavy trials and yet always smile. They do not ask everyone for sympathy. Let us learn to bear our little suffering for the love of God, without telling everyone about it.

St. Teresa of Avila   *July 9*

St. Teresa helped reform the Carmelites in Spain in her day. She insisted that penance is needed. We must not always be giving in to our bodies.

"Believe me", Teresa said, "once we begin to conquer these pampered bodies of ours, they will stop demanding so much." Put aside too much care of self and think of others. If we cry out at every little pain, we shall never do anything.

"Try not to fear death; abandon yourselves completely to God and let come what will", she said. Let us master the body and not be mastered by it. This is a tremendous help in getting through the battle of life. May God in his goodness grant us this grace. The war we wage is against ourselves. Our feelings often lead us to desire things we should refuse. Our feelings are like spoiled children and constantly want things we should not have. If we refuse to pamper ourselves, God helps us and grants many graces to our souls. We seek our ease. God wants us to work, to spread his love by being kind to others.

When we acquire the habit of refusing to follow feelings that are unhealthy, we are making progress. When our reason rules, we are on the right road.

An individual who truly serves God does not serve himself so much. We offer God our poor life and we work for him. A true person of prayer allows God to work through him, and does not allow his ease to come first. One is then numbered among Christ's intimate friends.

All lives are short. We should labor for the Lord while we can. We are not sure of a single day of life. It can all end this hour. Let us labor for the Lord. Let us spread the sunshine of kindness. Let us overcome our anger; there is already too much anger in the world. Every day can well be our last. Let us spread love.

St. Augustine   *July 10*

St. Augustine wrote, "And now thou didst 'stretch forth thy hand from above' and draw up my soul out of that profound darkness because my mother, thy faithful one, wept to thee on my behalf more than mothers are accustomed to weep for the bodily deaths of their children. For by the light of the faith and spirit which she received from thee, she saw that I was dead. And thou didst hear her, O Lord, thou didst hear her and despised not her tears when, pouring down, they watered the earth under her eyes in every place where she prayed. Thou didst truly hear her."

For by this time, Augustine in his pride had become enmeshed in the false Manichean philosophy. But he came to see that it was untrue. And he drew away from this group, largely because they could not answer his questions. Still he lived in sin. He wrote, "O madness that knows not how to love men as they should be loved! O foolish man that I was then, enduring with so much rebellion. Thus I fretted, sighed, wept, tormented myself, and took neither rest nor counsel, for I was dragging around my torn and bloody soul." He was unhappy. Following his lustful ways made him miserable, but he would not give them up. "When my soul left off weeping, a heavy burden of misery weighed me down."

St. Augustine continued his story, one of the greatest conversion stories ever written. "Thou didst so deal with me, therefore, that I was persuaded to go to Rome and teach there what I had been teaching in Carthage." He was highly successful in Carthage and thought he would become famous in Rome, the capital of the empire. But at this, St. Monica, his mother, was heartsick, for Rome was a far more wicked city even than Carthage.

St. John Chrysostom   *July 11*

St. John Chrysostom was one of the best known of the Doctors of the Church. He was the Bishop of Constantinople in the fifth century. He was one of the most famous orators of Christianity. In one noted homily he spoke of Christ's prophecy concerning the Eucharist.

Jesus called himself "living bread" because he welds together for us this life and the life to come, Chrysostom said. It is Christ's body that strengthens our souls. He told the people that their forefathers wandering in the desert with Moses had received manna from heaven. Jesus said, "Your fathers ate the manna in the desert and have died." He would give a much greater food from heaven. Jesus said, "If anyone eat of this bread, he will live forever." He went on, "And the bread that I will give is my flesh that I will give for the life of the world." And many of his disciples turned back, saying, "This is a hard saying. Who can listen to it?"

Jesus did not tell them to come back, that they had misunderstood him, that he was only speaking in figurative language. He went on to say again and again that he would give them his Body as food for their souls. We must accept this wondrous sacrament in all its mystery, said St. John. Jesus has given us this food as a great gift "because he desires to prove the love which he has for us. It is for this reason that he has shared himself with us and has brought his body down to our level so that we might be one with him as the body is joined to the head. This, in truth, is characteristic of those who greatly love. . . . Christ has done this to spur us on to greater love. And to show the love he has for us he has made it possible for those who desire him not merely to look upon him but even to touch and consume him and to be commingled with him. Let us then come back from that table like lions breathing out fire, thus becoming terrifying to the devil, and remaining mindful of our Head and of the love which he has shown for us."

St. John Chrysostom   *July 12*

St. John Chrysostom said, "Awe-inspiring, in truth, are the mysteries of the Church; awesome, in truth, her altar. A fountain sprang up out of paradise, sending forth sensible streams; a fountain arises from this table, sending forth spiritual streams. Beside this fountain there have grown, not willows without fruit, but trees reaching to heaven itself, with fruit ever in season and incorrupt." He goes on to recount the blessings that the Church gives to us, especially the great gift of the Eucharist.

St. John said, "Let us who enjoy such blessings, beloved, take heed to ourselves, and when we are tempted to utter a sinful word, or when we find ourselves being carried away by anger or some other such passion, let us reflect on what privileges we have been granted, what Spirit it is whose presence we enjoy, and this thought will check in us the unruly passions. How long, in truth, shall we be attached to present things? How long shall we remain asleep? How long shall we not take thought for our own salvation? Let us remember what privileges God has bestowed on us, let us give thanks, let us glorify him, not only by faith, but also by our very works, in order that we may obtain blessings also in the world to come, by the grace and mercy of our Lord Jesus Christ with whom glory be to the Father, together with the Holy Spirit, now and always, and forever and ever."

He said of the Eucharist, "Since it is such a great and wonderful thing, if you approach with purity you come unto salvation, but if with conscious unworthiness, unto punishment. Scripture says, 'For he that eats and drinks unworthily, eats and drinks judgment to himself.'"

194

Receive the Eucharist with love so that Christ may adorn your soul.

St. Bonaventure $\qquad$ *July 13*

St. Bonaventure went about preaching. He taught the beautiful things that Jesus did and said. These are the most wonderful things that anyone has ever heard. Jesus brought the message of heaven to earth. "How great was this loving Shepherd's solicitous care for the lost sheep. And how great his mercy", he said. He told of the love of Christ for sinners in the parable of the lost sheep. Jesus went out and searched everywhere and at length found the lost sheep and brought him back joyfully.

Jesus showed his love by traveling through towns and villages, thoughtless of self, to tell the people the good news. Unfortunately, some thought the news too good to be true.

Jesus spent days of labor and nights of watchful prayer; he experienced anxiety and need. Unafraid of the critical Pharisees, Jesus was most kind to sinners, saying that he had come for the sake of the sick. He opened his arms of divine mercy to all. He said to the sinful woman who washed his feet with her tears that she should go in peace and sin no more.

Bonaventure wrote, "To pour out the sweetness of a supreme love, Jesus wept for us sinful creatures." He wept because of the misery of human weakness in those who do not look to him in their blindness of mind and hardness of heart.

"O stubborn heart, insane and irreverent, pitiable because devoid of true life, why is it that in your wretchedness you laugh and rejoice like a madman, while the wisdom of the Father weeps over you?" wrote Bonaventure, who is called the Seraphic Doctor.

On Palm Sunday Jesus went into Jerusalem mounted on an ass so that amid the very applause of these men who threw palms and spread their garments before him, he gave a great example of humility.

Said St. Bonaventure, "Among all the memorable events of Christ's life, the most worthy of remembrance is the Last Supper." At this sacred feast he gave us spiritual nourishment. "Wonderously glowed the tender love of Christ" as he gave us this tremendous gift.

"Stupendous was the example of humility when the King of Glory, girt with a towel, stooped to the task of washing the feet of the fishermen—even the feet of the betrayer. And illimitably rich was his generosity when he gave us his very Body and Blood as food and drink."

In giving us the glorious Eucharist, he gave to the Church food to sustain souls on their journey. Otherwise we would perish and fall by the wayside.

In the Mass he gave to the Church a sacrifice pleasing to God. This was his gift the very night before paying the priceless price for our redemption. His intense love is beyond our comprehension. How wonderful his love, how full of delight. Let us run to him with all ardor of heart, crying out with the psalmist, "As the deer longs for running water, so my soul longs for you, O Lord!"

During the Last Supper Judas got up and went out into the night. "This man was so filled with the poison of deceit that he betrayed his Master and Lord. He burned with the fire of greed." And so he sold out the Savior. He accepted for Christ's priceless Blood the price of a cheap reward. He was so ungrateful that he betrayed the one person who loved him the most. Hard of heart, he did not hear the sweetness of Christ's words.

All this the meek Jesus allowed so that he could rescue us from sin.

St. Bonaventure continued telling about the last days of Jesus. He related what happened after the Last Supper.

He led his apostles out to pray. But this night, with the agony of death close at hand, when the flock which the gentle Shepherd had so tenderly nourished was about to be scattered and left leaderless, Jesus prayed so intensely that in his anguish he sweat blood.

Then the mob came. Judas led them. Hoping for him to repent, Jesus did not refuse Judas' kiss with lips full of malice.

The mad mob laid their cruel hands on the King of Glory, binding him like a captured animal.

"What a shaft of pain must have pierced the hearts of the disciples as they saw their beloved Master betrayed by one of their own company, and led away toward his death", Bonaventure said. When the Shepherd was captured, the flock scattered. The disciples all ran away.

Jesus was taken before the evil-minded Council. Because he told the truth, in shameless infamy they condemned him to death.

His face, worthy of all human reverence and angels' desire, his face which fills heaven with joy, was spat upon and struck with cruel blows. Yet his countenance remained calm, quiet and humble. He mildly endured all hardships.

"O Jesus, all truthful and all kind, how could any soul that loves you, beholding your blood and hearing the insults, refrain from tears", Bonaventure wrote.

St. Bonaventure   *July 16*

St. Bonaventure, deeply spiritual, tells of the Passion of Christ.

The soldiers, like fierce animals, convulsed with rage and boldly beat him mercilessly.

The priests had dragged Christ before Pilate and clamored for his crucifixion, he who knew nothing of sin. He was falsely accused; they shouted for his death who was the Author of life, while they saved the life of a murderer and cruel criminal. In folly they preferred "the wolf to the Lamb, death to Life, darkness to Light".

Bonaventure said, "O sweet Jesus, who could be so pitiless as not to cry and groan in spirit while hearing their fiendish cries."

Pilate was fully aware that it was not for the sake of justice, but out of the depth of their hatred, that they had delivered him up. He publicly admitted that he could find in Jesus nothing deserving of death. Yet he yielded to human fear and delivered this all-good man over to the soldiers to crucify.

The barbarians, not content just to crucify him, first humiliated him with mockery. Sadistically, they played games and struck him ruthlessly and pressed down upon his sacred head a hideous crown of thorns that filled him with pain.

The godless men then made him carry his Cross to Calvary. "They threw him roughly upon the wood, pierced him with sharp nails and raised up the nailed figure on the Cross."

The mob ridiculed him, while in sweet kindness he prayed for them.

"As the deadly darts of extreme suffering multiplied in every limb", he looked upon his beloved Mother and thought of us and gave her to us to be our Mother.

St. Bonaventure   *July 17*

St. Bonaventure prayed to the Blessed Mother at the foot of the cross: "O Virgin blest, what tongue could utter, what mind could grasp, the heaviness of your sorrow! This sacred and most holy flesh you had so chastely conceived, so tenderly nourished and sustained with your milk, so often held in your arms and kissed with your lips, so often gazed upon with your loving eyes, you now see torn by the blows of the scourging, pierced with the cruel thorns, battered and bloody in body, transfixed with nails, mocked by the mob and his side opened with the spear.

"You saw him enduring every bitterness, trembling in body, filled with fear and weariness, now in the throes of agony, in anguish to the depths of his being; oppressed by the most dreadful sorrow, partly from pain, partly from pity for wretched sinners. And, in part, in compassion for you, O dearest Mother, as he looked upon you with tender eyes. He knew that your heart was more severely wounded by the sword of compassion for him than if you had suffered it in your own body."

Now all was fulfilled and Jesus, God and man, with a loud cry and tears to manifest the mercy of his heart, commended his soul into the hands of the Father and bowed his head and died.

"O you, redeemed man, see who is hanging for you on the Cross", Bonaventure said. "How great he is whose death revives us from the death of sin. Heaven and earth lament. O human heart, if you are not moved to pity, riven with sorrow, softened with love — you are harder than the hardest rock."

When his side was opened there flowed out blood and water. Jesus was covered with blood, crimson everywhere.

His body was taken down from the Cross.

Then at dawn on Sunday they went out to the tomb but the tomb was empty. The Power and Wisdom of God overcame death and vanquished sin. Jesus rose from the dead to show us the path of life.

St. Francis of Assisi   *July 18*

St. Francis of Assisi brought Christ to the people in simple truths. Francis saw the truth that no man may be assessed according to what he has, but according to what he is, what God sees him to be. God esteems one by his likeness to Christ. As St. Paul said, "Christ being rich, for our sake made himself poor."

As the end approached Francis was almost blind. The doctor said he had to cauterize. He knew how terrible the pain would be, but Francis said simply, "I will gladly take what God sends me."

The doctor heated the dreaded irons. Francis said, "O Brother Fire, who have so often warmed me and lighted my way in darkness, and ever been so helpful and cheerful, be gentle with me now."

He heard the hiss of the hot iron against his flesh at his temples and offered up the great pain. The cauterization did no good. He accepted this without complaint.

His health continued to degenerate, until it was evident he

was dying. They carried him back to Assisi and the Portiuncula, the little church where the community had started. He whispered, "There is no other place where I think the narrow path to paradise is so straight and so sure."

He was suffering a good deal but he sang. One Brother said, "People thought it strange to hear singing coming from a room where a saint is dying."

"I have nothing to do now but wait for the light step of my sister, Death, and the summons to my Master's presence."

The Little Brothers about his bed said, "Give us a word, Brother Francis, that we may keep in our hearts always." But he was past speaking.

He was able to tell them to take him out and lay him on the ground, naked, to die. He blessed them all. Then Francis cried out cheerfully, "Welcome, little Sister Death."

St. Benedict   *July 19*

St. Benedict was the patriarch of Western monasticism. He said that we must pray in order to praise God and obtain from him the graces we so desperately need; we must labor in order to cooperate with the graces received and merit the heavenly glory that awaits those who persevere to the end.

He told his monks that by the labor of obedience one can return to God by whom one was made. One should do battle under the Lord Christ, the true King, by taking up the strong and bright weapon of obedience. He wrote, "Whatever good work you begin to do, beg of God with most earnest prayer that he will perfect it, that he who has now deigned to count us among his sons may not at any time be grieved by our evil deeds."

He said, " 'Now is the hour for us to rise from sleep.' Let us open our eyes to the deifying light, let us hear with attentive ears the warning which the divine voice cries daily to us, 'Today if you hear his voice, harden not your hearts.' And again, 'He who has ears to hear, let him hear what the Spirit says to the churches.'

And what does he say? 'Come, my children, listen to me; I will teach you the fear of the Lord. Run while you have the light of life, lest the darkness of death overtake you.' "

St. Benedict reminds us, "And the Lord, seeking his laborers in the multitude to whom he thus cries out, says again, 'Who is the man who will have life, and desires to see good days?' And, if hearing him, you answer, 'I am he', God says to you, 'If you will have true and lasting life, keep your tongue from evil and your lips that they speak no guile. Turn away from evil and do good; seek after peace and pursue it. And when you have done these things, my eyes shall be upon you and my ears open to your prayers; and before you call upon me, I will say to you, "Behold, here I am." ' "

St. John of the Cross   *July 20*

St. John of the Cross, the Spanish Carmelite mystic, was a very simple, pleasant person, easy to talk to and easy to live with. He was not a grouchy and melancholy puritan who pretended to be a saint.

St. Teresa of Avila paid him the highest compliment. When a nun was complaining, she wrote her, "I am really surprised, daughter, at your complaining when you have with you Padre Juan de la Cruz, who is a divine, heavenly man. I can tell you since he left us here I have found no one like him in all Castile, nor anyone who inspires others with so much fervor on the journey to heaven. You would not believe how lonely his absence makes me feel. You should reflect that you have a great treasure in this holy man. Our Lord has given him a special grace for directing souls."

St. John of the Cross said that the love that Jesus has for us urges us on. On Good Friday he was bruised and bloody and in terrible agony, his body torn by pain. He underwent humiliation and betrayal; he was blindfolded, buffeted and derided, and insulted, defiled and outrageously tortured. Why did he endure all this? His reply is, "Because I love you."

His death made up for our sins. Men dragged him out to the hill and hung him upon the Cross. Blasphemy and sadistic sarcasm surrounded him. He suffered all in silence. In doing so he made up for our weakness. We are too powerless to save ourselves. Jesus had to save us.

Many in our world live sordid lives. But let us follow not our own way but the way of Christ. Jesus said, "I am the Way." It is he who truly leads us to our heavenly home.

St. Gertrude *July 21*

St. Gertrude was a mystic. Jesus assured her that whoever humbly exposes his defects, with contrition, would be forgiven.

Jesus took delight and pleasure in dwelling in her soul, for she was devout and humble. He took joy in helping others through her. Happily he rejoiced in giving others new hope.

He said that she was not to complain of her weakness but that she was to approach him and receive his love. And he opened to her both hands and he took her hand and touched it to his Sacred Heart. He said, "Each time you acknowledge your unworthiness of my gifts and confide fully in my mercy, each time you acquit yourself of the debts you owe me for your benefits, I love you."

Gertrude said to Jesus, "When you showed your most adorable Face—the source of all blessedness—a light of inestimable sweetness passed through my inmost being. When you embrace me and your holy eyes look into mine, into all my parts with admirable sweetness and power, I am happy."

St. Gertrude learned from these revelations that she was to endure some trials in order to increase her merits. She began to fear her human weakness, but the Lord had compassion on her infirmity and gave her his most merciful Mother, the Queen of Heaven, to be her mother and helper. This was so that when the burden of her grief appeared beyond her strength, she might always have recourse to the Mother of Mercy and by her loving intervention obtain relief.

She prayed to Mary, Mother of the Afflicted, and her heavenly Mother replied, "Give freely what you possess, for my Son is rich enough to repay all that you expend for his glory."

St. Benedict *July 22*

"What can be sweeter to us, dear brothers, than the voice of the Lord inviting us?" asked St. Benedict of his monks. He pointed out that Jesus was calling them to walk with him. Others he calls also, but they are called in a most special way to be his special friends. "Behold," he said, "in his loving kindness the Lord shows us the way of life." He told them they were to have faith and grow in faith through prayer and they were to do good works so that they could walk in the path of Jesus by the guidance of the gospel. Then one day all will see Christ who has called them to his Kingdom.

He told them to listen to the Lord and cast away their temptations from the malicious devil. He said, "It is they who, fearing the Lord, do not pride themselves on their good observance, but, convinced that the good which is in them cannot come from themselves and must be from the Lord, glorify the Lord's work in them."

Having assured us that he will help us, the Lord is waiting every day for us to respond by our deeds to his holy teachings, St. Benedict said. Let us amend our evil ways, for the Lord who is merciful said, "I desire not the death of a sinner, but that he should be converted and live."

St. Benedict said, "We must prepare our hearts and our bodies to do battle under the holy obedience of Christ's commands; and let us ask God that he be pleased to give us the help of his grace for anything which our nature finds hardly possible. And if we want to escape the pains of hell and attain everlasting life, then, while there is still time, while we are still in the body and are able to fulfill all these things by the light of this life, we must hasten to do now what will profit us for all eternity."

St. Peter Julian Eymard, who lived in France in the last century, founded the Blessed Sacrament Fathers, whose first duty is perpetual adoration. He also formed the Blessed Sacrament Confraternity to promote devotion to the Eucharist among the faithful.

He wrote, "How good is the Lord Jesus! How loving! Not satisfied with having become our Brother by his Incarnation and our Savior by his Passion, not satisfied with having delivered himself up for us, he wants to strain his love to the point of making himself our Sacrament of life!

"With joy he prepared this great and supreme gift of his love!

"With what happiness he instituted the Eucharist and bequeathed it to us as his last will!

"Let us observe this divine wisdom at work preparing the Eucharist and let us adore his power, exhausting itself in this act of love."

St. Peter Julian then related how Jesus revealed the Eucharist beforehand. He promised this Food from heaven to the people. Then at the Last Supper, the night before he died, at this most solemn time, he gave us the Eucharist, gave us himself for our spiritual food.

"The time for the institution of the august Sacrament had come. What a moment!" wrote the saint. "The hour of love had struck. The Bread of Life, the Bread from heaven was substituted for the manna in the wilderness. Jesus sat down at table with a grave simplicity. A deep silence came over them all. The apostles looked on most attentively.

"Jesus became meditative. He took some bread in his holy hands, raised his eyes to heaven, gave thanks to his Father for this hour he had so desired. He consecrated the bread and wine and gave it to them for nourishment for their souls."

St. Philip Neri was very gentle when he asked a Father of his community to do something. He would say, "This is what I would like you to do—but if it seems too hard I will do it for you." His ordinary rebuke was to fix his eyes sternly on the other. It was enough.

As is always the case with every work of God, opposition does not fail to arise. But Philip had many more admirers than opponents. With the assistance of his supporters he was able to weather the conflict.

The spreading of his congregation was not Philip's intention. He was so humble that he never even thought of such a thing. He only wanted the word of God preached daily in a simple way. Everything else was subsidiary. His ways may have seemed haphazard, but they were very effective. And he would not change; on this he was firm.

His influence, especially toward the end of his life, was enormous. This seemed so because he did not set out to influence people, only make them better Christians. He did not have to work at being interested in people. It was natural for him to be interested in everyone he met. One Father at the Oratory asked, "Who could resist the charm of his personality and the vehemence of his prayers combined?"

Philip often said to others, "I want you never to commit sin, but to be always happy and cheerful of heart." One of his favorite sayings was, "A cheerful and glad spirit attains to perfection much more readily than a melancholy spirit."

Philip liked people. He liked to laugh and joke. Merely to look at his shining eyes was enough to cure another's depression. He lifted the spirits of others, and they walked away with good cheer.

The Fathers of the Oratory, one or two at least, asked him to deport himself with more dignity, but dignity is something he knew nothing about.

St. Martin de Porres was a humble Dominican lay brother in Peru. When he was a boy he could not pass a church without going in to pray. These visits to Jesus made him strong in faith. He dedicated his days to helping the homeless and the orphans.

Martin's father was Spanish, a nobleman; his mother was a beautiful black woman. For eight years the proud Spaniard refused to acknowledge him. His mother had to struggle alone to support her family, Martin and his sister; she did the washing for the rich people. She worked so hard that she was very unhappy when she would send little Martin to the market for food and he would give half of it away to poor people there.

At the age of twelve Martin became an apprentice to a barber. In those days such a person not only cut hair but also was a surgeon and a druggist. Martin eagerly learned how to set broken bones and brew herbs and bind up wounds. With these skills, he could help people, and he could especially help the poor who could not pay.

He stayed in a rooming house. The landlady wondered why there was a light on in his room so often late at night. So she peeped through the keyhole. Martin was praying.

He attended the Dominican church in Lima, where he lived in the early days of that Spanish colony. In time he asked to be accepted as a lay brother. The Dominicans debated for a long time, for all their Fathers and Brothers were Europeans. Finally he was admitted. He did all the hard things, sweeping, cleaning, scrubbing, washing. The fact is, he preferred these humble tasks. Most of all, for long hours Martin prayed before the Blessed Sacrament.

One evening one of the other Dominicans chanced to come upon Brother Martin in his cell kneeling before the crucifix, his arms extended in the form of a cross, his eyes intently fixed on the figure of the suffering Christ. Another time he was seen lying on the floor of his small room saying the Rosary. The Dominican who saw him said that he had never seen anyone pray the way Martin prayed.

As a youth Augustine tried to change from his sinful ways. He heard a voice within say, "Do not follow your lusts and refrain yourself from your pleasures." But he did not.

Later he went to Rome to teach and become famous, but despite his move to Rome he did not become famous. He started a school there but it did not prosper as had his school in Carthage. Then he became ill. He wrote, "Lo, I was received in Rome by the scourge of bodily sickness; and I was very near to falling into hell, burdened with all the many and grievous sins I had committed against thee, myself and others—all over and above that fetter of original sin whereby we all die in Adam. For thou had forgiven me none of these things in Christ, neither had he abolished by his Cross the enmity that I had incurred from thee through my sins."

He continued, "My fever increased, and I was on the verge of passing away and perishing; for, if I had passed away then, where should I have gone but into the fiery torment which my misdeeds deserved, measured by the truth of thy rule?"

He felt disordered when he recovered. He didn't know what to do. He felt God had restored him, but he was confused. Sometimes he tried to think of the Catholic Faith of his mother but every time "I was cast down, since the Catholic Faith was not what I judged it to be", said St. Augustine.

Since his school was not successful, when he learned that a teacher of rhetoric was needed in Milan, he went there. It was in Milan, according to Providence, that Augustine met the outstanding Bishop St. Ambrose. And this changed his way of thinking.

St. Peter Julian Eymard *July 27*

St. Peter Julian Eymard was most devoted to the Holy Eucharist. He wrote, "At the Last Supper, while the apostles were filled with respect, not daring to ask the meaning of this mystery, Jesus pronounced those beautiful words as powerful as the creative word of God: 'Take ye and eat. This is My Body. . . . Drink ye all of This. This is My Blood.' "

Father Eymard wrote, "The mystery of love was consummated. Jesus had fulfilled his promise. He had nothing more to give but his mortal life upon the Cross. He would give it and would rise again to be our perpetual Host of propitiation, the Host of our Communion, the Host of our adoration.

"Heaven was enraptured at the sight of this mystery. The Most Holy Trinity contemplated it with love. The angels, struck with awe, adored it. And with what a frantic rage were not the demons seized in hell!

"Yes, Lord Jesus, all is consummated. Thou hast now nothing more to give man to prove him thy love. Thou mayest die now; thou wilt not leave us, even by dying. Thy love is perpetuated on earth. Go back to the heaven of thy glory; the Eucharist will be the heaven of thy love."

St. Peter Julian said, "O Body of Christ, O divine fire which Jesus kindled on Mount Sion, burn, spread thy flame and set the world on fire!

"Heavenly Father, thou wilt always love men; they possess Jesus Christ forever! Thou wilt not lay waste the earth anymore with storms and floods, the Eucharist is our rainbow. Thou wilt love men since thy Son Jesus Christ loves them so much!"

The saint said, "What love our good Savior has for us. Did he not love us enough to deserve our greatest gratitude? Do we require further proof of our Lord's love?"

St. Thomas Aquinas   *July 28*

The brilliant St. Thomas Aquinas wrote, "The Catholic Church is one body, having many members. The soul that quickens this body is the Holy Spirit. The holy Church is the assembly of the faithful, and the individual Christian is a member of the Church, of which it is said, 'Draw near to me, ye unlearned, and gather yourselves together into the house of discipline.' This holy Church has four marks in that she is one, holy, catholic (universal) and apostolic."

He points out that the Church is one and that the heretics who break away are not members. The unity of the Church arises from the unity of the faith, from the unity of hope and from the unity of charity. All true members of the Church believe the same, all have hope in the same goal and gain that goal by love for God and others. Each one, he said, must be of service to his neighbor. We must make use of the grace God gives us to assist others in need.

No one, he wrote, should think it of small account or allow himself to be cut off from the Church. There is but one Church wherein men have the faith given us by Jesus. We must be steadfast in the truth; thus one is loyal to Christ. The Blessed Mother is our example.

We must beware, since we were created for the happiness of heaven, and watch over our souls, lest by sin we are defiled. The Church was established by Jesus to make us holy. Countless saints show us this.

The Church is for all. Jesus came to save souls. His Church is not for one group but for all people. And the Church was founded by Christ with the apostles the first teachers and leaders. The apostles taught what Christ taught, and the Church, down through the centuries, continues to do so.

St. Thomas Aquinas   *July 29*

St. Thomas Aquinas had a gifted mind and a humble heart. This is why he spoke so wonderfully of our faith. The saints are wiser by far than those who are only knowledgeable.

A person of sublime thought, Thomas nourished his soul constantly with prayer, spiritual reading and contemplation. Everyone remarked on his humility. So many who are learned become proud. Aquinas who might well be called a genius remained like a humble little boy all his life. In a moment of confidence he said to Father Reginald of Piperno, "Thanks be to God, my knowledge, my title of Doctor, my scholastic work, have never occasioned a single movement of vainglory, to dethrone the virtue of humility in my heart." He would never accept an office in the Dominicans. He could have been the Lord Abbot of Monte Cassino, but he refused. One Pope, Clement IV, tried to offer him the red hat of the Cardinal but he would not accept it. And at his death he said, "Thank God, I die a simple religious." This insightful statement in itself shows his profound wisdom.

He loved poverty. All his many long journeys he made on foot, as was the rule of the friars. Another Dominican mentioned that when Thomas was writing his profound *Summa Contra Gentiles* he was so dedicated to poverty that he wrote it on scraps of paper, although he could have had as many copybooks as he wanted.

As to obedience, it was one of his sayings that an obedient man is the same as a saint. Thomas obeyed his local superior just as readily as he obeyed the Pope.

The depth of his love for God, is known only to God. But love showed constantly in his daily kindness. No harsh statements were ever made by him. As a fellow friar put it, "He could slay an argument, yet spare a foe."

St. Thomas Aquinas   *July 30*

St. Thomas Aquinas stated that the Church is here to make us holy. Christ has "loved us and washed us from our sins in his own blood. Jesus, that he might sanctify the people by his own blood, suffered outside the gate."

Jesus died to save us from sin and to reopen the gates of heaven to us. The Church gives us the graces and blessings of Jesus.

One of the great gifts the Church gives to us is the forgiveness of our sins. This sacrament takes away our sins; it expresses our belief that the apostles received the power to forgive sins: wherefore we must believe that the ministers of the Church, who derive this power from the apostles, who received it from Christ, have power in the Church to bind and to loose, and that there is in the Church full power to forgive sins.

Thomas stated that in addition to the forgiveness of sins there are other sacraments, seven in all. The power of Christ's Passion operates through the sacraments of the Church, which bestow grace upon us. The first of the sacraments is baptism, which is a spiritual regeneration: for just as man cannot live in the flesh unless he is born in the flesh, even so a man cannot have the spiritual life of grace unless he be born again spiritually.

Thomas wrote, "Another sacrament is confirmation. For just as those who are born in the body need to be fortified in order that the body becomes operative, even so those who are reborn in the spirit need to be fortified by the Holy Spirit. Another sacrament is the Eucharist. As in the life of the body, after a person is born and grows, he requires food that his life may be preserved and sustained, so also in the spiritual life, after being fortified, he requires spiritual food." Then there are the sacraments of holy orders for the priesthood and matrimony for married life. And finally the sacrament of the anointing of the sick.

St. Francis Xavier   *July 31*

St. Francis Xavier travelled throughout Asia. A companion, Francis Mansilhas, wrote, "I knew Father Francis in Portugal, and I went about with him for six or seven years on the Fishery Coast. No human being could have done what he did or live as he lived without being full of the Holy Spirit. Indeed his life was more of a saint and angel than of a man. . . . Many a time, out of his love for God and our holy faith, he offered himself to martyrdom in the midst of his incessant labors and sufferings. . . . If he could find time in the night, as he never could during the day, he gave himself completely to prayer. Day and night he consoled people. He had nothing of his own, and on himself never spent a cent. As much as one could dream of a man doing he did, and more."

On his journeys he came across numerous Hindu temples with their false gods. He encountered opposition from many sides and often labored alone, a lonely missionary of the Lord. He had been promised help but none came. That was almost the story of his life.

He prayed, "May the grace and love of Christ our Lord befriend us and stand by us always." Here and elsewhere he was laying the foundations for Christianity, but many Christians, including some Jesuits, thought he was off on a wild-goose chase.

Francis was humiliated for Christ every time he came across money-grubbing "Christians", white merchants who seem to have left their faith back in Europe. He wrote a woeful letter about these heathen "Christians" who cheated the natives mercilessly. He could not stop their vicious activity. They only laughed and said "business is business". They were, in truth, far more uncivilized than the natives, though in their pride they thought themselves far superior. Francis wept with Christ.

St. Martin de Porres *August 1*

St. Martin de Porres was appointed the infirmarian in the Dominican House in Lima, Peru, where he lived. As the infirmarian, he took care of the Dominicans who were sick. He was always kind and cheerful, even when some of the old priests were cranky. When natural remedies failed he prayed.

An epidemic raged in Lima. More than sixty of the Dominicans were stricken. Brother Martin waited on them day and night. With indefatigable solicitude he cared for them. He was an apostle of mercy. It was the first time that most of the Dominicans in the house realized how wonderful he was.

One who had a severe fever recalled that he was certain he was going to die; at one o'clock in the morning he looked up and beheld Martin standing beside his bed. The sick Brother's clothes were saturated with sweat, but Martin assured him that he would not die. This greatly consoled him and he relaxed and fell into a deep sleep that broke the fever.

One day while walking down the street Brother Martin saw a poor old man abandoned and covered with sores. Martin, a big strong lad, picked him up, carried him back to his own bed in the monastery and took care of him. He daily bathed his sores until he was healed.

After the poor patient left, another Brother came along and, seeing the soiled blankets, said that the old man might have a contagious disease. Martin replied quietly, "My dear Brother, it is more important to have Christlike charity toward your neighbor than to worry about clean blankets. The stains here can be washed out with soap and water, but those that blot the soul for lack of love can be washed out only with tears."

St. Augustine   *August 2*

St. Augustine, while teaching oratory in Milan, often went to hear the great Bishop Ambrose, who was famous for his preaching. He tells us, "I took no trouble to learn what he said, but only to hear how he said it", since he was instructing others in eloquence. But gradually, some of the things that St. Ambrose said begin to sink into his soul.

St. Augustine wrote, "O Hope from my youth, where were thou to me and where hadst thou gone away? . . . Yet I was wandering about in a dark and slippery way, seeking thee outside myself and thus not finding the God of my heart. I had gone down into the depths of the sea and had lost faith, and I had despaired of ever finding the truth."

St. Augustine knew that his mother was praying for him. "Nor had I come yet to groan in my prayers that thou wouldst help me. My mind was wholly intent on knowledge and eager for disputation. Ambrose himself I esteemed a happy man, as the world counted happiness, because great personages held him in honor." Ambrose was happy and Augustine was miserable, but he still did not accept the faith of Ambrose. He was filled with doubts. He said, "Still, from this time on, I began to prefer the Catholic doctrine." It was far better than the old false philosophies he had held. He must be honest. He began to believe more, sometimes more strongly than at other times. However, he admits,

"I was still eagerly aspiring to honors, money and matrimony; and thou didst mock me. In pursuit of these ambitions I endured the most bitter hardships, in which thou wert being the more gracious the less thou wouldst allow anything that was not thee to grow sweet in me. Look into my heart, O Lord, whose prompting it is that I should recall all this, and confess it to thee. Now let my soul cleave to thee, now that thou hast freed me." He no longer held his past false notions, but he seemed unable to move ahead.

St. Augustine *August 3*

"By now, O my Helper, thou hadst freed me from those fetters", Augustine said. He now knew that physical things were not evil, as the Manicheans contended. He said to the Lord, "There is no health in those who find fault with any part of thy creation; as there was no health in me when I found fault with so many of thy works. And because now my soul dared not be displeased with my God, it would not allow that the things which displeased me were from thee."

Augustine continued to reflect. He had read of the conversion to Christ of a famous orator and philosopher. This moved him greatly. "O my God, let me remember with gratitude and confess to thee thy mercies toward me." He was certain that God had influenced him to read this account. Now Christ was much more important to Augustine. "But as for my temporal life, everything was uncertain, and my heart had to be purged of the old leaven. 'The Way'—the Savior himself—now pleased me well, but as yet I was reluctant to pass through the straight gate."

Augustine said that he went to a priest, the spiritual director of St. Ambrose. The holy priest was kindly. He "encouraged me to copy the humility of Christ, which is hidden from the wise and revealed to babes". Augustine went on to say that he steadily gained spiritual strength from reading and inquiry, and came to fear lest he should be denied by Christ before the holy angels if he now was afraid to confess Christ before men.

"Go on, O Lord, and act: stir us up and call us back; inflame us and draw us to thee; stir us up and grow sweet to us; let us now love thee, let us run to thee", wrote Augustine. "With increasing anxiety I was going about my usual affairs, and daily sighing to thee." He asked to be freed from the burden under which he groaned.

St. Augustine   *August 4*

"Grant me chastity and continence, but not yet", Augustine sighed to the Lord. He waged, he said, a vehement quarrel with his soul in the chamber of his heart. Raging inside him, in his inner soul, was this conflict that so agitated him. He was sick and tormented, reproaching himself more bitterly than ever. Deep reflection drew up out of the secret depths of his soul all his misery and heaped it upon him. He gave way to tears and lamentations. He said, "The streams of my eyes gushed out an acceptable sacrifice to thee." He went to the back garden so others could not see his tears. He flung himself down under a fig tree. He cried out, "And thou, O Lord, how long? How long, O Lord? Wilt thou be angry forever? Or, remember not against us our former iniquities." For he still felt enthralled by them. He cried out again, "How long, how long? Tomorrow and tomorrow? Why not now? Why not this very hour make an end to my uncleanness?"

He said, "I was saying these things and weeping in the most bitter contrition of my heart, when suddenly I heard the voice of a boy or girl—I know not which—coming from the neighboring house, chanting over and over again, 'Pick it up, read it; pick it up, read it.' Immediately I ceased weeping and began most earnestly to think whether it was usual for children in some kind of game to sing such a song, but I could not remember ever having heard the like. So, damming the torrent of my tears, I got to my feet, for I could not but think that this was a divine command to open the Bible and read the first passage I should light upon. I snatched it up, opened it, and in silence read the paragraph on which my eyes first fell: 'Not in rioting and drunkenness, not in chambering and wantonness, not in strife and envying, but put on the Lord Jesus Christ, and make no provision for the flesh to fulfill the lusts thereof.' "

This experience changed his life.

St. Augustine   *August 5*

St. Augustine, after reading the Scripture, closed the book and now had a tranquil countenance, for the first time since he could remember. He told his mother, Monica, who was with him in Milan, what happened, to her great joy. She blessed God who is "able to do exceedingly abundantly above all that we ask or think". For his mother saw the hand of God here. She saw that God had granted her far more than she had ever dared to ask for in all her countless pitiful and doleful lamentations. "For", said Augustine, "thou didst so convert me to thee that I sought neither a wife nor any other of this world's hopes, but set my feet on that rule of faith which so many years before thou hadst showed her in her dream about me. And so thou didst turn her grief into gladness more plentiful than she had ventured to desire, and dearer and purer than the desire she used to cherish."

St. Augustine now wrote, "O Lord, I am thy servant; I am thy servant and the son of thy handmaid. Thou hast loosed my bonds. I will offer to thee the sacrifice of thanksgiving. Let my heart and my tongue praise thee, and let all my bones say, 'Lord, who is like unto thee?' Let them say so, and answer thou me and say unto my soul, 'I am thy salvation.' "

St. Augustine continued; "Thou hadst pierced my heart with thy love, and changed thy servant from night to day, from death to life."

The saint left Italy and returned to his native town in North Africa. He became a priest; others joined him and they formed a small religious community. Later he was named the Bishop of Hippo. He wore himself out for the Lord. At the end of his life Hippo lay under siege to the barbarians. It looked like the light of faith and learning was going out in the places where Christianity was established. And yet Augustine continued to pray and have hope.

St. Gertrude

Prostrating herself at the feet of Jesus, St. Gertrude implored him to make known his will to her and to give her the desire to accomplish it. Jesus told her that what she suffered would add brightness to her crown in heaven. He showed her a small, narrow garden filled with many beautiful flowers. He said, "Would you prefer the pleasure which you might enjoy here to me?" She answered, "Assuredly not, Lord." Then he told her never to distrust him.

St. Gertrude at another time realized as if she were present there that Jesus, broken in body, hung on the Cross for love of us. In this he rescued us from our selfishness and sin and we should thank him with all our hearts. She implored him to help her draw closer to his holy heart. She asked his holy Mother to assist her, for we know at the wedding feast of Cana he could not resist her pleading. We beg her then to help us be more like Christ.

St. Gertrude said that our Lord appeared to her looking very weary because he carried so many people to heaven.

We come to Christ in our sins. He does not cast us out. We have his divine assurance for this. He embraces us and we are greatly consoled. Jesus said, "Come to me all you who labor and are weary and I will give you rest." The Gospel writer said, "Having loved his own, he loved them to the end." Jesus said, "My sheep listen to my voice. I know them and they follow me. They are mine and no one can snatch them from my hands."

In our pampered souls we are weak and wavering. We need him. We must pray. It is prayer that makes our love spill over into kind deeds for the sake of Christ. And we have peace of soul, for no heart that loves his heart will ever be abandoned.

As death approached Gertrude could no longer speak, but she listened with the utmost attention when anyone spoke to her of

God. And so great was her fervor that she insisted on being brought every day to assist at the Holy Mass. When at last the happy day of release arrived, Jesus appeared to her with his divine countenance radiant with joy.

St. Benedict August 7

St. Benedict said to the monks that the first degree of humility is obedience without delay. This is the virtue of those who hold nothing dearer to them than Christ; of those who, because of the holy service they have professed, the fear of hell and the glory of life everlasting, as soon as anything has been ordered by the Superior, receive it as a divine command and do not suffer any delay in executing it. With these the Lord is most pleased.

Benedict wrote in his rule that the good monk should be aware of the words of Jesus, "Narrow is the way that leads to life." And so by obedience one can be humble and enter by the narrow gate.

Benedict said that exalting oneself is a kind of pride. Jesus told us, "Everyone who exalts himself shall be humbled, and he who humbles himself shall be exalted." The prophet proved to be on guard when he said, "Lord, my heart is not exalted, nor are mine eyes lifted up; neither have I walked in great matters, nor in wonders above me. . . . Rather have I been of humble mind than exalting myself; as a weaned child on its mother's breast, so you solace my soul."

Benedict said, "Brothers, if we wish to reach the very highest point of humility and to arrive speedily at that heavenly exaltation to which ascent is made through the humility of this present life, we must by our ascending actions erect the ladder Jacob saw in his dream, the ladder on which angels appeared to him descending and ascending. By that descent and ascent we must surely understand nothing else than this, that we descend by self-exaltation and ascend by humility. And the ladder thus set up is our life in the world, which the Lord raises up to heaven if our heart is humble. For we call our body and soul the sides of the ladder, and into these sides our divine vocation has inserted the different steps of humility and self-discipline that we must climb."

St. Thomas More   *August 8*

St. Thomas More tells us that it was pride that "threw down the devil out of heaven". So, he said, shall there never be anyone ascend to heaven without humility. The devil offers us only trifles. He gives us pleasure which ends in pain. Only the proud, who are blind, are deceived by the devil, for they judge on their own and do not in humility ask for divine assistance.

God in his goodness offers us grace, we must not continue to refuse it; we must not lose it.

"Holy Scripture is the highest and best learning than any man can have, it shows us the right way in learning." The Church must guide us in the Gospels and then the Gospels will lead us to Christ.

St. Thomas said many times to hold fast to the Faith. That is the most important thing of all. No matter how many are against you, with the Faith you are with Christ and you are right. "A faint faith is better than a strong heresy", he noted. Have faith and a good purpose and a humble heart and then you will walk with Jesus. There is nothing more important and more wonderful and more joyful than that.

On which road do we meet Christ? Prayer. It is prayer that makes us grow in faith. Those who seek only pleasure, who set out to make themselves happy, are on a fool's errand. Those, however, who, for Jesus, help others, know peace of soul and an inner happiness.

Kindness is the nobility of humans.

A true Christ-follower must, as Christ said, pray and do penance. We pray so that Jesus will help us. Even when weary of limb, Jesus had time for sinners. He shows the unutterable mercy of God. He outdistances every creature in love, generosity and humility.

Before St. Thomas was beheaded he said, "May we all merrily meet in heaven."

St. Thomas Aquinas wrote that life everlasting is the end of all our desires. Man is not of the same condition as the beasts. His soul does not perish with the body. The human soul is likened to God in point of immortality, whereas in point of sensuality he is like the beasts; so that when a man believes that his soul dies with his body, he abandons his likeness to God and becomes like a beast. God created man incorruptible, and to the image of his own likeness he made him.

In eternal life man is united to God: since God himself is our reward and the end of all our labors. This union with God consists in seeing him clearly. St. Paul said, "We see now through a glass in a dark manner, but then face to face." St. Augustine said that in heaven, "we shall love, and we shall behold and we shall praise." The Scripture says, "Joy and gladness shall be found therein, thanksgiving and the voice of praise." Eternal life, said Thomas, is the perfect fulfillment of desire, inasmuch as each of the blessed will have more than he desired or hoped for. The reason for this is because in this life no man can fulfill his desires, nor can any creature satisfy a person's craving; for God alone satisfies and infinitely surpasses man's desire, which for that reason is never at rest save in God. St. Augustine said, "Thou hast made us, O Lord, for thyself and our heart is restless until it rests in thee." In heaven our desires will be satisfied and our glory will surpass every expectation. Our Lord said, "Enter into the joy of the Lord." St. Augustine said of the souls in heaven, "Their whole joy will not enter into the joyful, but the joyful will enter into joy. I shall be satisfied when thy glory shall appear."

In heaven, whatever is delightful will be there in abundance, wrote Thomas Aquinas. It will be there superabundantly. Scripture says, "Then shalt thou abound in delights in the Almighty."

The founder of the Blessed Sacrament Fathers, St. Peter Julian Eymard, said, "Alas! If the love of Jesus in the Most Blessed Sacrament does not win our hearts, Jesus is vanquished. Our ingratitude must be greater than his goodness; our malice is more powerful than his charity. O no, my good Savior. Your charity presses me, torments me, binds me.

"I want to devote myself to the service and glory of thy Sacrament. By dint of love I want to make thee forget that up to this day I have been so ungrateful; by dint of devotedness I want to obtain forgiveness for having loved thee so late!"

The saint said that Holy Thursday, the eve of our Savior's death, the day on which he instituted the adorable Sacrament of the Eucharist, was the most beautiful day in our Lord's life. It was the greatest day of his love and tenderness.

Christ's love on the Cross was boundless, but when in the Eucharist he perpetuated his presence in our midst, he manifested openly that love. On Good Friday there came an end to his suffering, but in the Eucharist there is no end to his love, until the end of the world. Jesus in the Holy Sacrament makes himself the Sacrament of Love forever.

On Holy Thursday Jesus was about to die. He would return to the Father, yet he wanted to remain with us. So he instituted the Eucharist. He gives himself to us day and night. He remains with us though he goes to heaven. Only a divine mind could be so ingenious and so generous and gracious and warm in his love.

Jesus in the Eucharist gives us himself. He does not give us a "thing". He is present here. He was poor when on earth. He had no possessions to leave us. He did far more. He left us himself. He is here.

As God, Jesus was master of his sacred humanity. He gave it to us, and with it all that he was.

St. Teresa of Avila said that self-denial helps us control our lives. It gives us satisfaction. So watch your desire always to please yourself. Our greatest duty is not comfort for ourselves but pleasing God. We are often too self-centered.

May the thought of Christ on the Cross, she said, keep us from constant self-gratification. Banish thoughts of pride and vanity. If they get hold of a person they become a plague.

Appeal to Jesus, pray more fervently to overcome pride, for that is the source of a soul's ruin. Pride does not permit a person to enjoy the graces God gives, which are our delight. Let God and his infinite wisdom lead us.

Be humble, be prayerful. Perfect prayer takes away our defects. Penance helps us make progress in prayer and enjoy the true fruits of prayer. Prayer assists us to see there are greater things than worldly honors. There is friendship with Jesus, and having this we need nothing else. As we are humble, so do we make spiritual progress.

When one looks back over his life and sees how little he has done for Jesus, he must be humble; he realizes that because of the little he has done, he has a great debt to Christ. Jesus abased himself, suffering great humiliation, in order to leave us an example of humility. The soul gains great humility when a person looks at his sins.

God deliver us, she prayed, from anyone in religion who is proud. He is like the Pharisees. Such a person loves honors and fears dishonor. But consider how foolish that is, for in religion there is only one thing needed—to be close to Christ. Honor is lost by seeking it, especially by desiring positions; there is no poison in the world so deadly as pride.

St. Bernard of Clairvaux *August 12*

St. Bernard of Clairvaux did a great deal as a peacemaker in his time, but he looked upon his successes as arbitrator among nations as mere scum and dross. What was important were spiritual things, "the love of the divine Love". His love and enthusiasm for Mary spread everywhere. Bernard's ardor was derived from the Bible, of which he had made a profound study. The Scripture was deeply impressed upon his mind and heart. His passion for Holy Scripture was such that he made it a part of his being. Figures from the Bible surged through his mind, stimulated his imagination and inspired him daily. His memory never failed to supply him with the Scripture text when he spoke, enforcing the meaning of his words. He wrote, "Lord, it is my delight that I feed in your pastures; that I am nourished by you, through the law, the prophets and the psalms." The Scripture was the source of his boundless love for Mary. He said that she is the flower that rejoices the heart of God. To him Mary was the channel through which the waters of heaven are carried to us.

St. Bernard wrote, "God knows that all I say and feel, my message as it appears in my writings, the foundation of my philosophy, is Jesus and Jesus crucified. I do not ask where he pastures his flock, for I contemplate him as he hangs on the Cross, the Savior of the world."

He spoke out forcefully against pride. He said that the boastful man "must talk or burst. He is so full of speeches he feels the need for expansion. He anticipates questions, giving replies which he has not been asked for, puts questions and provides the answers. . . . His vainglory is evident from his loquacity. He avoids performance and speaks of it instead."

St. Augustine   *August 13*

St. Augustine wrote masterful essays on the spiritual life. In one he said that he who loves himself with a wrongful love also loves his neighbor in the wrong way.

There are vile and sinful loves—the loves of adulterers and seducers—impure loves. Shun such unlawful loves. Despise them.

You will find no one more worthy of love than God. If you do not offend him, there is nothing in which he can offend you.

There is nothing or no one so fair and sweet as he. We should love our neighbor for love of him. Begin to love God and you will love your fellow man because of him. Do not abandon him who made you and love that which he made. You are most ungrateful if you desert him who made you. The soul that loves creation, leaving the Creator abandoned, is wicked. For there is no love more pure and more to be desired than the love of God. To desert God and to embrace the world is a defilement.

"O soul, that you may be worthy of his embrace, cast out the world and cling gladly to him. The psalm says, 'But it is good for me to adhere in my God.' This is called grace, for it is a gratuitous act. When you begin to love God willingly, you are secure. For then your love for your neighbor is willing and spontaneous and you love him that he may love God with you."

Why is a state of well-being so transitory, so delicate, so short-lived, so vain? St. Augustine notes that St. James said, "For what is life? It is a mist that appears for a little while." What is life everlasting? This is true well-being. Pray for those close to you in this life so that they will be close to Christ and be saved. Since you long for salvation, which is eternal, you love your friends best by desiring this for them. You love to conduct your life under God and so desire your friends to conduct their lives under God. You love life everlasting, and so you wish that they will reign with you in eternity.

St. Bernard of Clairvaux   *August 14*

St. Bernard of Clairvaux, like all the saints, said pride is blind.

Pride grows even more deadly when one feels that he is bearing superhuman hardships and must be a saint. One is tempted to vainglory, his tongue is poisoned and he talks of his great suffering, which in reality is quite small.

When a proud person confesses some guilt he exaggerates his guilt but adds circumstances so incredible or impossible that you doubt what you considered to be the truth. He conceals the fault, of which he is guilty, by these inventions, which he knows will not be believed. He bows his head, prostrates himself and, if he can, squeezes out a few tears; his confession is interrupted by sighs and groans.

In speaking of self-denial, Bernard said that this should be practiced with discretion. But the body that is used to soft living should do penance. He said the body is a good and faithful companion to the soul; its passions and feelings must be kept under control. However, practice self-denial in secret. "Witness our Lord's condemnation of the Pharisees for taking pride in their fasting", he said.

One seeks union with God in love. This is perfected only in the life to come, but a union can be attained here.

Love is the condition of the knowledge of God since God is Love. Man resembles God in works of love. If we must have love in order to know God, it is he himself who must give it to us. The spiritual life is a sharing of the divine life. The presence of the Holy Spirit within us is a substitute for the sight of God, of which we are deprived in this life. We love God because he loved us first and for all eternity.

Assumption of Mary   *August 15*

All the saints had a great love for the Blessed Mother. On this day we remember that she was taken to heaven. We cannot begin to imagine the joy of the reunion of Mother and Son. They must have embraced with all their hearts, rejoicing with a happiness beyond words.

When Jesus was to depart this world he asked his Mother to remain behind. How heartbreaking it was for her not to go to heaven with him, and yet she never for a moment thought of refusing. All her life it was the same: whatever God wanted she wanted. All her life her one thought was, "Be it done unto me according to thy word."

She loved Jesus so much. Her heart was his heart. She had been with him for so long. And now he was leaving her. How could she endure it? It must have been like cutting her heart in two. But she knew that she must stay in the world to be an example for the apostles, who were very weak. Her courage and her prayers would make the infant Church possible. Without this the apostles would no doubt run away completely.

She stayed with the apostles and gave them the spiritual strength that they needed. Would the Church ever have begun without her sterling example and wonderful prayers? No wonder we call her Mother of the Church.

What sustained her until it was her turn to go to heaven and join her Son? Surely it must have been the Eucharist. She was with John, a priest. He offered Mass. It almost seems unnecessary to say that all of her time, other than her duties, was spent in praying to Jesus. He was gone, but he was in her heart. He had supported and sustained her when he walked in the world, from the time he was born to her in the cave at Bethlehem, until the day he returned to the Father. He sustained and supported her still, especially in the Eucharist. She knew he was truly present. It was only because of the Eucharist that she had the courage to stay behind and give courage to the apostles and the young Church.

St. Augustine   *August 16*

St. Augustine was constantly writing to encourage the Christians. Whenever you find affliction in the souls of others, you beg God to help them, he said.

Our Lord suffered and through his suffering he brought forth love among men. Our Lord loved us first and wishes to be loved by us.

"It was that no one might fear to die in his name that Jesus died first for all of us. It was that he might create love in the hearts of men that he cast out the devil. It is evil desire that summons the devil into the hearts of men, and it is Godly love that casts him out", Augustine wrote.

He said that when men proudly claim as their own the intelligence God has given them, they lie. St. Paul wrote of the proud,

"While professing to be wise, they have become fools." We should hide from pride.

The proud study creation with countless disputes and ingenious inquiries, but have no concern for the Creator. Others know God but do nothing to glorify him or thank him.

It is the humble whom God loves. God reveals himself to them. If we are humble we are blessed by God and we come to know Christ. Jesus said, "All these things have been delivered to me by my Father." The humble know Jesus and his teaching. The grace of Christ blesses us and reveals to us what is hidden from the proud.

As we become more devout, we learn more of Christ. He tenderly speaks to his little ones, whom he allows to know him. He permits the humble to see his way. They glimpse the vision that is to come.

The Savior says to the humble, "I know what it is you desire. You little ones will receive this great blessing." You will know Jesus and you will know the road to heaven.

St. Peter Julian Eymard   *August 17*

St. Peter Julian Eymard devoted his life to the Blessed Sacrament. He wrote, "In this testament of love our Lord included everything, all his graces, even his glory.

"We can say to our heavenly Father: 'Give me the graces I need, and I will pay thee with Jesus Eucharistic.'"

St. Peter Julian said that Jesus gave the Eucharist to us in trust. Priests are the guardians of the Blessed Sacrament. The first guardians were the apostles. The apostles handed it over to priests, who bring it to the people. They give the consecrated Host to us. "There is neither past nor present nor future for Jesus Christ." He is with us always in the Blessed Sacrament.

He said, "Our Lord's only purpose in coming to us is to do us good. How good our Savior is." Let us therefore take this heavenly Bread. Our Lord gave it to us. What an honor!

He wrote, "John the Baptist's mission on earth was to announce the coming of the promised Savior, point him out to men, and prepare the way for him.

"The Church fulfills the same mission with regard to Jesus in the Eucharist, a more extensive and lasting mission, which takes in every age and country. She carries out her mission by manifesting Jesus in the Blessed Sacrament, by preaching him by word, and also by the testimony of her faith and works—a silent preaching, but just as eloquent as the first.

"The Church presents herself before us with the words of Jesus on her lips; she repeats and explains them with an authority equal to that of the Savior: 'This is my Body. This is my Blood.'

"She tells us and we must believe this: that by the divine power of these sacramental words Jesus Christ becomes truly present on the altar."

St. Benedict

St. Benedict wrote, "The first degree of humility is that a person keep the fear of God before his eyes and beware of ever forgetting it. Let him be ever mindful of all that God has commanded; let his thoughts constantly recur to the hell-fire, which will burn for their sins those who despise God; vices whether of the mind, the tongue, the hands, the feet or the self-will; and let him check also the desires of the flesh.

"Let a man consider that God is always looking at him from heaven, that his actions are everywhere visible to the divine eyes and are constantly being reported to God by the angels. This is what the prophet shows us when he represents God as ever present within our thoughts, in the words, 'Searcher of minds and hearts is God' and again in the words, 'The Lord knows the thoughts of men.' And again he says, 'You have read my thoughts from afar' and 'The thoughts of men will confess to you.'

"In order that he may be careful about his wrongful thoughts, therefore, let the faithful brother say constantly in his heart, 'Then shall I be spotless before him.'"

St. Benedict said, "We must be on our guard, therefore, against evil desires." In humble prayer we gain strength against the evil one.

To show our faithfulness the monk ought to endure difficulties for the Lord. Be patient. Let the Brother know that God is almighty and we can do nothing without his help. Through humility a person comes to God. The humble love God with a great love. They will love Christ and be grateful to him for dying for our sins and for reopening the gates of heaven to us. We would be lost without Jesus, our Savior, our Redeemer.

St. Augustine
August 19

St. Augustine was great in mind and heart but he always emphasized humility.

The Father makes known the Son to the humble. The proud, however, are spiritually blind and cannot see him. You recognize the Son because of the grace of the Father. Thus when you look upon Jesus with the eye of the mind and the eye of faith, you will know him as the Son.

Our sins keep us apart from God. But if we beg forgiveness he turns his face to us.

Let us listen to the call of Christ while we sweat beneath the burdens of our hearts. Jesus said, "Come to me all you who labor." Where do you labor if not in your longing for Jesus?

The great St. Augustine was probably the most influential early Christian writer and one of the greatest of all times. Augustine says humbly that he has feeble powers but that his love for Jesus makes him want to treat of him. "For Jesus was the Son of God, the only-begotten of the Father, God everlasting, a man because of us, a creature of his own creation—for he who made man was made a man", Augustine stated.

The Son praised the Father. And he instructs us to praise the Father, the God of mercy. In the Scripture it says, "Magnify his name, and give glory to him, and you shall say in this manner: all the works of the Lord are exceedingly good." Both in extolling God and reproaching yourself for your sins, you are praising God.

Jesus praised God "that thou didst hide these things from the wise and prudent and didst reveal them to the little ones".

Augustine asks, "What is it that he hid from the wise and prudent and revealed to the little ones?" The wisdom to follow Jesus.

St. Augustine   *August 20*

St. Augustine emphasized the great need to be both wise and prudent.

St. Paul said, "Where is the 'wise man'? Where is the scribe? Where is the disputant of this world? Has not God turned to foolishness the 'wisdom' of this world?" Many dispute much about God and speak falsely—they are inflated with their own learning and are least able to find and know God. Some of them, in place of God, whose essence is incomprehensible and invisible, assign divinity to pagan objects like mountains and great trees.

The book of Wisdom, the saint points out, proved that God's reproach is intended for those who do not discern the Creator from creation. Such people do not seek out the Creator who is ever near at hand but study the course of the stars far away.

St. Augustine wrote, "Love him who is the Creator because he made you to his own image. He also made you to love him. Some take heed of God and some do not. The proud do not; the humble do."

St. Augustine told us to love Jesus, for it is he who guides us. Life is a struggle and we need the daily assistance of Jesus. Jesus rescues those who turn to him. We need the strength of soul that Jesus gives us so we can resist the evils of the world.

Prayer leads to Christ. In troubled times we must have him at our side. He comes to us when we pray. It is necessary to face life without losing heart. Christ is our hope. Fidelity to him gains us the graces we need. Through persevering prayer the way is revealed for us; it unfolds for us. Life is a mystery, but Christ is our teacher. It requires courage to take brave steps in the darkness. But we are not alone. Jesus is with us. With him we are safe.

St. Bernard of Clairvaux

St. Bernard of Clairvaux said, "You wish me to tell you why God should be loved, and in what way or measure we should love him. I answer then: the reason for our loving God is God; and the measure of that love is none. Is that enough to say about the matter? For a wise man most probably it is, but I am under obligation to the foolish also; and though I may have said enough for those with understanding, I must have due regard for others too. For those less apt, then, I gladly will explain what I have said more fully, if not with greater depth.

"I might have said there was a twofold reason for our loving God solely for himself. First: nothing can be loved more justly. And, second: nothing can be loved with so much profit to ourselves. The question Why should God be loved? includes both of these; first, it may mean either What is his claim upon our love? or What benefit shall we derive from loving him? My former answer stands in either case: there is no other worthy cause for loving God except himself. As to his claim upon our love, he surely merits much from us who gave himself to us, unworthy as we were: what better gift could he have given than himself? If, then, it is his claim we have in mind when asking Why should God be loved? the first and foremost answer is, 'Because he first loved us'."

St. Bernard said that most plainly is God worthy of our answering love, especially if we consider who he is and who thus bestows every good thing upon us. How great is his love for us.

God shows to us a selfless love. He loves us freely though we are sinners. He who is Almighty stoops down to love us who are weak. He helps us in our misery. We owe him all the gratitude we can give him.

St. Martin de Porres

In the streets, St. Martin de Porres, the humble Dominican Brother in Lima, Peru, saw so many poor who were sick that he opened a hospice for them. Returning from it to the Dominican House one night he found an Indian lying in the street. He had been stabbed with a knife and was bleeding badly. St. Martin carried him to the residence and put him in his own bed and nursed him until he was well.

Sometimes Martin would arrive at a home with help just when the family was on the point of despair. No one knew how he was aware of their sad plight.

He constantly visited the poor Indians and blacks who labored long and were no more than slaves on the huge plantations of the wealthy Spanish. Because he was black he was always welcomed by the laborers.

Lima was overrun with orphans, deserted and lost boys and girls who were homeless. These small outcasts suffered terribly. They were used and abused by heartless adults, the prey of every sort of evil influence. The problem seemed hopeless, but Martin did not think it hopeless. Saints never do. He awakened the public conscience, and gifts began to pour in and he established the Holy Cross school and orphanage.

One religious in the house was very hard to please and was always complaining. Everything that Martin did for him was wrong. He told Martin, as the humble Brother waited on him hand and foot, that Martin was a hypocrite. Martin continuously thanked him for correcting him, and added that if he found any other faults in him he should let him know.

One day Martin saw the superior taking an expensive holy painting to town to sell it so they could pay some of their bills. The humble Brother ran after him and offered to be sold into slavery so that the holy picture could be saved. Fortunately, neither happened.

St. Frances Xavier Cabrini   *August 23*

Mother Cabrini loved the words of St. Paul, "I can do all things in him who strengthens me." And these words were so true in the life of this little Italian nun. Though frail and often ill, she with her Sisters came to America and worked tirelessly with Italian immigrants and others. She later became an American citizen.

She arrived in New York with almost no money. Worse still, the letter from the Archbishop telling her not to come at this time did not reach her. He was unprepared. He had originally invited her, but then there was a prejudice against immigrants that broke out in New York, so he wrote again saying not to come. He was surprised to see her in New York, and he first suggested she return to Italy. Fortunately, she did not heed his advice. She worked wonders in America, building schools, orphanages and hospitals—her work extended across the country.

The ship that she was on arrived in New York on the last day of March 1889. With this tiny, fragile looking woman, who had a will of steel, were six of her Sisters, some of them already homesick for Italy. In Rome Mother had knelt before the Holy Father, Pope Leo XIII, and told him that she wanted to be a missionary to India, like St. Francis Xavier. But the Holy Father, all in white, tall and old and thin, looked at the little lady and said gently, "Not to the East, my daughter, but to the West". He had heard of the need of the Italian immigrants in the New World. Always obedient, Mother Cabrini went to America. She and her Sisters spent the first night in a poor dirty room in a tenement hotel. There were so many bed bugs they could not sleep in the beds. But from that humble beginning she went on to do wonderful works in many parts of the United States.

She was canonized in 1946.

St. Teresa of Avila   *August 24*

St. Teresa said, "Our nature is so wretchedly weak we think small pain is great suffering." When others sympathize we feel it is even greater and we are convinced of our greatness. The soul thus loses the opportunity to gain merit.

God deliver us, she wrote, from thinking often of injustices we have suffered. Jesus suffered unjustly so much more on the Cross, and without complaint. The Cross is given us to make up for our sins. Do not mention the injuries you have endured. We wish to share happiness in the Kingdom of Christ with him; we then should share in the insults he endured on earth.

May God preserve us from pride. Proud people often think they are treated unfairly. The humble Blessed Mother, Queen of the Angels, was unjustly treated many times. We must not be unlike her and make her ashamed of us because of our pride. Let us, rather, be her faithful, loving children. Carefully uproot your pride and serve your Savior; humbly and prayerfully show his kindness.

With humility, St. Teresa wrote, "Look at the disorderly way I write. It indeed betrays a person who does not know what she is doing."

She continued, "The fault is yours, my Sisters, since you command me to do this. And if you find it bad, throw it into the fire. The work requires leisure and I have so little time."

The chief gain, she wrote, is to imitate Christ. "O my Lord, when I consider the many ways in which thou didst suffer and how totally undeserved thy sufferings were, I do not know what to say for myself", she wrote.

St. Teresa said, "You ask me to explain to you how one begins to pray. I know no other way than this. Nothing makes Jesus surrender as quickly as humility. His humility brought him down from heaven to be born of the Virgin. And by our humility we easily draw him into our souls. You may be sure that the humblest person will possess him most."

St. Teresa of Avila   *August 25*

St. Teresa of Avila emphasized humility, as did all of the saints. She said that there cannot be humility without love. No matter how abandoned one may feel, if he is humble, Christ is with him. But the King of Glory will never come into our souls in such a way as to be united with them unless we strive for humility. The "joy of the angels" delights in a humble soul. And he draws it to him. And he pours forth his favors upon that person. When one is in his arms, the Lord comforts him and delivers him from his difficulties.

"God once commanded that the world be made, and it was made", Teresa wrote. Do not be afraid that he will abandon you. Consider the wonderful exchange: his love for ours. He can do everything, and we can do nothing at all, except as he gives us the power.

"O Lord, all our evil comes from not keeping our eyes fixed on thee. And so we often stumble and fall and stray. Help us please." To follow Christ is the sole reason for our lives. Let us give glory to God. Never be discouraged, for God helps the valiant.

If you are humble there is nothing to fear. Humility consists chiefly in a willingness to be satisfied with whatever the Lord wishes, considering oneself unworthy to be called Christ's servant. What does it matter whether we serve him in one capacity or another? It is not for us to choose, but for the Lord to give. Let the Master of the house do as he pleases. He is the wisest of all. He knows what is best for us. What better proof of friendship than the fact that Jesus desires more than anything to lead us to heaven. "May he lead each of you by a safe road to the port of light", St. Teresa said.

St. Teresa of Avila   *August 26*

St. Teresa of Avila, in her reforms, brought many souls to Christ. It all began with prayer. She constantly urged people to pray more faithfully. "May God grant me the grace to help people to pray", Teresa wrote. Some are restless at prayer. They must pray for patience. We must look to the Lord to overcome our distractions.

The Lord has different paths by which we go to him. If we are humble, he provides for us. May we always be so blessed. He gives drink to those who desire it. No one need fear that he will die of thirst along the road. Make the effort to pray and Jesus will come to you. He will do the rest. He will never fail you.

Be resolved to pray, and you will pray. Pray for yourself and the welfare of souls; these are the graces that you must always beg of our Lord. To pray for a friend or a relative is truly to love that person. There is nothing more splendid that we can do on earth than pray.

Begin with a firm resolution to be devoted to prayer. This is the royal road to heaven. "Great is the treasure to be gained by traveling this road. Everything else", St. Teresa said, "is worthless in comparison."

When a person prays, Christ comes to him. Prayer is visiting with Christ. In this way we draw closer to him and we think more like him and love more like him.

We cannot, if we are thinking people, be indifferent to God. We are in profound need of his graces every day. How sad that many adults are immature and live by slogans and do not pay much attention to God.

What love was in our dear Savior's heart when he suffered and died for us. How can we ignore him? How can we be ungrateful to him? Let us serve the Lord; let us serve the Lord with gladness.

St. Frances Xavier Cabrini

August 27

When the Archbishop of New York suggested that Mother Cabrini return home to Italy, she said simply, "No, your excellency, we cannot do that." The Archbishop was surprised at this answer and looked stern. He was used to having people do his every wish. But Mother took out some letters from her purse and showed that Rome wished her to engage in this mission. He immediately changed. She had letters from the Vatican.

Mother Cabrini set to work among the poor immigrant Italians. Soon a well-to-do Italian lady urged her to open an orphanage. She would give her a house on Fifth Avenue where the rich people lived. The Archbishop did not like this idea. He thought it would disturb the wealthy people. But Mother Cabrini contended it would do the rich good to see the poor children. And she won out.

In Italy, when she was young, Mother Cabrini had applied to be a Sister in a nearby convent, but she was refused because they said her health was not good enough. Again, some time later, she applied and was refused. In the light of all that she later accomplished throughout Italy and Europe and North and South America, it is evident that God did not want her just to live and die in one remote convent in her native land.

She became a teacher, and then the parish priest told her she should go to a nearby village where an orphanage was being badly run by some women who wore the religious habit but were not officially Sisters. He told her she would have to stay there only for six weeks. She stayed for six years. Every time she wanted to leave, and this was often, for she was ill-treated by the women, she thought of the children, and she could not abandon them. The children loved her dearly, but the women were jealous of her and made life miserable. And yet because she was devoted to prayer, she stayed, even though at night many times she cried herself to sleep.

St. Bernard of Clairvaux   *August 28*

St. Bernard of Clairvaux said that when we love one another, for all men are brothers in Jesus Christ, then we are near God. There is an absence of fear, for love casts out fear from the soul and replaces it with confidence. We know God sustains and protects us because of his love for us. We must have hearts of stone if we are not moved by the goodness of God who protects us day and night, we must show gratitude.

God makes himself known to us little by little, he said. When we have experienced his kindness, when we have tasted and found how sweet he is, we grow in our love for him. Our will becomes fused with the divine will.

St. Bernard wrote, "O pure and holy love, O sweet and most tender affection; O complete submission of the will to God, all the nobler in that there is no thought of self; most sweet and loving is it that the soul's whole feeling is divine. As a tiny drop

237

of water appears to vanish when mixed with a large quantity of wine, since it takes on its taste and color, so it is with the saints. Their natural affections seem, in some way, to melt into and become entirely transformed into the will of God."

He went on, "This love can be expressed without words. It is a cry of the heart. It is a love as intoxicating as wine. Love returns to the fountain-head." Love is the only gift man can give his Creator similar in kind to God's gift to him. In his love, God asks only to be loved in return, knowing that in this way those who love him will find happiness.

If we love God to the best of our ability, we will be happy, Bernard tells us. In this life we are unable to look continually on the divine countenance. We suffer from worry and apathy because our faculties are servants of our frail bodies, which are prey to suffering.

St. Bernard of Clairvaux   *August 29*

St. Bernard of Clairvaux saved many souls. Like Christ, he was interested only in this goal.

St. Bernard wrote, "When you feel you are becoming apathetic, lukewarm or indifferent, do not lose confidence. Continue your spiritual exercises and strive to cling to him who can help you. Beseech Jesus to draw you after him. Aroused to activity by grace, you will find you are able to advance along the path to God. . . . We all complain because we have not been given the grace of devotion, but we have no right to complain because, more often than not, the fault is ours. In fact, this grace, which we desire, will come to us if our hearts are in the right disposition to receive it; but whoever closes the door of this inner sanctuary, will effectively prevent it from entering into him."

In prayer the saint said we should present ourselves to God full of respect, with attention, not in a state of indifference or indolence. We are free to do this, if we will. He said, "The will is a rational impulse which rules the senses and the appetites. Whenever the will is in control, it has reason as its helper and, to some degree, as its servant. When a person allows himself to be guided by wisdom he does well." Man "resembles" God inasmuch as he is free, but in sin he becomes a slave of bodily desires. His soul is then dominated by "the law of the members which is repugnant to the law of the spirit". And man no longer resembles God. He is caught up by the love of lower things.

The Son of Man came on earth to reform mankind. He who "was made flesh and dwells among us should dwell in our minds and hearts" so that the soul can "bring forth fruit, will be a star in the darkness, will be visited by the Holy Spirit".

St. Bernard of Clairvaux   *August 30*

St. Bernard of Clairvaux would go anywhere to save a soul. He said, "Astonishing indeed is the charity of a God who calls back to him the soul who has defied his authority.... Sin, to some degree, destroys the likeness of the soul to God. When sin is wiped out, creature and Creator become one in spirit, each can behold the other, each can love the other." Bernard continued, "I salute you, Jesus, whom I love. You know why I wish so ardently to cling to your Cross. Give yourself to me! From the Cross upon which you are raised, look at me, my Beloved: draw me to yourself and say to me, 'I have cured you, you are forgiven.' As I embrace you in a transport of love, I am very conscious of my unworthiness."

Christ visited Bernard and he was caught up in ecstasy. He told the monks that he would reveal his experience for their benefit. If they did derive profit from his words, Bernard said, "then I shall be consoled for my imprudence. If not, I shall openly acknowledge my folly." He went on, "I admit—and I speak as if it were in foolishness—that the Word has visited me not once, but many times. But although he has often come into my soul, I have never been conscious of the exact moment of his coming. I have been aware of his presence within me. I could remember afterward that he had been present. I have even had a presentiment that he could come, yet I have never been able to sense the moment of his entry or of his departure. But looking within myself, he was more interior than the very center of my being. Blessed is the soul in which he dwells, which lives for him, and is moved by him.... You will now want to know how I knew that he was present within me, since his ways are unsearchable. I answer that the Word of God acts with rapidity and efficaciously. The moment he entered, he awoke my slumbering soul. He touched my heart and softened it and wounded it. He began to root up and pull down, to build and to plant, to water what was dry, to light up what was dark." Bernard said that happy was the soul that was privileged to experience the sweetness of such an embrace.

St. Bernard of Clairvaux   *August 31*

St. Bernard, the abbot of Clairvaux, loved justice and truth. Bernard had enthusiasm for the Lord and the temperament of a fighter; he shared the frustrations of those whose petitions go unheard; quick, impulsive, generous, he was always ready to bear witness to the truth. He refused to compromise with evil in any form. He was, as one observer noted, possessed of Messianic impatience. His was the type of humor that prevented him from being overawed by the splendor of the established order.

He was constantly torn between his joy of prayer in the monastery and the need to go out and help the Church in distress. He had the conflict of Mary and Martha in the Gospel. He said, "While the bride is absorbed by the sweetness of the Word, at the same time she is required by her neighbors in trouble; on the one hand there are the kisses of the Bridegroom and on the other the children's cry for help. It is the nourishment which the Bridegroom gives that enables the person to look after the children."

But at length the conflict was over. He wrote, "I shall await tranquilly and in silence the hour of my passing. My life is ebbing away drop by drop. In truth, I am not worthy to die quickly and enter into life immediately."

Now that he knew the end was near, that his work was over, that he had fulfilled his duties, it was good for him to be back at the monastery among his brothers. And while his spiritual sons wept and prayed for their Abbot, Bernard, who had labored so hard, suffered so much, so loved the only true Love, passed out of life.

This twelfth-century saint heralded the coming of the thirteenth century, the epoch of St. Francis of Assisi, St. Dominic, St. Thomas Aquinas and other great saints.

St. Bernard of Clairvaux   *September 1*

St. Bernard of Clairvaux gave his life for Christ. He fought rationalism, anti-clericalism, realism and a host of other false philosophies in what was called "an epoch which was one of the most troubled the world has ever known". His one goal was to bring in as many stray sheep as he could. Mediator, diplomat, advocate, judge, witness to the truth at all times, comforter—this great saint righted numerous wrongs, remedied injustice, championed the innocent, pleaded the cause of the poor and rebuked tyrants. But in all this activity, the spirit of prayer, which gave him a closeness to Christ, never left him. "My weapon is prayer", he said. Prayer gave him courage, and he had plenty of that. "He lent himself to the world," said the author Michelet, "but he never belonged to it; his heart and his treasure were elsewhere." His writings were permeated by the Holy Spirit.

Above all else he was a Knight of Mary. From her he received the strength and the humility which enabled him to do so very much. His face radiated ineffable happiness as he sang the praises of our Lady. It was she, the Queen of Heaven, for whom he burned, as Dante wrote of Bernard.

St. Bernard wanted all men to know Christ and to love him. And devotion to the Blessed Mother helps us do this. For Mary's one great thought is to make her Son known.

If we were wiser, we would know that we gain our inspiration from Jesus. He feeds and heals our souls. He teaches us that it is the humble who truly do great things in life. Humility is the foundation of all the other virtues. The Blessed Mother was the most humble of the saints and the greatest.

St. Francis of Assisi   *September 2*

In his rule St. Francis of Assisi said to the Little Brothers, "The friars to whom God has given the grace of working should work in a spirit of faith and devotion and avoid idleness, which is the enemy of the soul, without however extinguishing the spirit of prayer and devotion, to which every temporal consideration must be subordinate."

He said about preaching: "I advise and admonish the friars that in their preaching, their words should be examined and chaste. They should aim only at the advantage and spiritual good of their listeners, telling them briefly about vice and virtue, punishment and glory, because our Lord himself kept his words short on earth."

Francis wrote, "Every day Jesus humbles himself just as he did when he came from his heavenly throne into the Virgin's womb; every day he comes to us and lets us see him in abjection when he descends from the bosom of the Father into the hands of the priest at the altar. He shows himself to us in this sacred bread just as he once appeared to his apostles in real flesh. With their own eyes they saw only his flesh but they believed that he was God, because they contemplated him with the eyes of the spirit. We too with our own eyes see only bread and wine, but we must see further and firmly believe that this is the most holy Body and Blood, living and true. In this way our Lord remains continually with his followers, as he promised, 'Behold, I am with you all days, even unto the consummation of the world.'"

Francis pointed out that knowledge very often brings pride and one thinks that what he knows comes from himself alone. It is only the humble who truly learn and, especially, learn about God and the things of God.

St. Clare of Assisi *September 3*

St. Clare was from a wealthy family of Assisi. She heard St. Francis preach and she determined to follow him. "She fled in the night from her father's home by a side door. She left her family, home and riches and went to Francis." He welcomed her. When her flight was discovered, her family members, and in particular her father, were furious. They thought it a scandal. But her strong will prevailed. She was determined to serve Christ. Her family and father and relatives begged her to come home, but she would not.

At the altar in the chapel she made her profession. She said, "I want only Jesus Christ, and to live by the Gospel, owning nothing, to live in chastity." To seal her vow Francis cut off her long fair hair and she was clothed in a poor, coarse habit and veil. She gave up all for Christ. Francis first took her to live with the Benedictine Sisters until a convent could be found for her new Franciscan Sisters. For soon other young women joined her. They then took over the church of San Damiano, where Francis had first gone after his severe illness to work and ponder. The residence there became their convent. St. Francis said, "What are the servants of God but his singers whose duty it is to lift up the hearts of men and women and move them to spiritual joy?" And this is what Clare and her Sisters did.

St. Clare wrote, "Thus by the will of God and our blessed father Francis, we came to dwell at San Damiano, where soon the Lord, in his mercy and grace, multiplied us in order that what had been foretold by his holy one, should be fulfilled; for we had sojourned in another place, but only for a short time."

With prayer and penance the Sisters of Clare grew in goodness and richness of soul.

St. Thomas Aquinas *September 4*

St. Thomas Aquinas wrote about eternal life. He said, "It consists in perfect security. In this world there is no perfect security, since

the more one has, and the higher one's position, the more reason one has to fear, and the more one wants; whereas in eternal life there is no sorrow, or toil, or fear. The Scripture says, 'He shall enjoy abundance without fear of evils.'

"It consists in the pleasant companionship of all the blessed, a companionship that is replete with delight: since each one will possess all good things together with the blessed, for they will all love one another as themselves, and, therefore, will rejoice in the happiness of others' goods as their own, and consequently the joy and gladness of one will be as great as the joy of all. Scripture says, 'The dwelling in thee is as it were of all rejoicing.'

"The saints in heaven will have all these things and many more that surpass description", Thomas said. He continued, "The wicked, on the other hand, who will be in everlasting death, will have no less sorrow and pain than the good will have of joy and glory."

St. Thomas wrote, "Thus we can realize the difference between doing good works and doing evil deeds: seeing that good works lead to life, while wicked deeds drag us to death. For this reason man should frequently call these things to mind, since thereby he is urged to good things and drawn away from evil. Thus significantly the Creed ends with the words: 'Life everlasting', that it may ever remain more and more impressed on the memory. To this life may we be brought by our Lord Jesus Christ, who is God blessed forever and ever."

Thomas urges all to do as Jesus wishes for our own good, our happiness here and our eternal happiness in the life to come.

St. Augustine   *September 5*

St. Augustine wrote, "Let me, O my God, remember with thanks to thee and confess thy mercies upon me. Let my bones be pierced through with thy love, and let them say, 'Who is like unto thee, O Lord? Thou has broken my bonds. I will sacrifice to thee the sacrifice of praise.' How thou has broken them I shall tell and all who adore thee will say as they listen: Blessed be the Lord of heaven and earth, great and wonderful his name."

St. Augustine wrote his *Confessions* in greatest gratitude to thank God for freeing him from the slavery of sin.

He speaks to God, "Your words have rooted deep in my heart and I was fenced about on all sides by you. Of your eternal life I was now certain, though 'I saw it in a dark manner and as through a glass.' All my former doubts about an incorruptible substance from which every substance has its being was taken from me. My desire now was not to be more sure of you but more steadfast in you."

He had turned to God after having avoided him for many years. Here was true happiness he found, and he rejoiced and could not thank God enough for this great grace.

He told how his heart had to be purged of the old leaven. He said that our Savior delighted him but that he was fearful of walking a way so straight.

Augustine recalled his conversion, how before he had been unhappy with his life of sin; still, then he had been weak and returned to his sin. He had been a slave of his passions. But in his change of heart he wanted to be a servant of Christ. And by the grace of God all this came about.

St. Patrick   *September 6*

St. Patrick, the great missionary to Ireland, said, "I give unwearied thanks to God, who kept me faithful, so that today I can confidently offer him my soul as a living sacrifice—to Christ, my Lord, who has saved me out of all my troubles. Thus can I say, 'Who am I, O Lord, and to what hast thou called me, thou who didst assist me with such divine power that today I constantly exalt and magnify thy name?' "

He said that in his difficult days in bringing the Faith to Ireland God was his great support, his guide, his protection, his all. God heard his prayers because he trusted him. He would never have undertaken so difficult a work, if God had not been with him. He preached his Gospel with the help of God. And "so we have seen it, and so it has been fulfilled: indeed, we are witnesses that the Gospel has been preached unto these parts beyond which there lives nobody."

He continued, "Now it would be tedious to give a detailed account of all my labors or even a part of them. Let me tell you briefly that the merciful God often freed me from dangers. God is my witness, who knows all things even before they come to pass, as he used to forewarn even me, poor wretch that I am, of many things by a divine message."

Patrick said, "I am very much God's debtor, who gave me such great grace, and many people were reborn in God through me and afterward confirmed and that clerics were ordained for them everywhere. All this was for a people just coming to the Faith, whom the Lord took from the utmost parts of the earth."

He said, "For this reason we ought to fish well and diligently for souls, so that many may be caught for God and that there be clergy everywhere to baptize and exhort a people in need and in want."

St. Catherine of Siena   *September 7*

St. Catherine of Siena was a mystic. She tells that through humble prayer we are lifted up.

She wrote, "The soul, who is lifted by a very great yearning and desire for the honor of God and the salvation of souls, begins by exercising herself, for a certain space of time, in the ordinary virtues, remaining in prayer in order to know better the goodness of God toward her. This is because knowledge must precede love, and only when she has attained love, can she strive to follow and to clothe herself with the truth."

We must first know Christ. To know him is to love him. We delight in following the one we love. Knowledge of Christ comes through prayer. Prayer is the all-important first step. And so Catherine says, "In no way does the creature receive such a taste of the truth, or so brilliant a light therefrom, as by means of humble and faithful prayer, founded on knowledge of herself and of God; because prayer, exercising her in the above way, unites with God the soul that follows the footprints of Christ Crucified. Thus, by desire and affection, and union of love, Christ makes her another himself."

St. Catherine said that Jesus told us this in the Scripture, "To him who loves me and will observe my commandment, will I manifest myself, and he shall be one with me and I with him." She said, "So it is through the effect of love that the soul becomes another himself." She stated that God does not want to conceal but wishes very much to reveal the great love he has for us. He is able to do this in prayer. He says, "Open the eye of your intellect, and gaze into me, and you shall see the beauty of me." And in prayer, faithful and fervent, God adorns us with beauty, many virtues, which make us pleasing in his sight.

St. Frances Xavier Cabrini   *September 8*

Mother Cabrini, as a young woman helping in an orphanage, endured every humiliation from the women who ran it because they were jealous of her popularity with the children. She would not leave for fear the children would be without a friend. One of these women even tried physical violence. Then, worse, the bishop made Mother Cabrini, then Francesca, the superior. The women spread false rumors and gossip about her. The bishop tried to dismiss them but they owned the orphanage. At length he gave up. He dissolved the orphanage and quasi-convent. Francesca took the orphans to another building, and she and some of her helpers formed a pious society. From this came Mother Cabrini's religious community. They established other convents in Italy and then as missionaries went overseas.

After coming to New York City she was soon looking for another house. The Jesuits offered to sell at a very low price an estate they had in the upper Bronx. They were selling it because there was no water on the place. Upon seeing the site, Mother Cabrini said she had seen this estate in a dream, and she purchased it. Everyone thought she was foolish. The Sisters had to go a long way down to the Hudson River and back for water. Mother

Cabrini continued to look around the spacious grounds. One day she spotted a damp place on the hillside. She said a well should be dug. After that, they had all the water they wanted.

She went to New Orleans, and she left some of the Sisters there. They had nothing; they had to beg. Mother Cabrini told them when they saw any promise of success they were to let her know, and she would come and open a convent. One day they collected $17.30, so they wired, "Success! Please come." Soon after, she arrived. For a convent the Sisters started with three rented rooms in the poor district. Soon they were able to establish a real convent and a school and settlement house.

St. Frances Xavier Cabrini   *September 9*

It came as a distinct shock to Mother Cabrini in New York when she was asked to take charge of a hospital. She had always thought only in terms of schools and orphanages. She knew nothing about hospitals. But a small Italian hospital under the direction of some priests was failing. Either the Sisters had to take over or it would close. Mother Cabrini hesitated, and she prayed very much. Then in a dream she saw the Blessed Mother with her sleeves rolled up and her skirt pinned back caring for the sick. And Mary, Mother of the Afflicted, said to Mother Cabrini, "I am doing what you refuse to do."

Mother Cabrini woke up and no longer hesitated. She took the hospital and made it prosper.

America was greatly blessed when Mother Cabrini came to this country. She and her Sisters built and staffed fine institutions of mercy in New York, Illinois, Pennsylvania, Colorado, California, New Jersey and in Washington state, as well as around the world in Europe, South America, Canada and Australia. Wherever she went the first thing she did was place in the chapel a statue of the Sacred Heart of Jesus. Only a woman of boundless courage and great confidence in God could have done all this. And as a youth she had been refused more than once when she wished to join a convent because she was told that her health was not good enough.

She said, "If anyone wants to know what is in me—let him look at a glass of water." She did not believe in introspection, and she did not think she had any special gifts. All things came from God. She liked cheerfulness, never talking of her troubles, and she did not like the Sisters to complain, even about the weather.

St. Thomas More   *September 10*

St. Thomas More was put in the Tower of London by the weak-minded monarch, Henry VIII. All that Thomas had done was serve the king with great faithfulness, but he would not swear an oath that Henry was the head of the Catholic Church in England. Since the king always had his way, this was called treason.

More's daughter, Meg, was allowed to come and see him. The conditions in the Tower were so poor she pitied him. He, however, did not complain. Rather, he prayed with her and cheered her up.

Then, in an effort to make him give in, it was ordered that his family could no longer visit him, and he was put in a dungeon cell. But since no one at court had any integrity, they did not know the integrity of Thomas. He would never say that anything false was true, especially when it had to do with God.

He wrote a treatise on the four last things. He meditated on these for he knew that his days were numbered. He prayed a great deal. Yet his sense of humor did not leave him. He stated that he often laughed at the devil. The devil, he said, being a proud spirit, "cannot endure to be mocked".

Thomas was sent people from the court to urge him to give in and then his fine home and good life and much more would be restored to him. But he only smiled. He could not, he would not, give up honesty for the world. He would remain faithful to Christ and faithful to the truth. His wife was even allowed to beg him to give in. But Thomas told her that if he did, he could not live with himself.

The court was full of hypocrisy. Thomas More, though now bent from suffering, was one of the few men in the whole kingdom who stood tall.

St. Elizabeth Seton   *September 11*

St. Elizabeth Seton was a convert. Shortly after the Revolutionary War, she married a wealthy merchant, William Seton of New York City. She and her husband had five children, and the family was loved by many.

After her husband's death and her conversion, Elizabeth was poor, but she said it was all right because she no longer had to go to parties and could spend more time with her friends. When she entered the Church she wrote a loyal friend about the event, "I professed my belief in the Church, rejoicing with my Savior in heart. I was light of heart and cool of head for the first time in many long months, but not without begging our Lord to wrap my heart deep in that opened side seen in the crucifix, or lock it up in the little tabernacle where I shall rest forever.... I set out on a new life—a new existence itself." She said, "All the confusion of the past, all the sorrow of soul and bitterness are behind me."

St. Elizabeth wrote after her first confession, "I felt as if my chains fell, as those of St. Peter at the touch of the divine messenger. My God, what new scenes for my soul. Now I shall be made one with him who said that unless you eat my flesh and drink my blood you can have no part of me."

Preparing to receive her First Communion, she said, "I count the days and hours, yet a few more of hope and expectation. How bright was the sun and the morning walk to church. Deep snow or smooth ice, all to me were the same. I see nothing but the little bright cross on St. Peter's steeple." After her First Communion she said, "At last, God is mine and I am his. I have received him."

In time Elizabeth founded the American Sisters of Charity. She and her Sisters had their motherhouse at Emmitsburg in

Maryland. They so helped people that they were called the angels of the mountain. They soon had Sisters teaching and caring for the sick in many towns and hospitals.

St. Elizabeth Seton   *September 12*

St. Elizabeth Seton is fondly called Mother Seton, for she was the first superior of the Sisters of Charity in America. When as an adult convert she received her First Communion she had to put down the fears of not having done enough to prepare for this great event. She put all her confidence in God's goodness.

She said, "My God, to the last breath of life will I not remember this night of watching for the morning dawn, the fearful beating heart so pressing to be gone, the long walk to church, every step nearer the tabernacle, nearer the time he would enter the poor, poor little dwelling so all his own. And when he did, the first thought I remember was, let God arise and let his enemies be scattered, for it seemed to me my King had come to take his throne. Instead of the humble, tender welcome I had expected to give him, it was a triumph of joy and gladness that the Deliverer had come, and was my defense and shield and strength and salvation for this world and the next."

Elizabeth went on, "Now all the excesses of my heart found their play and it danced with fervor. I was far richer than the prophet and more honored than he.

"Truly I felt all the powers of my soul held fast by him who came with so much majesty to take possession of his poor little kingdom."

As superior of the Sisters of Charity later in life, Mother Seton wrote a Sister, "Often I shall say in prayer to God that you are with him. Every moment, Lord, she will be serving you and loving you with me.

"Be a friend and comfort and support for the other Sisters; let them see that you do all in faith. Love your Blessed Mother above.

"If you suffer, so much the better for your journey to heaven.

251

The work in the vineyard here is of warfare and crucifixion. May you enjoy true peace in him. He will take us home at last. Be faithful to our Faithful One. Courage, dearest child of Eternity. The things of this life have eternal consequences. We must be careful to meet our graces. When we go to a place for which we have a dreadful aversion, in that place there is a store of grace waiting."

St. Elizabeth Seton   *September 13*

Mother Seton often wrote her Sisters very beautiful letters. To one she said, "Providence is with us. Its grace falls on us. It often makes the black clouds that we see pass by harmlessly. It can break the forces of a storm. You have been in the storm clouds again. May they soon disperse. May God guide and direct and control and comfort you. I carry you before him continually in my heart. It is all I can do. Let me hear from you soon that your dear heart is quiet.

"We are all tempted. God is our Father, trust in his goodness for his resistance. Be faithful. Love to the Lover brings sorrow for our sins. Trust him." Some trials, Mother Seton said, are sent to us just to prove how little we can do in this world and that we must put all our faith in God.

Mother Seton knew many sorrows. Not only had her husband died, but later she lost two daughters. At the grave of her daughter Elizabeth, she, crying, begged Mary to behold her Son and plead for the girl's mother and the other Sisters. To Jesus she prayed, "Behold your Mother and pity this mother, this poor, poor mother, who is so uncertain." She said that after saying this her soul was quieted by the loneliness of the falling leaves in the cemetery. They seemed to cry, " 'From eternity to eternity, you are God. All shall perish and pass away, but you remain forever', and then the thought of our dearest Jesus stretched on the Cross and his words came powerfully to me. Jesus' eyes lifted to the high heavens and crying out, 'Forgive them, they know not what they do.' "

In a talk on Jesus she pointed out that Jesus taught the people, no matter how many rebukes and contradictions he endured. His apostles were often unable to comprehend him, but he repeated and explained patiently his teachings again. She said that we must ask ourselves, "Have I been as my blessed Lord; have I learned to bear with the weakness of others? They are obliged to bear with mine."

St. Peter Julian Eymard   *September 14*

St. Peter Julian Eymard had a beautiful devotion to the Blessed Sacrament. He founded the Blessed Sacrament Fathers to honor the Eucharist.

He wrote that ever since the Last Supper the Church has been proclaiming the Eucharist. Her apostles have had but one voice, her teachers but one doctrine, her children but one belief, one love for the Eucharist. How majestic is the voice of all Catholic people through the centuries. How touching and beautiful is the love of the people for the Blessed Sacrament. He wrote, "Every true child of the Church wants to bring to the feet of the divine King present on the altar a tribute of homage, a token of his affection—one brings gold, another myrrh, and all bring incense. Every one wants to have a place in the court and at the table of God in the Eucharist."

St. Peter Julian said that we believe in the Eucharist because we believe in the love of Jesus and we know that nothing is impossible with God.

"To the testimony of her words the Church adds the testimony of her example and practical faith", he said. "As John the Baptist, after having pointed out the Messiah, cast himself at his feet to prove the liveliness of his faith, so the Church devotes solemn worship to the Eucharist. She adores Jesus Christ as God, present and hidden in the divine Host. She pays him the honor due God alone; she prostrates herself before the most Blessed Sacrament like the heavenly court before the majesty of God. Distinction of rank is not in order here: great and small, kings and subjects, priests and people instinctively fall to their knees before God in the Eucharist.

"It is the Good God!

"The Church is not content to attest to her Faith by adoration alone; to that she adds public and magnificent honors."

St. Elizabeth Seton   *September 15*

Mother Seton wrote in her journal, "Our God, our God, such friends you give me, so miserable a one and a poor sinner. The mystery of infinite Goodness. I try to repay him praying at the tabernacle.

"I feel on the high seas with rolling bellows up to the heavens and down to the deep, our God! O my infinite good Master!"

She said that she hoped at the resurrection that she and the Sisters would be able to lay hold of their crucifixes so that they could hold them up in defense. "Our God, when will I be good and look at death and judgment as I ought?"

Later, she wrote concerning receiving Holy Communion, "Most precious Communion—how Jesus loves and welcomes the poor and desolate. Peace, silence. His will forever."

In a talk she instructed her Sisters, "God, infinitely happy in himself, gave us our free will, which is our noblest gift from God. Some choose to serve themselves and are separated from God. But we are made in his image, to be like him, our first and last and only end. Our first parents departed from the end of their creation and many of the redeemed depart from it. God in his goodness did not leave souls in their miserable state after the fall; he promised immediately a redeemer, saying that I will recreate you, I will go myself and dwell with you. I will take on myself their humiliation and abjection. I will show them the horror of sin and the means of reparation. Yet, by blood and death, I will redeem them.

"We are all destined to share God's bliss. We Sisters are set apart from the world to serve our King. We are his servants. We draw near to his person, we dispense his favors, promote the Kingdom, and spread his love.

"The charity of our Blessed Lord should be the model for our conduct. His gentleness always appeared. His forbearance and moderation in all things are shown, for he had to endure the grossness and ignorance of the crowd. He accommodated himself to serve them."

St. Thomas Aquinas

September 16

St. Thomas Aquinas tells us, "Truth, the object of the intellect, is not pragmatic, not a personal convenience, but something which imposes itself on the mind. The object of the will is good, not as a personal delectation or for utility, but as it is in itself." The good is man's end. The good appeals to man, and the greatest good, God, is man's final goal.

The thing that is desired as end is that which constitutes happiness, Thomas said. The final end, God, constitutes complete happiness. We may know a degree of happiness here on earth but we will be fully happy only in heaven, where we have attained the greatest good, God himself. In life we seek ourselves, and in seeking ourselves we seek God. "Man tends to his own good because he tends to the divine likeness, and not vice versa." It is the love of God which draws us on, but we are unconscious of this most times. Without ceasing, we follow after the first Truth and the final Good, even though in actuality we pursue here and now lesser truths and goods. It is our own blindness that makes this so. Otherwise we would be aware of the love that guides us.

Finite objects compel us but do not compel assent. We can always say no. We are free to do a thing or not to do it, because there are various objects of attraction. Men should do what God wants, which is always right and best, but oftentimes they seek a lesser good.

We can come to know God by an ascent through creatures to the knowledge of the Creator, Thomas said. Or there can be a descent of divine truth by revelation, God making known things to us, truths that exceed human understanding, truth accepted because God says it is so. God speaks through the prophets and, most wonderfully, through his only Son, Jesus, whom he sent into the world to guide us to heaven.

St. Augustine   *September 17*

In the *City of God* St. Augustine wrote his masterpiece. In his day one persistent rumor was that Christianity had sapped the strength of the Roman empire and that it was the cause of its falling. A Roman official in North Africa wrote this to the Bishop of Hippo. The first ten sections of the *City of God* constitute Augustine's answer to this charge. He shows that Christianity gives strength and courage to a people.

The *City of God* ranks among the classics of all literature. Its main theme is that Christianity seeks to make all men good and to create a society where there is goodness and peace.

Rome fell but the Church survived. The capture of Rome by the barbarians made a deep impression upon the entire empire. It seemed like the end of the world. But that Christianity kept going, even after the fall of Rome, is a lesson not easily forgotten. Augustine tells us why. Christ seeks love and harmony and not discord and chaos. Christianity is the triumph of love over hatred.

St. Augustine wrote, "From this earthly city issue the enemies against whom the City of God must be defended. Some of them, it is true, abjure their worldly error and become worthy members in God's City. But many others, alas, break out in blazing hatred against it and are utterly ungrateful, notwithstanding its Redeemer's singular gifts. For they would no longer have a voice to raise against it had not its sanctuaries given them asylum as they fled before the invaders' swords, and made it possible for them to save that life of which they are so proud.

"Have not even those very Romans whom the barbarians spared for the sake of Christ assailed his Name? Many of those whom you see heaping impudent abuse on the servants of Christ would not have escaped the ruin and massacre had they not falsely paraded as servants of Christ. Now, with ungrateful pride, impious madness and perversity of heart, they work against that holy Name."

St. Clare of Assisi   *September 18*

St. Clare's community of nuns followed the rule of St. Francis. One observer wrote, "Wishing her order to bear the name of poverty, Clare made a petition to Pope Innocent III begging for this privilege. He was greatly gladdened at the fervor of this virgin, and said that no one had ever asked the Holy See for such a singular privilege." He granted her the privilege of poverty, and for the rest of her life she took her stand upon it. She had come from a wealthy family. Perhaps she had seen firsthand what quarrels money creates.

When St. Francis was in Assisi he often visited St. Clare, giving her holy counsel. In this way he guided the Sisters on their journey to heaven.

Clare and her Sisters acquired the name "Poor Ladies of San Damiano".

Clare was noble by birth, but still more noble by grace. Though still young she was mature in her mind, fervent in the service of God, endowed with rare prudence and deepest humility. She fully agreed with Francis who said, "Poverty was Christ's faithful companion from his birth in a stable to his death and burial. O who would not love Lady Poverty above all things; of thee, O Jesus, I ask to be signed with this privilege, I long to be enriched with this treasure, I beseech of thee, O most poor Jesus, that for thy sake it may always be the mark of me and mine to possess nothing of our own under the sun." He said, "He has never perfectly renounced the world who keeps hidden in his heart the treasure of his own will."

St. Clare wore a long tunic of cheap, common, harsh cloth with a very common cloak that gave little warmth, and an equally common black veil, and she wore no shoes. She fasted often; the community kept two Lents during the year, which for Clare meant bread and water.

St. Augustine   *September 19*

St. Augustine said of the fall of Rome, "Many Christians have been led into captivity. This would be lamentable, indeed, if they had been led to a place where they could not find God. But Holy Scripture gives us instances of great consolations bestowed even in such calamity. God did not abandon the Prophet Jonas even in the belly of the monster. He did not desert his faithful ones in the power of a barbarous people."

The reward of the good Christian is not the possession of earthly things, he stated. We owe all to God. We daily owe our survival to God.

Augustine wrote about the final goal of humans. To obtain the supreme good is the end for which one should strive. This has been the aim and effort of all who have professed a zeal for wisdom in this world of shadows. Eternal life is the supreme good and we should live rightly in order to obtain it.

He said, "Those who think that the supreme good is to be found in this life are mistaken. They seek in vain whether they look to serenity, to virtue, or both; whether to pleasure plus serenity, or to virtue, or to all three; or to the satisfaction of our innate exigencies. It is vain that men look for beatitude on earth or in human nature. Divine Truth, as expressed in the Prophet's words, makes them look foolish: 'The Lord knows the thoughts of men' or, as the text is quoted by St. Paul: 'The Lord knows the thoughts of the wise that they are vain.' "

This gifted thinker and humble saint continued: "For what flow of eloquence is sufficient to set for the miseries of human life? . . . This much, however, we can do with the help of God — not yield by surrender of the spirit and be dragged into sin willingly."

Augustine knew the difficulties of this world. We must look to God for divine assistance. We are too weak to live well by our own efforts. But if we pray and beg for aid, Christ will be with us.

St. Patrick *September 20*

St. Patrick said, "I ought unceasingly to give thanks to God who often pardoned my folly and my carelessness, and on more than one occasion spared his great wrath on me, who was chosen to be his helper and who was slow to do as was shown me and as the Spirit suggested. And the Lord had mercy on me thousands and thousands of times because he saw that I was ready, but that I did not know what to do in the circumstances. For many tried to prevent my mission; they would even talk behind my back.

"You know and so does God know how I have lived among you from my youth in the true faith and sincerity of heart. Likewise, as regards the heathens among whom I lived, I have been faithful to them, and so I shall be. God knows it, I have overreached none of them, nor would I think of doing so, for the sake of God and his Church, for fear of raising persecution against them and all of us."

St. Patrick, ever humble, though the primate of Ireland, related how he had baptized thousands of people. He expected nothing in return. "But I see myself exalted even in the present world beyond measure by the Lord, and I was not worthy nor such that he should grant me this", Patrick said. "I know perfectly well, though not by my own judgment, that poverty and misfortune become me better than riches and pleasures. For Christ the Lord, too, was poor for our sakes, and I, unhappy wretch that I am, have no wealth even if I wished for it."

He stated, "If ever I have done any good for my God whom I love, I beg him to grant me that I may shed my blood with those exiles and captives for his name."

Mother Duchesne was an outstanding pioneer missionary Sister in America. She has been canonized for her heroic life of prayer and sacrifice.

She lived in the last century in Grenoble, France, and wished to be a nun, but her father violently opposed the idea. One day she went with an aunt to visit the convent—and she stayed. The aunt went rushing back to report this. The parents all but ran up the hill to the convent to get Philippine. But she would not see them. Her angry father was flabbergasted, but there was nothing he could do. In the meantime Philippine was in the chapel with tears in her eyes praying to Jesus in the Blessed Sacrament.

But then, in the aftermath of the French Revolution, the convent was closed and Philippine had to return home. She busied herself rounding up the orphan children who were living in the streets as a result of the war. She rented a house and started an orphanage. In time she was able to get her wealthy father to lease the old convent for the orphanage. She expected the nuns who had been dispersed to return, but only a couple of them did. So she and her women workers in the orphanage started a pious society. Then Philippine learned of a new order of Sisters in France. She wrote the priest founder and he came to visit the orphanage. All during the visit he said little. She related, "I followed him to the door when he was leaving, unable to detect what he thought or intended to do, for he was very reserved." Finally, she asked outright if they could become a part of his order. But he replied vaguely that God works in a slow way.

"Surely not," Philippine exclaimed, "for the Scripture speaks of him as a giant running his course—and what would St. Francis Xavier have done in ten years if he had been so slow?"

The priest laughed and said she was right. In time he admitted them to his order, the Religious of the Sacred Heart, and he sent them his saintly superior, Mother Barat, to train them.

St. Rose Philippine Duchesne

Mother Barat, Madeleine-Sophie Barat, also a canonized saint, arrived at the orphanage at Grenoble, where saint met saint, and Philippine and Mother Barat warmly embraced one another. Two who had such great love for Christ had a great love for each other all their lives.

Philippine fell to her knees and kissed Mother Barat's feet. Mother was taken by surprise, but for Philippine it was the end of thirteen years of waiting, hoping and praying. They at the orphanage were a real convent again.

Both hearts of these great women had a beautiful love for the Blessed Sacrament. They worked together wonderfully. Philippine was back to being a novice again, she who had been the superior, and she loved it. She was so humble and obedient Mother Barat hardly had to tell her anything. Philippine was able to tell Mother of her lifelong dream to be a missionary to the Indians in the New World. Mother did not laugh at her, as others did about this, but said she also had yearned to be a missionary.

But it seemed Philippine, now Mother Duchesne, would never have her dream fulfilled, for she was, in time, Mother Barat's secretary in Paris. One day, however, a missionary bishop from America came to the convent. Mother Duchesne hurried to Mother Barat to announce the bishop and added, "Do not miss this opportunity—the time has come." The other said, "If the bishop asks for us to go to Louisiana, Philippine, I will take that as an indication of God's will."

Not that day but the next day the bishop did ask for Sisters. Mother Duchesne was chosen to be superior of the little group that would go to America.

St. Rose Philippine Duchesne

It was most difficult in the early days in America. After a most difficult sea voyage and much travelling, Mother Duchesne and her Sisters were taken to a log cabin near St. Louis where they were assigned. It had five small rooms and a larger area that was their chapel. They started a school. The children were to pay a penny a day, but most were so poor they could pay nothing. In fact, many times for weeks, the Sisters gave their food to the children to eat and they lived on hot carrot juice and bread. She still longed to go to the Indians, but there was much work to do with the poor people right here.

The Sisters struggled and endured great hardships. They were, at times, cold, hungry and sick. But their school thrived and they were able to start other schools. Later quite a number of American girls joined the community. Mother Duchesne prayed constantly. The chaplain said that he never went to the chapel to get the Blessed Sacrament to go on a sick call without seeing Mother Duchesne praying in the shadows.

When Mother Duchesne was quite old, a missionary priest from Kansas asked the Sisters to go there and take over a school for the Indian children. If they did not, the mission would have to close up. It was a long journey from St. Louis, but Mother Duchesne, who had dreamed so often of this, went as superior with the few Sisters.

She could not learn the Indians' language, but she impressed the Indians far more than the Sisters who taught. Every day she went to the log cabin chapel to pray. It was very hot in summer and very cold in winter, but she prayed there almost all day. The Indians greatly admired her. Sometimes they would sneak into the chapel to touch this holy woman. Her old face was alight with fervor as she prayed.

The Indians called her "Duah-kah-ka-num-ad", "the woman-who-always-prays".

St. Elizabeth Seton   *September 24*

The handful of Sisters of Charity headed by Mother Seton suffered many difficulties in their primitive home at Emmitsburg. The first night the local priest had to go to the village for cups and saucers so supper could be served. They started growing carrots at once, and for a long time they had carrot juice to drink instead of coffee. The Sisters got up at five for meditation and then walked a mile to the village church for Mass. They said the Rosary on the way. Back home they went about their daily chores. When the creek was high they had to take off their shoes and stockings to wade across to Mass. They did the washing in this same creek. And yet they were happy.

However, a new priest was assigned to direct the Sisters and he almost destroyed the community. He thought he knew more about nuns than the Sisters did. It got so bad that he wrote to Mother Seton that he was removing her as superior. She did not mind for herself, but she knew the new religious order would fall apart. She did the only thing that she could do. She prayed. Fortunately, she was not removed and, as it turned out, the priest was sent elsewhere.

Elizabeth's sister-in-law Harriet Seton came to the convent at Emmitsburg, joining her sister Cecilia who was there. Also there were Elizabeth's three daughters. Her two boys were at boarding school with the Jesuits.

There was great joy when Archbishop John Carroll, seventy-four years old and failing, made his first visit to the Sisters of Charity. But shortly after there was sadness, for Harriet was seriously ill. She had always seemed strong and healthy, but she was seized with a fever and she died four days before Christmas. Cecilia, who was ill most of the time, kissed her sister goodbye at her bedside.

Their school grew. They soon had nearly fifty students. Mother Seton, ever joyful, cheered up the others every day.

St. Jean de Brébeuf   *September 25*

St. Jean de Brébeuf was a Jesuit missionary who was martyred by the Indians in the New World.

He was born and grew up in Normandy in France and was tall, well built and friendly. He attended a Jesuit school and decided to enter the Society of Jesus. He was a good student, but suddenly he became ill with tuberculosis. His huge frame shrunk until it looked like a skeleton. He suffered a good deal and was going downhill so fast that his superiors were alarmed. Since by this time he was finishing theology, they decided to ordain him a priest, because they were certain he would not live long. He was ordained and offered his first Mass though he was very weak.

But suddenly his health started to improve to the extent that he was able to take on some duties in the treasurer's office at the Jesuit college. He gave himself over to prayer. He had always longed to be a missionary to the Indians in New France (Canada) but that now seemed impossible.

In time, because his health was, inexplicably, continually improving, he thought that perhaps the realization of his dream might be possible. In fact, though he felt he had only a small chance of being selected, he volunteered for the missions. One day not long afterward he was handed a sealed letter. When he opened it he could not believe it. He had been chosen to go.

With other Jesuit priests and Brothers they left by ship to cross the wild North Atlantic. The frightening journey at length came to an end. Father de Brébeuf never felt such peace of soul when finally he stepped off the ship on the soil of New France.

St. Francis Xavier   *September 26*

St. Francis Xavier on his missionary adventures in Asia was often humiliated by the greedy Europeans. He wrote, "It is a permanent bruise on my soul, an overwhelming sorrow ever to me. These cruel, ruthless Portuguese not only snatch their goods but snatch their women as slaves." One high official was actually selling horses to a wild tribe for great profit so that these pagans could make war on the Christians. The warriors descended on Francis' people, slaughtering, pillaging and enslaving his defenseless natives. It broke his heart. They came sweeping in on swift Arabian horses supplied by detested Portuguese profiteers.

Francis became a beggar, in the hot summer sun, going everywhere seeking food and clothing for his war victims. Sometimes he felt the wretched survivors were worse off than those who had been killed, so pitiful were the ruins. Someone said, "He was utterly fearless, denouncing the tribe of the war raiders face to face, condemning them openly." Had he not been on hand, his native Christians would have been totally exterminated.

In time he continued his missionary journeys. He was on the move, going farther afield, assessing opportunities for missionary work, translating prayers and instructions into the natives' languages. In ships that were always uncomfortable, he crossed the Bay of Bengal to Malacca, then passed to the dense jungles of the Malayan peninsula and the island of Java. It is reported that, no matter what the hardship, grimness never replaced his bright charm. He carried on, one observer mentioned, with laughter in his mouth. He said, "If one takes these hardships for the sake of him for whom we should bear them, they will turn into sources of great refreshment. . . . It is my belief that the man who knows how to carry the Cross of Christ will find rest in these labors."

St. Catherine of Siena   *September 27*

St. Catherine of Siena was a mystic. Her first love was to pray in silence, contemplating Christ and begging him to help his people. So much suffering was caused by offenses against God. It caused her great sorrow. She prayed for peace among men.

Jesus said to her, "I have shown thee, dearest daughter, my great love for you. . . . Very pleasing to me, dearest daughter, is your willing desire to suffer for the salvation of souls."

Jesus said, "Up to the present, I have taught thee how a person may serve his neighbor, and manifest, by that service, the love which he has toward me. Now I wish to tell thee further that a person proves his patience on his neighbor when he receives injuries from him. Similarly, he proves his humility on a proud man, his true hope on those who despair, his justice on the unjust, his kindness on the cruel, his gentleness and benignity on the irascible. Good people produce and prove all their virtues on their neighbor." Our neighbor gives us an opportunity to show

265

our virtue. And the more difficult they are to deal with, the greater we grow in virtue.

"The humble man extinguishes pride", Jesus said to her. "A proud man can do no harm to a humble man. Neither can the infidelity of a wicked man, who neither loves me, nor hopes in me, when brought forth against one who is faithful to me, do him any harm. His infidelity does not diminish the faith or the hope of him who has his faith and love in me; rather, it fortifies it and proves it in the love he feels for his neighbor."

Jesus told Catherine to observe the virtues of fortitude and perseverence; these virtues are proved by the long endurance of the injuries and detractions of wicked men, who, whether by injuries or flattery, constantly endeavor to turn a man aside from following the true road and the true doctrine.

St. Ignatius Loyola   *September 28*

St. Ignatius said that closely following Christ calls for humility. Only this can bring union with Christ through prayer. Prayer gives us a freshness of vision so that spiritual truths are appreciated more. Prayer brings special insights into spiritual principles, and it lights up the mind.

The saint said that the contemplation of the life of Christ makes us more Christlike. By reading the Gospels and praying over them, one becomes absorbed in Christ. What is God's plan for you? In prayer there is a shifting of emphasis. The soul depends less on itself and more on God. A simplification takes place. God challenges the soul, which finds new strength to go forward.

The first Jesuit urges us to think of the scenes in the life of Christ. At the Annunciation, for example, we should see Mary and the angel who greets her. God sent the angel because he said, "Let us work for the redemption of mankind."

When we look at the world with all its crimes and sins, we know well that it needs those who will work for Christ and be his ambassadors. We should say, "I will ask help according to the need that I feel within myself, so that I may more closely follow and imitate Christ", and engage in his work.

St. Ignatius stated that Jesus gave us the Church to guide us to heaven. When we follow the Church we are on the true road to eternal life. In the Church, with the Mass, the sacraments and her other great gifts, we can know true happiness and spiritual joy.

St. Teresa of Avila   *September 29*

Our good Master has bestowed countless blessings upon us and we should be grateful with all our hearts, said St. Teresa of Avila. God is our Father and what a wonderful, generous, gracious and kindly father he is. No human father, no matter how good, can begin to compare with our heavenly Father. God fills our hands with blessings daily, hourly. He bestows such tremendous graces upon each of us. Most of all, he sent his Son to us. May we pray faithfully so that we may understand and appreciate this magnificent gift more. "O God," she prayed, "how is it that you give so many gifts to us and then you give us your Son?"

God bears with us, we who are weak and wayward, with great, great patience. He pardons and comforts us continually. He supports us every second of every day. He gives us all we have and are. He is far, far better than all earthly fathers. Consider the love he has for us. Let us honor him and thank him. We are sinful, but let us not be so sinful as to forget where all our gifts come from.

St. Teresa pointed out that the love of God is shown especially in the Son. He came to earth for our good. He redeemed us, who could not redeem ourselves. On earth he praised the Father. Teresa prayed, "O my Jesus, like a darling Son, you praised him for yourself and for us. Blessed forever be you, O my Lord, who are so desirous of giving." Jesus spent his life giving honor to God the Father, and he spent his days helping men in need. Most especially did he help souls. Saving souls was his chief concern, and it should be ours.

She said that we should pray to Jesus who was meek and humble of heart and who asks us to be more like him in all that we say and do.

St. Peter Claver   *September 30*

St. Peter Claver was a Spanish Jesuit who gave himself to the service of Christ among the slaves in the Caribbean islands in the early days in the New World. For more than forty years he labored tirelessly, calling himself "the slave of the slaves". He was their apostle, father, physician and friend. He fed them, nursed them with tenderness, taking care of their loathsome diseases, and he worked endlessly to ease their oppression and to soften the hearts of their harsh masters.

Whenever he heard of another slave ship coming into the harbor, he was there. He was ever comforting the woebegone slaves, even though he was bitterly criticized by slave owners, who put many difficulties in his way. His reply was, "The humble ass is my model. When he is evilly spoken of, he is dumb. Whatever happens he never complains, for he is only an ass. So also must the servant of God be."

As a young man, Peter graduated with distinction from the Jesuit college in Barcelona and then joined the Society of Jesus. He was sent to study philosophy in a Jesuit college on the Spanish island of Majorca. There Peter met and was most impressed by one of the Jesuit Brothers, the old assistant gatekeeper, Alonso Rodríguez. Alonso, then seventy-three, was ignored by some of the professors, but Peter saw in this saintly, gentle old man a great wisdom. About life he was much wiser than the faculty. He had profound spiritual insights. The aged porter said to the people as they departed the college, "May the three adorable Persons of the Blessed Trinity accompany you."

It was he who interested Peter in the missions in the New World.

St. Clare of Assisi

St. Clare of Assisi and her Sisters had great devotion to the Blessed Sacrament. They prayed endlessly. They also shared St. Francis' idea of work. He hated idleness as much as he did money.

One day Francis went to visit the Sisters. He spoke to no one but went straight to the chapel and stood there for some time silent, with uplifted arms, while the Sisters waited for a word or sign. At last he turned and asked for ashes, and when they were brought he sprinkled them on his own head and all around. He intoned the *Miserere* (Lord, have mercy on me), after which he left hastily and in silence.

Francis at that time was fighting for poverty for his Little Brothers. Church officials were trying to get the Franciscans to own buildings and live there and to stop going around begging every day. He lost this struggle. If the Little Brothers were forced to change their lifestyle, the Sisters of St. Francis were not. They lived in great poverty all their days.

When Francis died the funeral procession up to Assisi was one of triumph, with songs and the waving of olive branches. Many had lighted candles. When it reached San Damiano, Clare's convent, the Brothers paused and "at the grating through which the handmaids of the Lord were wont to receive the Sacred Host, the Brothers lifted the sacred body of little Francis from the bier, and held it in their raised arms in front of the window as long as Sister Clare and the other Sisters wished for their comfort."

Of all people, she and her Sisters knew well the triumph of their spiritual father, yet, "who would not be moved to tears when even the angels of peace wept so bitterly?" one spiritual writer wrote. "Never again shall they have speech with him who will not now return to visit them for his feet are turned into another way! Therefore with sobs and groans and tears they would not be checked in gazing on him and crying, 'O Father, why hast thou abandoned us and left us desolate?' "

St. Bernard of Clairvaux

St. Bernard of Clairvaux, the great reformer of the Middle Ages, wrote that we owe everything to God and any person of character cannot be ungrateful. He is most worthy to be loved by us and to be thanked by us. How can people be ungrateful when all have received countless blessings from our heavenly Father? He gives us food and light and air and innumerable other good things. It is foolish even to try to make a list of all the things he has given us. They are numberless. And many of his gifts are higher blessings for our souls. He gives us dignity as men, for we have the gift of free will. It is the possession of the power of choice that renders man superior to all other living creatures on earth and sets him in dominion over them. He gives us an intellect so that we can have knowledge, the power by which men recognize their dignity and at the same time know this gift is given us by God. He helps us to grow in virtue, the gift that makes a person seek ardently him from whom he derives his being, and cleave to him most steadfastly when found.

St. Bernard reminds us of the words of St. Paul, "What have you that you have not received? Now if you have received it, why do you glory as if you had not received it?" So people are blameworthy when they think they have given to themselves all good things. All things come to us as gifts. If we think at all, we know this. Worse are individuals who glory as if they were their own in the very gifts that God has given them. This is folly. Such people senselessly behave as though all the good they have they did not receive from the Father. This kind of glorying, Bernard said, is rightly called vain or empty, because it fails to rest upon the solid rock of truth. He remarks that St. Paul says, "He that glories, let him glory in the Lord." This is the truth of the matter.

St. Thomas Aquinas

St. Thomas Aquinas, one of the most gifted thinkers who ever lived, tells us that it can be demonstrated that God exists. He quotes the Epistle to the Romans, "The invisible things of him are clearly seen, being understood by the things that are made." A painting needs an artist, a book needs an author, creation needs a Creator.

St. Thomas wrote, "When an effect is better known to us than its cause, from the effect we proceed to the knowledge of the cause. And from every effect the existence of its proper cause can be demonstrated, so long as its effects are better known to us; because, since every effect depends upon its cause, if the effect exists, the cause must pre-exist. Hence, the existence of God, insofar as it is not self-evident to us, can be demonstrated from those of his effects which are known to us."

St. Thomas goes on to explain that the existence of God and other truths about God, which can be known by natural reason, are not articles of faith but are preambles to the articles, for faith presupposes natural knowledge. Reason judges that our faith is reasonable.

When the existence of a cause is demonstrated from an effect, this effect takes the place of the definition of the cause in proving the cause's existence. This is especially true, he said, in regard to God, because, in order to prove the existence of anything, it is necessary to accept as the middle term of the syllogism the meaning of the name, and not its essence. We do not have to know what something is to know that it exists. We can never know what God is. This is beyond human knowledge. But with human knowledge we can know that God exists. Once we know God exists, we know that we must honor him, for he has given us everything. After we know of the existence of God we must praise him. This is worship.

St. Teresa of Avila   *October 4*

St. Teresa of Avila was one of the greatest reformers in Spain. She was a Carmelite and a mystic.

She wrote to her Sisters, "For the love of God, daughters, be not at all anxious for high favors: let each one endeavor to do her duty, and if the superior does not approve of it, you may be sure our Lord will accept it and reward you. We do not have to have a reward in this life. Let our thoughts be fixed upon that which endures forever, and let us not be overly concerned about the things here below, since even they do not continue on, for today you may be going on well, but tomorrow we do not know. Do not be much disturbed about little things. Your kingdom is not of this world."

St. Teresa said that by the Cross our souls grow, and no matter what happens the Lord is with us. Your Master is always with you; he will not be lacking to you. He is most compassionate and never fails to help the afflicted and troubled, if they trust in him. So David said, "Mercy shall encompass him that hopes in the Lord." Either you believe these words, or you do not: if you do, why do you worry? "O my Lord, did we truly know you, we should not be anxious about anything, for you give so plentifully to those who wish to trust in you. Believe me, friends," Teresa wrote, "if we understand the truth, it will be of great assistance toward enabling us to discover that the favors of this world are small; sometimes they even hinder the soul."

Realize that you are in the company of Christ, she said. Enjoy his presence. This is paradise. If we pray, Christ comes to us with his graces. That is why we should pray faithfully and fervently.

St. John of the Cross   *October 5*

St. John of the Cross helped St. Teresa of Avila in the reform of the Carmelites in Spain in the sixteenth century. He was put in a small cell for nine months by members of his own order who did not want reforms. He endured many hardships and yet, at the same time, in his prison he composed some of his great mystical poems.

He wrote that we must be humble and God will help us to grow spiritually. To make progress in virtues we have to pray and beg for the grace of God. And God will come to us with his consolation and sweetness. God gives us tranquility of soul and quietness of heart, so that we are not restless and discontented. Then we can make progress in the sight of God.

We must do penance, he said. This purifies our hearts. He who loves God wishes to be fashioned by him. Such a person is like a stone that must be polished. This is not pleasant, but it is the only way to grow spiritually. Thus we improve in virtue and character. It is tiresome and troublesome to deny ourselves, and yet this is the only way. And thus we are fashioned by God and made worthy of heaven. The faithful soul does not seek honor, comfort, credit or ease. He seeks Christ and wishes to follow Christ, and Christ carried his Cross up the hill to Calvary.

Let the soul striving to come closer to Christ be humble. With humility there is interior quiet and joy. Seek Christ in humility and you will learn from him. "Learn from me, for I am meek and humble of heart", Jesus said. God sometimes lets us fail. Accept this humbly and start anew. It is a form of penance. With self-denial he purifies us, as gold is purified with fire. Without the fire one never has pure gold. Trials and temptations cleanse our hearts. Bear difficulties with patience and trust in God. Unless we do this we are constantly put to shame and confusion.

St. Francis de Sales　　　　　　　　　*October 6*

St. Francis de Sales, the greatest preacher of his day, was also a masterful spiritual director. He wrote to one person, "As soon as the children of this world perceive that you desire to follow a devout life they will shoot at you a thousand arrows of mockery and detraction. The most malicious will calumniate your change as being hypocrisy, bigotry and artifice. They will say that the world has frowned on you and that being rejected by it you turn to God. Your friends will make a world of objections which they imagine to be very wise and charitable. They will tell you that you will fall into a melancholy state of mind; that you will lose credit in the world; that you will make yourself insupportable; that you will grow old before your time; that your domestic affairs will suffer; that you must live in the world as one in the world; that salvation may be had without so many mysteries; and a thousand similar trivialities."

He went on to relate that all this is nothing but foolish and empty babbling. He quotes the Savior, who said, "If you had been of the world, the world would love its own; but because you are not of the world, therefore the world hates you." He goes on to say that we have seen gentlemen and ladies pass the whole night, even many nights, at chess or cards. Is there any concentration more absurd, stupid or gloomy than that of gamesters? Yet worldly people do not say a word, nor do their friends ever trouble themselves about them. Should we, however, spend an hour in meditation, or rise in the morning a little earlier than usual in order to prepare for Mass, everyone runs for a physician to cure us of our illness.

He states, "We can never please the world unless we lose ourselves together with the world." But who wants to be so foolish?

Our Lady of the Rosary   *October 7*

This is the feast of the Holy Rosary. This wonderful devotion to the Blessed Mother has brought countless blessings to people everywhere in every century. It was St. Dominic in preaching to the heretics in southern France who spread this beautiful devotion to Mary, and not just a devotion to Mary but to her Son. The Rosary is a very good way to think about the life of our Savior, with the various mysteries—Joyful, Sorrowful and Glorious—reminding us of how much Jesus has done for us, how much he suffered and sacrificed for us, as did his holy Mother.

This feast was established in thanksgiving because the Holy Father Pope St. Pius V had called on the people of Europe to get down on their knees and pray the Rosary so that they would be saved from the vicious Turks. At that time the Turkish armies had invaded a good deal of the continent and a great naval armada was preparing to come by sea and destroy this part of the world called Christendom. The people in terrible fear did as the Pope asked.

The Christians were disorganized but at length Don John of Austria was able to put together a small fleet to sail out into the Mediterranean Sea to meet the powerful enemy. It seemed impossible, and yet, as the two naval units came near to one another, a great storm arose and all but destroyed the great Turkish fleet. And Christendom was saved.

Pope Pius V, knew of this victory even though the messengers from Don John did not arrive with the triumphant news until many hours later. The Pope was certain of the sea victory, and he proclaimed that ever after this day would be set aside to honor Mary, who had saved the Christians from disaster. The Blessed Mother worked a great miracle to avoid the catastrophe of the destruction of the Christian world and Western civilization. This feast was first called Our Lady of Victory. In 1573 the name was changed to Our Lady of the Rosary.

St. Peter Julian Eymard   *October 8*

At every opportunity St. Peter Julian Eymard pleaded for a greater devotion to the Blessed Sacrament. If Christ is present with us, as we believe, then we must honor him.

He said that if there were a gathering of saints in a church they would be on their knees praying and proclaiming, "There is more than Solomon, more than an angel here!" Jesus Christ is here, before whom every knee bends, of those that are in heaven, on earth and under the earth. In the presence of Jesus Christ in the most Blessed Sacrament, all greatness disappears, all holiness humbles itself and comes to nothing. Jesus Christ is here.

St. Peter Julian wrote, "The Eucharist is the work of a measureless love that has at its service an infinite power, the omnipotence of God. St. Thomas calls the Eucharist the wonder of wonders, the greatest of miracles. To be convinced of this we need but meditate on what the faith of the Church teaches us concerning this mystery."

The saint bemoans the fact that in most places the Blessed Sacrament is not honored. He said, "Alas, it is but true: our Lord in the most Blessed Sacrament is not loved." Many are too busy to visit him. They are out running around doing trivial things. "Must I not then at least try to love Christ for them, in their stead? What is the reason for the forgetfulness and coldness of people in regard to this beautiful Sacrament? Is it that they do not know the goodness of the Lord? Is it that they do not know the sweetness and delight of loving him?"

Many, he said, have no idea of the extent of Christ's love for us in the Blessed Sacrament. They are busy about many things, and they ignore Jesus. Their faith is lifeless and superficial. It does not reach their hearts. Many Catholics live as real pagans, as if they hardly have heard of the Eucharist. How sad that is. For devotion to the Blessed Sacrament brings joy to our souls.

St. Thérèse of Lisieux   *October 9*

St. Thérèse of Lisieux, the Little Flower, was told by her superior to write about her "Little Way" to heaven. She was still a young Carmelite nun, full of love.

And so in obedience she told the story of her soul. "O how peace comes flooding into the soul, when once it learns to rise above its natural sensitiveness. To be really poor in spirit—there is no joy like it. You ask, with complete unconcern, for something you really need, and the other person not only refuses, but wants you to hand over something you've got already." She said that you ask for something and the other person wants your coat. And you take it off and give it to him and now you find you can run better into the arms of the Lord.

The Little Flower wrote that when you do a service to others they ought to get the impression that you are grateful and honored to have the opportunity to help them. You look glad, and in so doing find peace.

Jesus had given her light, she said, and she saw that charity needs to be deep-rooted in the soul. For this we must have

Christ's help. Without his loving grace, we wouldn't be able to understand love and kindness and do acts that reveal them. Thérèse said that she was like the donkey carrying a relic. All the reverence is shown the relic, but the silly donkey thinks the honor is being paid to him. It is Jesus who feeds our souls. And with the strength that comes from him, we must assist others.

The Little Flower lived in the convent less than ten years, yet now her writing about her soul is known and loved all over the world. When she died her final words were, "My God, how I love you."

Following Thérèse's death, her story of her soul was sent to other Carmelite convents. Others loved it so much, they had it printed. Millions of copies now have been sold all over the world.

St. Peter Claver   *October 10*

It was the old Brother Alonso Rodríguez, the lowly porter, who urged St. Peter Claver, the outstanding young philosophy student, to go as a missionary to the New World "where the harvest is abundant, but there are few workmen". The old man said, "How many souls in America might be saved by a zealous missionary. The savages there are like unpolished diamonds who can be brightened into things of beauty." Alonso added, "If the glory of God's house concerns you, go to the West Indies and save those perishing souls."

And so Peter did. When he departed, Brother Alphonsus gave the young Jesuit a farewell gift that he was to treasure all the rest of his life. It was a few pages of spiritual reflections that the old Brother had written down.

On the long sea voyage to the new land Peter won all hearts by his devotion to the sick.

He landed at Cartagena, an important city of the Spanish Caribbean. There he spent the rest of his life helping the slaves.

When he arrived at Cartagena, the chief center of the slave trade, he kissed the ground. It was hot, humid, with insects everywhere. The slaves suffered much. These poor wretched people who were so ill-treated came under the care of Peter.

Whenever a slave ship arrived with a new cargo of Africans, sick and full of terror, Peter was there to meet the boat. The blacks had endured a most horrible crossing; many of them had died on the way and were tossed overboard. In terrible conditions they had been secured with chains. Great epidemics of disease had broken out. Also, the slaves were in anguish at having been taken from their families and tribes, and many on the ship tried to commit suicide.

Peter was one of the few who tried to help them.

St. Francis of Assisi   *October 11*

St. Francis of Assisi would often "invite all the elements to praise the Lord". One of his sermons says, "Bring to the Lord glory unto his name; bring your own bodies and bear his holy Cross, and follow his most holy precepts unto the end." He had a great love for Christ on the Cross. And in his last days his own body was sealed with the wounds of Christ.

When he looked at the crucifix he said, "I am weeping over the sufferings of my Lord Jesus Christ, and I will not be ashamed to wander around the whole world and weep for them." The sight of the crucifix sent him into a transport of love and compassion; "then he would sing, so full was his soul of melody. He would begin softly," a Little Brother said, "and then the song would become louder. He would pick up two bits of wood, and pretend they were a violin and he would sing songs of love to Christ. His crucified love so overcame him that he broke into piteous sobs and lamentations, and forgetting his make-believe violin, he would fling himself down on the ground in an ecstasy."

"Within thy wounds hide us", Francis would say like a little child. Looking at the crucifix he was so very aware of the horror of the death of Jesus. And he knew that this death was caused by our sins.

St. Bonaventure wrote of St. Francis, "One day there appeared to him Jesus Christ crucified, and at this sight his soul was so filled with love, and the memory of Christ's Passion was so impressed on his heart that henceforth he could not think of Christ and the Cross without breaking into tears." Francis from that hour was so penetrated with compassion for the Crucified that ever afterward he carried in his heart those stigmata which later were to appear in the wounds on his own body.

St. Francis Xavier *October 12*

St. Francis Xavier, after striving to save souls in Japan, returned to Goa in India, the Portuguese colony. He was distressed to find that the college he had started for the natives was seriously harmed by the superior. Among other things, the young Jesuit in charge had hurried through their studies a number of Portuguese students and had them ordained priests, but they turned out to be more trouble than help. These ill-trained Europeans, ordained despite their lack of a deep spiritual life, proved worthless. And he dismissed still more Indian students, the very ones whom Francis had looked to for native priests.

Also Francis learned that one of the ablest Jesuits had been murdered by the Muslims. This was a great loss. And now he found that the young superior at the college had crushed his fellow Jesuits with his stern military ways. All was in great confusion. There was all but open revolt.

Francis did what had to be done. He removed the superior and sent him elsewhere. But the young priest was very popular with the politicians, who let out a great cry. Francis knew he had done the right thing, however, and would not bow to them. This firmness gave them all the more reason not to like the saint, and it was too late to save the college.

Francis, after settling things here, was now able to set out on another missionary journey, his last. He never returned. Francis visited many areas of Asia, always teaching about Jesus. At last he was near China. It was the greatest country in Asia and he felt it was ripe for the message of Christ.

He died, however, before a ship would take him there.

St. Francis Xavier   October 13

Francis Xavier wished to enter China, but it was a closed country. He would have to be taken in by night under cover of darkness. The voyage would be dangerous. Yet he was determined. He would do anything to tell others of Christ. He had with him two servant boys, one of whom was Chinese and would act as an interpreter.

They ran into a terrible storm at sea and everyone thought they were going to sink. Much of the cargo had to be thrown overboard. Father Francis alone remained fearless. He said our Lord would save the ship. He prayed to the Holy Trinity to have mercy on them and the winds died down and the storm abated.

They put in at the port of Cochin on the Fishery Coast. The official there would not let the ship go to China. Francis tried to argue, but in vain. And then Francis found that when the ship sailed it would not go to China but to San-cian, an island six miles away from the Chinese coast near Canton. Here the Chinese coast was guarded day and night by Imperial police boats.

The saint prayed. Finally he was able to get a small Chinese junk. The master said he would slip him into China at night. He had to pay a very high price in advance. The Portuguese merchants on the island said Francis was foolish. Going to China would mean sudden death, or that the crew would push him overboard even beforehand. Francis paid the man and waited. He and his companions built a little shelter, a thatched roof with no walls. They waited. The boat did not come. Francis stood in the rain. "Heaven is crying", said one of the boys. The next morning Francis was so sick he could not get up. The European officials avoided him. He said, "Never in all my life have I endured persecution like this, not even from the pagans or Mohammedans."

The cold and icy wind was merciless, piercing his bones. The shelter had no sides. He got worse. He could hardly speak. Early on the morning of the sixth day he spoke. It was a single word, "Jesus". And he died.

St. Jean de Brébeuf   *October 14*

St. Jean de Brébeuf arrived in New France, now Canada, to work with the Indians. As the sailing ship he was on made its way up the St. Lawrence River, the Indians were fascinated by the vessel. And they were particularly taken with the Blackrobes on board and Father de Brébeuf in particular, for he was as tall as a young tree.

The Jesuits stayed with the Franciscans who were already there, but they were near despair. The neighboring Indians were now hostile because of the way they were cheated by the French fur traders. So it was decided that the Jesuits would be better off going farther west, away from the French traders, to a more promising tribe, the Hurons.

The Hurons came down annually to trade, making the long journey from their land around the Great Lakes. Father de Brébeuf and a companion then left for the most distant French outpost to the west which the Hurons visited. It was a journey of three days from Quebec. Not long after they arrived there the Huron canoes could be seen coming down the river. These natives were larger men than those around Quebec. They were sturdy and proud, with painted faces. Curious, like all Indians, they were particularly fascinated by the tall, broad-shouldered Father Jean. In his black robe and black boots and with his black beard, he was a commanding figure. He tried to gain the approval of the Hurons, so they would take him back with them, by attending the council, feast and dancing.

There was, however, a discordant note. The Indians arrived without the Franciscan Father they were supposed to bring back with them. They claimed he had drowned when the canoe he was in hit some white-water rapids. The French agents at the post were suspicious that they had thrown him out of the canoe in the middle of the large lake. They were known for their terrible tempers. Relations were strained. Still the Jesuits persisted in their efforts to go back with the Hurons.

St. Jean de Brébeuf   *October 15*

The agents were against the Jesuits going with the Hurons since they felt they had purposely gotten rid of the Franciscan Father. You can't trust them, they told the Jesuits. St. Jean de Brébeuf still wished to go. But the Hurons, sensing the French suspicion, would not take him. The Jesuits had to return to Quebec. There Jean went with the neighboring Indians for the eel season when the natives spent the nights fishing, spearing and netting the eels by the hundreds. They ate them until they were bloated; the rest the squaws sliced and cleaned and smoked and rolled into bundles to carry with them and eat on their winter hunts.

He also went with them on their winter hunt that year. It was a hard, cold winter. First of all he had to live like they did in their huts so they would accept him. Lice and filth were everywhere. Also he had to eat out of the common, unwashed kettle in which each person dipped his dirty hand. Staying with these people was also difficult because of their sexual promiscuity. Yet, despite these hardships, Jean de Brébeuf remained with them because of his love for Christ. He hoped that he could somehow teach them about Jesus. He had a phenomenal ear and memory and soon he had learned their language and knew what they were saying. He also learned their customs. On the hunt the men wore robes of animal skins and carried only their snowshoes, bows and arrows and clubs and spears. The squaws and girls were loaded down with great packs like beasts of burden. On the hunt the men moved quickly, trotting on the trail, while the women and girls tried to keep up as best they could. Jean jogged with them. They were always accompanied by the dirty white dogs with pointed ears and wolflike snouts.

They made their way through the underbrush and tangled vines. Every day Father de Brébeuf's legs and back ached terribly, but he would not give up. At the campfires in the evenings, if the

Indians were in a good mood he would ask them words and names and jot them down. If the hunt had been bad, the braves were sullen and wild.

Father de Brébeuf endured many hardships to bring Christ to these people.

St. Peter Claver   *October 16*

One of St. Peter Claver's works during his priestly years was to bring comfort to slaves. When they arrived in Cartagena, the Spanish slave port in the Caribbean, the Africans were frightened and greatly confused. On the slave ship they had been chained and put down in the stinking hold where they were forced to lie on their sides on shelves. There was no room to stand up or even sit up. It was extremely hot in the hold. Blood, dung and mucus were everywhere. The slaves were treated worse than animals. Father Claver met these ships. He and a few helpers seemed to be almost the only ones to think of the blacks as humans. He was nearly alone in his interest in their souls.

He went among the slaves when they arrived, soothing them, nursing them and comforting them. In the city he walked from house to house to beg food for them. He said that he spoke to them with his hands before he was able to speak to them with words. His tenderness was like a healing ointment to their troubled bodies and minds. Sometimes he carried the sick ashore from the ship. He hauled the ill in a little cart to a shelter and dressed their sores. Many were bloody from the sadistic beatings by the crew. It was heartbreaking work, but he did it with a reckless disregard for his own health.

Peter instructed many of the slaves, telling them about Jesus and baptizing them. It was not an easy task to change their outlook to a Christian one. He went often to the slave barracks and to hospitals and prisons to do this work.

Then in his old age Peter came down with the plague, contracted from serving the sick in the disease-stricken area. During his illness he who had helped so many was grossly neglected. A former slave was employed to look after him but did not do so, knowing the saint would never complain. Now the slave of the slaves was dying. Peter stretched out his arms to meet and embrace the Lord, as he left this "valley of tears" for the joy of heaven.

St. Elizabeth Seton   *October 17*

Mother Seton held her Sisters of Charity together despite many difficulties. Their school grew, and it seemed like Mother was always encouraging the children. She would write little notes to them. She said to one, "Mother begs our Lord to bless our dear Mary that she may be an ever-blossoming rose in his garden."

But then her sixteen-year-old daughter Anna became sick. In those days medicine was primitive and illness widespread. Anna had entered the Sisterhood, but it was soon evident that she was dying. The girl kept her eyes fixed on the crucifix. She suffered greatly and died bravely. Elizabeth was desolate, yet even in this terrible grief she prayed and God gave her the grace to go on.

Then her daughter Rebecca became ill, and soon everyone knew she was dying. She was never out of Elizabeth's arms. The day before her last Rebecca said, "I have just been handing our Lord my little cup. It is not quite full. He will come for me." And he did.

What faith and courage Mother Seton had when she lost in a comparatively short time two daughters and two beloved sisters-in-law. What grace God gave her to keep her from despair!

One bright spot was that the Sisters of Charity were able to start an orphanage in New York City. This city which had treated Elizabeth with such shabby prejudice, she paid back with an institution of mercy.

By the time Mother was forty-five she was worn out. She had three years left. She was bedridden many days, and yet she never let a day pass without praising God and encouraging the others. She was ever thankful and always cheerful, even when in pain.

As death approached she received a letter from her saintly friend Bishop Cheverus of Boston. He said, "I do not pity you; I envy you, running now to embrace him who loves you."

St. Alphonsus Liguori, the founder of the Redemptorist Fathers, wrote, "God has conferred so many blessings on me, thereby to draw others to love him, but many do not even acknowledge him as Lord."

He pointed out that if Jesus had not redeemed us we would have been lost. Also, he might have redeemed us without suffering, but no, he willed to free us from eternal death by his own death. How great is his love! And yet many ignore him. Many are too busy even to think of him and all that he does for us.

Though Jesus was able to save us in a thousand ways, Alphonsus said, he chose the most humiliating and painful way by dying on the Cross of pure suffering to purchase for us freedom from the slavery of sin. The only cause for his most sorrowful death was the love that he has for us.

St. Alphonsus prayed, "Ah, my Jesus, may that love which made thee die for me on Calvary destroy in me all earthly affections and consume me in the fire which thou art come to kindle on the earth. I abhor the shameful Passion which cost thee so much pain. I repent, my Redeemer, with all my heart for the offenses I have committed against thee. For the future help me not to offend thee; I wish to do all that I can to please thee. Thou hast spared nothing for my love; neither will I spare anything for thy love. Thou hast loved me without reserve; I also without reserve will love thee. I love thee, my only good, my love, my all."

St. Alphonsus wrote that we can never comprehend the love that God has for us. The extent of his love is beyond our understanding, so great that he sent his Son to die for us, so that lost man might be saved. And who would ever have been able to bestow on us this gift of infinite value but a God of infinite love?

St. Alphonsus Liguori said, "I thank thee, O Eternal Father, for having given me thy Son to be my Redeemer; and I thank thee, O great Son of God, for having redeemed me with so much suffering and love. What would have become of me, after so many sins that I have committed against thee, if thou hadst not died for me? Ah, that I had died before I had offended thee, my Savior. Make me feel some of that detestation for my sins which thou hadst while on earth and pardon me. But pardon is not sufficient for me. Thou dost merit my love; thou hast loved me even to death, unto death will I also love thee. I love thee, O infinite Goodness, with all my soul: I love thee more than myself; in thee alone will I place all my affections. Do thou help me; let me no longer live ungrateful to thee, as I have done hitherto. Tell me what thou wouldst have of me, for, by thy grace, all, all will I do. Yes, my Jesus, I love thee, my treasure, my life, my all."

St. Alphonsus said that God has loved all mankind from all eternity. St. Bernard wrote, "Before the Incarnation of the Word the divine Power appeared in creating the world, and the divine Wisdom governed it." However, it was only when Jesus came that men were able to see truly the love that God has for them. After seeing Christ go through so afflicted a life and so painful a death, we would be offering him an insult if we for a minute doubted the great love that he bears us. Yes, he does surely love us, the saint said. And because he loves us, he wishes to be loved by us. "Christ died for all, that they also who live may not now live to themselves, but for him who died for them and rose again", St. Paul said.

"Ah, my Savior, when shall I begin to understand the love which thou hast had for me?" prayed St. Alphonsus. "Hitherto instead of loving thee I have repaid thee with offenses and disregard for thy graces, but since thou art infinite in goodness I will not lose confidence."

St. Alphonsus Liguori *October 20*

St. Alphonsus Liguori said that the Incarnation is our greatest joy. If Jesus had not come to save us we would be in despair. But God in his great goodness sent his only Son and now all is different. He sent the angel to Mary to ask her consent that the Son of God should become her Son, and Mary gave her most gracious and generous consent. And what a tremendous difference that has made for all of us! We should every day thank God for sending his Son to rescue us as we were drowning in a sea of sin. Man in his stupidity and folly was destroying himself, but Jesus died and redeemed us.

Jesus came and suffered for us. St. Alphonsus said, "Behold what was the life of the Son of God made man, the most abject of men. He was treated as the vilest, the least of men. To what extreme meanness could the life of Christ be reduced than being crucified as a criminal?" St. Bernard wrote, "My Jesus, when I see you so humiliated for me, how can I wish to be esteemed and honored at all? A sinner to be proud! Ah, my despised Redeemer, may your example inspire me with love of contempt and of an obscure life; from this time forward I hope, with your help, to accept suffering for the love of you."

St. Alphonsus prayed, "Pardon me the pride of my past life, and give me love in its place. I love thee, O my Jesus. Go before me with the Cross; I will follow thee with mine, and I will not leave thee till I die crucified for thee, as thou didst die crucified for me. My Jesus, my despised Jesus, I embrace thee; in thy embrace will I live and die."

St. Alphonsus said that Christ's life was a life of sorrow. He suffered the ingratitude and the sins of men. Let us pray so that we may be grateful and so that we may overcome our temptations.

St. Jean de Brébeuf *October 21*

In the New World, St. Jean de Brébeuf went with the Indians on their winter hunt to gain their confidence and acceptance. When the tribe arrived at lakes or streams they fished and gorged themselves on their catch. Between these orgies, on the trail, they often had little to eat unless they could catch rabbits or squirrels. Their great delight was to kill beavers because the skins were prized and the meat was delicious. Higher up in the hills they searched for deer and moose, which now in the deep snow could not run away. Sometimes they killed a bear.

It was cold and on the narrow trails in the mountains they often made their way along the rim of a precipice, slippery with snow and ice. Father de Brébeuf went with them.

In their tents he almost suffocated from the stench and smoke. The family packed close together at night to keep warm near the fire, with the dogs piling on. They gulped down their food with loud noises and belches, eating ravenously until they were almost insensible. At other times, they nearly starved, existing on acorns, roots and the shreds of skinned trees.

The Indians were highly superstitious, and sorcerers abounded in every clan. These men had fantastic rituals with screeching and ear-splitting yells. They would work themselves into a frenzy as they contorted themselves horribly in magic dances.

Jean de Brébeuf lived that winter in the wilds with these people, who were so erratic and lived without restraint. Then back in Quebec he soon left for the remote Three Rivers trading post, hoping to be taken by the Hurons to their distant villages far to the west. The Hurons would not take him. Again the next year Hurons refused. However, on the eve of their departure, after trading with the French, one agent piled high the presents that would be awarded to the ones who would take the Blackrobe with them. One chief at last agreed. Seeing all the presents, he could not resist, but he would take only one, and he chose Jean.

St. Jean de Brébeuf   *October 22*

St. Jean de Brébeuf was called "Econ" by the Hurons. This is the way the Indians pronounced Jean. They agreed to take him back to their village near the Great Lakes.

Jean got in the canoe. The Indians warned him gruffly that he must paddle with them and he must never move or the canoe would upset. If this happened he knew well they would simply abandon him in the wilderness. Econ was strong and paddled well, even though he soon ached in every joint and the hot July sun beat down on him and his legs were numb from sitting on them and never moving. All his bones ached and his whole body was in agony, but he paddled on. He was determined to go to the Huron tribes and tell them about Jesus.

The journey was a thousand miles. They traveled up many rivers, down white-water rapids, across great lakes. They carried their canoes around waterfalls or where the rapids and rocks were too fierce to traverse. If Father de Brébeuf made the slightest mistake the Indians would fly into a rage. But they liked having him there when they had to carry their loads overland because he would carry for two.

When they passed through the land of unfriendly Indians they were always on the alert for an ambush. They had little food to eat and were pestered constantly by insects of every kind. But, finally, they came to Lake Huron and were only ninety miles from home. At length they reached their village. They were greeted with shrieking Huron women and shouting naked children and leaping, barking dogs. They could not understand why Echon knelt on the beach and spoke to someone they could not see.

The Blackrobe entered the longhouse of his host and the squaws handed him a bark platter of corn mush seasoned with pumpkin and fish. Here the priest was to live with these primitive people the rest of his life.

St. Augustine   *October 23*

St. Augustine wrote, "The angels are not the only rational or intellectual creatures whom we think should be called blessed. For no one will dare to deny that the first human beings in paradise were blessed before their sin, although they were uncertain about the duration or eternity of their happiness—which, in fact, would have been eternal had they not sinned. And even today we rightly regard as happy all those whom we see leading a good and holy life in the hope of future immortality, untroubled in conscience and with easy access to God's forgiveness for the sins which are due to the frailty of human nature.

"These saints, however, although certain of their reward if they persevere, can never be sure of their perseverance. For, no man can be sure that he will continue to the end to act and advance in grace unless this fact is revealed to him by God." Yet the saint feels an assurance that God will always take care of him. He puts all his trust in God and prays for perseverence and has peace within.

St. Augustine wrote, "The only meaning we can give to the constant refrain, 'God saw that it was good', in Genesis is God's approval of his work." What God saw was good, and he would not have made it unless he had seen that it was good before he did so. God did not have to create us. He did so out of love, because of his goodness, because he wished to share his love with us. We should be grateful forever. How generous beyond words God is. How gracious in his love for us.

The explanation of the goodness of creation is the goodness of God. He made the world, a garden where man can live, and he made men, who have the ability to be happy: happy here if they follow the rules God has given us; happy hereafter in heaven with God, our Father.

St. Thomas Aquinas   *October 24*

St. Thomas Aquinas said that finite beings can have no right to claim from God their existence. We have life because God in his goodness gave it to us as a pure gift. He is so loving that he wished to share his happiness with us, and so he created us. Thomas said that creatures below man must please God. Man is free. His will seeks goodness and the greatest good is God. Lower creatures please God by being and by instinctively striving to be the best they can be. They have no choice. But humans, being free, can choose to do God's will or to reject it. They can choose a lesser good instead of God.

God did not have to create creatures to be happy. He did so only because he wanted to make thinking and loving creatures to enjoy his happiness. The created universe, then, is the outcome of the divine goodness, Thomas wrote. The order in the created universe is based on its resemblance to the Divine Creator. He said that creation is multiple because it is fitting that the epitome of perfection, God, should be illustrated by a thousand-and-one splendors. Each creature, too, because it is of divine handiwork, is stirred in the depths of its being and drawn by the divine goodness. All that we have, all that we are is a wonderful gift from God. And not only did the Supreme Being make us, he sustains us every hour, every second of every hour. If for a single second God should withdraw his support from us, we could no longer live or exist. We owe everything to God. That is why we should be grateful.

St. Alphonsus Liguori   *October 25*

"The love of friends increases at the time of death, when they are on the point of being separated from those they love; and it is then, therefore, that they try more than ever, by some pledge of affection, to show the love they bear for them. Jesus during the whole of his life gave us marks of his affection, but when he came near the hour of his death he wished to give a special proof of his love." These are the words of St. Alphonsus Liguori. He said, "For what greater proof could this loving Lord show us than by giving his blood and his life for each of us? And not content with this, he left this very same body, sacrificed for us on the Cross, to be our food, so that each one who should receive it would be wholly united to him, and thus love should mutually increase."

The saint prayed, "O infinite goodness, O infinite love. Ah, my loving Jesus, fill my heart with thy love, so that I may forget the world and myself, to think of nothing but loving and pleasing thee. I give to thee my body, soul, will and freedom. Up to this time I too often have sought to satisfy myself. I am exceedingly sorry for my selfishness. Sin has crucified thee. My God, thou art my all, I wish thee alone and nothing more. Oh, that I could spend myself for thee, who hast spent thyself for me: I love thee, my only good, my only love."

Alphonsus quoted the words of Jesus, "My soul is sorrowful even unto death." These were the words that proceeded from the sorrowful heart of our Lord in the Garden of Gethsemane before he went to die. Alphonsus asks, "Alas, whence came this extreme grief of his, which was so great that it was enough to kill him? Perhaps it was on account of the treatment that he saw he should have to suffer? No; for he had foreseen these torments from the time of his Incarnation. He had foreseen them and had accepted them. His grief came from seeing the sins men would commit after his death. It was then, according to Bernardine of Siena, that he saw clearly each particular sin of each of us."

St. Alphonsus Liguori   *October 26*

"It was not, my Jesus, the sight of the scourges, of the thorns and of the Cross which so afflicted thee in the Garden of Gethsemane; it was the sight of my sins", said St. Alphonsus Liguori. "This is the recompense I have made thee for the love thou hast shown me by dying for me. Ah, let me share the grief thou didst feel in the garden for my sins, so that the remembrance of it may make me sad for all my life. Ah, my sweet Redeemer, if I could but console thee as much now by my grief and love as I then afflicted thee by my sins! I repent, my Love, with all my heart for having preferred my own satisfaction to yours. I am sorry, and I love thee above all things."

St. Alphonsus Liguori said, "A God taken and bound! What could the angels have said at seeing their King with his hands bound, led between soldiers through the streets of Jerusalem! And what ought we say at the sight of our God, who is content for our sake to be bound as a thief, to be presented to the judge who is to condemn him to death?" He quotes St. Bernard who laments, "saying, 'What hast thou to do with chains?' What have malefactors and chains have to do with thee, O my Jesus, thou who art infinite goodness and majesty? They should belong to us sinners and not to thee who art innocent and the Holy of holies. St. Bernard goes on to say, on seeing Jesus judged guilty of death, 'What hast thou done, my innocent Savior, that thou shouldst be thus condemned? O my dear Savior, thou art innocence itself; for what crime hast thou been thus condemned?' Ah, I will tell thee, he replies: 'The crime thou hast committed is the too great love thou hast borne for men. Thy sin is love.'"

St. Alphonsus says, "My beloved Jesus, I kiss the cords that bind thee, for they have freed me from those eternal chains which I have deserved. Alas, how many times I have renounced thy friendship and made myself a slave of sin." He begs Jesus for the blessings he needs to persevere.

St. Bernard of Clairvaux   *October 27*

"So you see that there are two things that we need to know— first, what we are; then that we are not such of our own selves. The former knowledge will keep us from glorying without any qualification at all, the latter will keep us from glorying without any foundation", said St. Bernard of Clairvaux. "We read in Solomon's Song, 'If thou knowest not thyself, go forth after the flocks of thy companions.' And that is just what happens, for when a man, being held in honor, has no understanding of that in which the honor consists, he is justly compared (by reason of his ignorance) with the beasts that perish, the creatures that like himself lie under bondage to death and to corruption. Not knowing itself, the creature distinguished by the gift of reason from the beasts confounds itself with them; not recognizing its peculiar glory, which must be formed within, it gets led astray by sensible and outward things." Pride makes us fools. Our pride makes us think that we are great when we are not. And our pride makes us think that when we are great all the glory should go to us. These ways of thinking are juvenile.

How can any thoughtful man be so ignorant as to credit himself for the gifts that God has given him? Many people do not seem to think at all. All honor and glory are due to the Creator. All that we have is a gift from the Maker. Childish individuals alone steal brazenly the honor that is due to Almighty God. Such foolishness. We cannot usurp the rights of God. This is an arrogance that is even worse than the ignorance of those who think they are self-made men.

It is pride that makes men fools. Pride ruins an individual. Pride blinds a person. Pride makes a person think he is far greater than he is. Pride poisons the heart and spoils all that we do.

St. Bernard of Clairvaux   *October 28*

St. Bernard of Clairvaux tells us that we must grow in virtue. This is the health of the soul. This is what makes us pleasing in the sight of God. As we grow in virtue we become more Christlike, truly the great goal of every man.

It is the humble who realize full well the need for virtue. Virtues glorify God. Without them we are servants who do not know what we are about. We must use our intellects for good and not use them to plan evil deeds. Knowledge without virtue leads to ruin, Bernard said. The man of virtue, the humble individual, says with the psalmist, "Not unto us, O Lord, not unto us, but unto thy Name be the praise." In other words, our knowledge is to please God who has given us everything. Let us take no credit for ourselves. Let us refer these gifts to the Giver.

St. Bernard said that even people without faith know quite well that food and light and air and all the things we need for life are not made by us. They come from the Maker. He makes the sun to shine and sends the rain and all good things. What man is so foolish as to think all the good we daily receive is not from God? Where do our gifts come from if not from the Lord?

Bernard tells us that since God is the giver, then he deserves to be honored. We should be grateful with all our hearts for his goodness to us. Only one who does not think is ungrateful. Justice demands that we thank those who help us. From God we have all that we have. He is our strength, our help, our hope. Let us praise him and give him glory. Unfortunately, selfish individuals think only of themselves. "All seek their own", the proverb states. But we must not do so. We must not wrench away from God the honor that is his due and treat his lavish gifts as our own.

St. Thomas Aquinas   *October 29*

St. Thomas Aquinas said that the first thing a Christian needs is faith, without which no man is a true Christian.

Faith unites the soul to God, because by faith the Christian soul is in a sense wedded to God: "I will espouse thee to myself in faith", the Scripture tells us. When we are baptized we begin by confessing our faith when we are asked, "Do you believe in God?" Baptism is the first sacrament. Hence Jesus said, "He that shall believe and shall be baptized shall be saved." Faith introduces into us a beginning of eternal life, Thomas stated. Eternal life is nothing other than to know God: thus our Lord said, "This is eternal life, to know you, the only true God." This knowledge of God begins in us by faith, and is perfected in the life to come, when we shall know him as he is.

Faith is our guide in the present life, since a man needs to know what is necessary in order to live a good life: and if, to discover all that is necessary for that purpose, he had to rely on his own efforts, either he would never discover them all or he would only do so after a long time. Now faith teaches us all that is necessary for leading a good life. We learn thereby that there is one God who is the rewarder of the good and who punishes the wicked. We learn too that there is another life besides this, and other similar truths whereby we are sufficiently enticed to do good and avoid evil. Before the coming of Christ none of the philosophers was able, however great his effort, to know as much about God or about the means necessary for obtaining eternal life as the humblest believer knows by faith since Christ came down upon earth. The Scripture says, "The earth is full of the knowledge of God."

It is by faith that we overcome temptations. "This is the victory that overcomes the world—our faith", St. Peter said.

St. Thomas Aquinas   *October 30*

St. Thomas Aquinas wrote, "Some will object that it is foolish to believe what one cannot see, and that a person ought not to believe what he sees not. This difficulty disappears, however, if we consider the imperfection of our intelligence; for if a man were able by himself to know perfectly all things, visible and invisible, it would be foolish for us to believe what we do not see: whereas our knowledge is so imperfect that no philosopher has ever been able to discover perfectly the nature of a single fly. Thus we are told that a certain philosopher spent thirty years in solitude in the endeavor to know the nature of a bee. If then our intelligence is so weak, is it not foolish to refuse to believe anything about God, except such things alone which we are able to find out by ourselves?"

St. Thomas stated, "We should believe what is of faith even more than the things we see: since man's sight may be deceived, whereas God's knowledge is never at fault." God tells us about himself and we believe it. We say, "I believe in one God." God is the provider and governor of all things. Seeing that nature is regulated, we look to the Ruler of Nature, the Creator. We believe that God governs and disposes all the things of nature. And God cares for all men. He sees all things. And he wants us to do good, so that we will grow in soul and increase the love in our hearts.

God is the Father almighty. Just as a good father cares for his children, God looks after us, for indeed we are his children. The nearer we are to God, the more we live according to his way, and the better we are and the happier we are.

St. Teresa of Avila says that we must remain with Jesus and never turn our backs on him. He is near; he is not far off. When we pray he is with us. He understands us and wishes to help us. He helps us to understand as well. He very much loves to deliver us from evil. How willing he is to give to us! How glad he is to be with us! Let us then pray frequently.

Our Lord teaches us the truth, that real happiness comes from following him who said, "I am the Way."

In prayer let us remind ourselves that we are visiting with Jesus. He is beside us. Let us speak to him and tell him our troubles. Let us thank him for his gifts and say we are sorry for our sins. Let us praise him. And also let us listen to him. He speaks to us especially when we read the Gospel slowly and prayerfully. It is then that Jesus speaks most intimately to us.

We should never separate ourselves from his good company. Let us not fail to pray frequently. We are continually in need of his holy blessings.

We must recall that Jesus prays to his holy Father in heaven for us. How beautiful that is. Surely we must thank him for his graciousness.

Jesus taught us to ask for graces. We should say, "Give us, Father, that which is expedient for us." Like Jesus we should resign ourselves to the will of the Father. "Not my will but thine be done."

God sometimes does not answer our requests; he gives us something much better than we ask for. We ask for material wealth and what he gives is spiritual riches. And when God is so good it is most important, and just common courtesy, to thank him truly for being so wonderful to us.

All Saints'   *November 1*

This is the Feast of All Saints. There are many wonderful saints that we know; and there are many more saints, small and hidden but so very good of heart, that we do not know. In the parish, most often it is not the big talkers—who get all the attention and publicity—who are the saints, but the people who pray faithfully. Scholars in theology know about Jesus, but people devoted to prayer know Jesus. They can become saints, for they are very close to Christ; they visit with him every day. And the most important thing in Christianity is to know Christ. If we know him we will love him and to love him is to follow him and be loyal to him.

How those in the parish who are faithful to prayer love Jesus! They put the rest of us to shame. We may feel important and have big plans and projects, but our programs go nowhere without prayer. Jesus prayed for thirty years before he began to preach. Jesus tells us that "without me, you can do nothing". We enlist his blessings in prayer.

The people who pray frequently hold the parish together, and our society as well. They have, like the saints, the wisdom of heaven. And there is nothing we need more in our sick, tired world. All the saints had wisdom about the things of importance gained from constant prayer, continually talking to Jesus. How else can one know what is best to do? You can't learn wisdom from a book or in school. True wisdom is a gift of God, which he gives to all who pray devoutly.

"Humility is the beginning of wisdom." Prayer is an act of humility. The proud do not pray because they ignore God. They are so self-centered they think they can do everything alone. And they end up making fools of themselves, like the Pharisees. Let us learn from the saints and pray so that we will have the wisdom to solve our difficulties. Today many have knowledge but precious few have wisdom. Many even lack common sense. And so our troubles grow.

The saints show us the better way.

All Souls' *November 2*

Today is All Souls Day, when we traditionally pray for those who have preceded us in death. So many people have helped us along the way in life, doing wonderful things for us, sacrificing very much for us, and we must remember them in prayer. How thoughtless are those — and we live in a thoughtless time — who do not thank parents, relatives and friends who have died by praying for them. Let us remember often the poor souls in Purgatory and, in particular, those who have helped us most in this life. And when our turn comes, we know well that they will pray for us in our hour of need.

After persons die we can no longer do things for them as we did when they lived here on earth. The only way we have of showing our love is prayer. Love does not stop at the grave; love is eternal. And it is prayer that goes beyond the grave. Prayer is our way of telling our loved ones who have left us that we love them dearly still and always will.

Sometimes we feel a person who died needs no prayers, and yet we pray for them. We want to show them that we love them still very much. And we know that if they are not in need of prayers, God will use our prayers for another soul in need. No prayer is ever wasted; no prayer is ever unanswered.

Prayer is the most powerful weapon we have to help ourselves and others. It is the most important thing that we do. And prayer is most truly a gift when we give it to the poor souls in Purgatory. How grateful they are for our kindness! As we never forget them, they will never forget us. And when they are in a position to help us, they will do so with all their hearts.

Too many Christians are talkers. They talk too much and do too little. They talk the faith but they do not do what is most important, pray. And they are so careless as to forget to pray for the dead. Yet in words they say they love the departed so much. How foolish they are!

St. John of the Cross, friend of St. Teresa of Avila and her fellow reformer, said that in prayer we find true humility, interior quiet and calm joy. In prayer we show honor to God, which is what the creature must do. And God gratefully loves us with a happy heart. This life quickly passes away, but our praise for God is eternal. Pray faithfully.

John prayed, "O my God and my delight, for your love I have also desired to give myself. Increase my virtue. Assist me on my journey."

He said, "The Lord has always revealed to men the treasures of his wisdom and his spirit, but when the face of evil more and more bares itself, so does the Lord bare his treasures the more." He prayed, "O Lord, my God, who will seek you with simple and pure love and not find you are all he desires, for you show yourself first and go out to meet those who desire you?" Though the path is plain and smooth for men of good will, St. John related, he who walks it will not travel far and will do so only with difficulty if he does not have courage and tenacity of spirit; these come from prayer.

"It is better to be burdened and in company with the strong than to be unburdened with the weak", he observed. "When you are burdened you are close to God, your strength, who abides with the afflicted. When you are relieved of the burden you are close to yourself, your own weakness; for virtue and strength of soul grow and are confirmed in the trials of patience."

St. John, a man of great prayer, endured many hardships. Toward the end of his life, his Carmelite order took from him all his high offices and sent him into exile to the most remote monastery in Spain. His reaction? He was grateful. He said, "Now I will have more time to pray."

"He who wants to stand alone without the support of a master and guide will be like the tree that stands alone in a field without anyone owning it. No matter how much the tree bears, passersby will pick the fruit before it ripens. A tree that is cultivated and guarded through the care of its owner produces its fruit at the expected time", said St. John of the Cross.

"The virtuous soul that is alone and without a master is like a lone burning coal; it will grow colder and not hotter", he said. He added, "God desires in you some suffering for love of him", and to God this means more than all possible consolations, spiritual visions and meditations you might have. To suffer for him is to show your true love. Visions and the like do not do this. "Deny your desires and you will find what your heart longs for. O sweetest love of God, so little known, he who has found you is at rest!"

The great Spanish Carmelite tells us that doing our own will brings bitterness, but doing God's will brings peace. "The person who in aridity and trial submits to the dictates of his reason is more pleasing to God than he who does everything with consolation, yet fails in submission", he wrote.

"God is more pleased with one work, however small, done secretly, without desire that it be known, than a thousand done with desire that men know of them. The person who works for God with purest love not only cares nothing about whether men see him, but does not even seek that God himself know of them. Such a person would not cease to render God the same services, with the same joy and purity of love, even if God were never to know of them. He who does a pure and whole work for God merits a whole kingdom. He who does not allow his appetites to carry him away will soar in his spirit like a graceful bird."

"How is it that our Lord is so little loved in the Eucharist?" asks St. Peter Julian Eymard, founder of the Blessed Sacrament Fathers, who honor the Eucharist day and night. One reason is that people are very distracted in modern society. They think they must always be on the go. They do not have time to visit their dearest Friend in the tabernacle. Catholics should be ashamed. From the way they pray or visit, adore and go to the tabernacle, few people would know that Christ is here present. He is here awaiting our visit, and he rejoices when we come to him. He is a prisoner of love, so that we can show our love to him and gain the graces all of us and our families so badly need. But in spite of his overwhelming love for us, many will not take time to show their love for him. Or, perhaps, we are so thoughtless we do not love him very much at all. As usual Jesus does everything for us, and we, who are ungrateful, do very little for him. It amounts to telling Jesus we do not have time for him. It amounts to saying that though he eagerly awaits us to give us great gifts and graces, we do not want them or do not need them, which is pure stupidity.

After we have received so many graces from our gracious Savior, if we have any gratitude at all, we will go to him and thank him from the bottom of our hearts. We say we love him, but do we?

St. Peter Julian said he could not understand why many who call themselves Catholics do not want to have a heart-to-heart talk with Jesus. The very core of Christianity is Christ. To know him is the heart of our faith. Why are people afraid of the love of Christ? Why do they avoid him? Why do they pass by his presence and not stop in to see him?

Is it ignorance? Is it thoughtlessness? Is it childishness?

It is most difficult to understand.

"Lord, God, my Beloved, if you remember still my sins in suchwise that you do not do what I beg of you, do your will concerning them, my God, which is what I most desire, and exercise your goodness and mercy, and you will be known through them. And if it is that you are waiting for my good works so as to hear my prayer through their means, grant them to me, and work them for me, and the sufferings you desire to accept, and let it be done. But if you are not waiting for my works, what is it that makes you wait, my most clement God? Why do you delay? For if, after all, I am to receive the grace and mercy which I entreat of you in your Son, take my mite, since you desire it, and grant me this blessing, since you also desire it." So wrote the mystic, St. John of the Cross.

He continued, "Who can free himself from lowly manners and limitations if you do not lift him to yourself, my God, in purity of love? How will a man begotten and nurtured in lowliness rise up to you, Lord, if you do not raise him with your hand which made him?

"You will not take from me, my God, what you once gave me in your only Son, Jesus Christ, in whom you gave me all I desire. Hence I rejoice that if I wait for you, you will not delay.

"With what procrastination do you wait, since from this very moment you can love God in your heart?"

St. John of the Cross speaks to his soul, saying, "Mine are the heavens and mine is the earth. Mine are the nations, the just are mine, and mine the sinners. The angels are mine, and the Mother of God, and all things are mine; and God himself is mine and for me, because Christ is mine and all for me."

St. John prayed, his soul enkindled with love, his soul humble, meek, gentle, patient.

St. Francis de Sales said, "Though light is beautiful and lovely to our eyes, nevertheless it dazzles them after we have been long in the dark. Before we become familiar with the inhabitants of any country we find ourselves at a loss among them, no matter how courteous and gracious they may be." And so entering upon the spiritual life is at first somewhat difficult, but we must persevere.

It at first is not easy to turn away from the world with all its pleasures. "It may perhaps be difficult at first to renounce that glory which fools and mockers brought to you in the midst of your vanities. In God's name, would you forfeit that eternal glory which God will assuredly give to you? The vain amusements in which you have hitherto employed your time in past years will again re-present themselves to allure your heart and invite it to return to them. Can you resolve to renounce eternal happiness for such deceitful trivialities? Believe me, if you persevere, you will not be long in receiving consolations so delicious and agreeable that you will acknowledge that the world has nothing but gall in comparison to this honey, and such that one single day of devotion is preferable to a thousand years of a worldly life."

He said that the mountain of Christian perfection is exceedingly high, and a beginner thinks that he shall never be able to ascend it. But with courage a person takes one step at a time up the hill. And in time he turns around and looks down at the valley and it is a sight of exquisite beauty, unbelievable in wonder, majestic in splendor.

St. Francis de Sales wrote that little by little we make progress in climbing the mountain. And then the steps become easier and soon there comes a time when we would never turn back, for this is glory.

St. Francis de Sales *November 8*

"The sorrow that is according to God worketh penance steadfast unto salvation, but the sadness of the world worketh death", said

St. Paul. St. Francis de Sales comments, "Sadness then may be good or evil, according to its different effects upon us. We should be sad for our sins and ask God's forgiveness. But God does not want us to be sad because of anxiety, sloth, indignation, jealousy, envy or impatience. This has caused the wise man to state, 'Sadness has killed many, and there is no profit in it.'" The saint says we must strive to be cheerful, for Christ is with us. And in his holy company, how can we be sorrowful?

The enemy makes use of sadness to make us dispirited, causing us to give up our efforts to do good. It is the devil who troubles us and disturbs the soul, exciting fear and creating a disgust for prayer and things spiritual. "In a word, it is like a severe winter, which lays low all the beauty of the country and devours every living creature", said the Bishop of Geneva.

He said, "Oppose inclinations to sadness. It is the enemy who seeks to make us sad so that we are weary of good works." We must be like St. Francis of Assisi and rejoice in the Lord.

Sometimes, of course, we feel dry in prayer. But this passes. Some days are cloudy and some are full of sunshine. This happens in the soul as well. Let us try to sail on an even keel, more cheerful when the day is cloudy, more reserved when joy fills our hearts. Tend always toward the love of God. Look to him for divine assistance. He will not forsake us. Never abandon him.

"As long as consolation may last, enjoy it", he said. Just as we enjoy good weather, for bad weather is coming. But do not be too disturbed about this either, for the weather of the soul, like the weather of the day, changes constantly.

St. Peter Julian Eymard   *November 9*

St. Peter Julian Eymard was forever urging people to be devoted to our Eucharistic Lord. He wrote, "How good is the Lord Jesus, and loving, to give us this wondrous Sacrament!"

When it was time for him to return to heaven, Jesus wanted to remain with us on earth. And so he instituted at the Last Supper the Blessed Sacrament, that divine wonder. Now he could return to the Father and still be with us.

He had promised this splendid Sacrament to the people, telling them that he himself would be food for the soul. Many could not or would not believe it. They turned away and walked with him no longer. Not only did he not call them back and say that he was speaking in poetic terms and that they should not think of this in a real way, but Jesus actually was willing to let the apostles go as well. "Will you also go away?" he asked. But Peter answered for them in inspired words, "Master, to whom shall we go, for we have come to know and to believe that you have the words of eternal life."

And so at the Last Supper, the night before he died, Christ consecrated the bread and wine, so they became his Body and Blood, and then told the apostles that they were to do this as he did it in memory of him.

Obedient to Jesus, the apostles consecrated as Christ consecrated. And they passed on this power to their successors, so that, as Jesus desired, he might always remain with us.

How we should rejoice in this supreme gift of his love! Jesus did not give us some *thing,* he gave us himself. What more could he give us? How incredible is his love for us! How then can we disregard the Blessed Sacrament? And yet most Catholics do. They say they believe, but they act as if they do not believe.

St. Alphonsus Liguori   *November 10*

St. Alphonsus Liguori wrote about the blow that Christ received after giving an answer to the High Priest on the night of his arrest. "One single blow suffered by this man-God was sufficient for the sins of the whole world." But this was just the beginning of his pain. Jesus was not satisfied with the blow. He loves us so much that he wished to endure far, far more to prove his love for us. He wished to be wounded and bruised for us. And so his flesh was torn from head to foot. As the prophet Isaiah said, "Yet we esteemed him stricken, smitten by God, and afflicted" (53:4).

St. Alphonsus prayed, "O wounds of my sorrowful Jesus, you are all living evidence of the love which my Redeemer preserves for me; with tender words do you force me to love you for the many sufferings that you have undergone for the love of me. Ah, my sweet Jesus, when shall I give myself to you, as you have given yourself to me? I love you, my sovereign good. I love you, my God, lover of my soul. O God of love, give me love. By my love let me atone to you for the sins I have committed in the past. Help me to drive from me everything that does not tend to your love."

Pilate treated Christ scornfully. He sent him to Herod who took him to be a false king and ridiculed him. Then Pilate's soldiers crowned Jesus with thorns and laughed at him and beat him mercilessly. They struck him and spit in his face.

"O my Jesus," prayed the saint, "this barbarous crown that encircles your head, this vile reed that is in your hand, this torn purple garment that covers you with ridicule, these make you known as a king, but you are a king of love. My beloved Redeemer, if others will not have you for their king, I accept you and desire that you should be the only King of my soul."

St. Alphonsus Liguori   *November 11*

St. Alphonsus Liguori wrote, "Behold the Savior of the world has now set out on his journey with the Cross on his shoulders, going forth to die in torment for the love of men. The divine Lamb allows himself to be led without complaining, to be sacrificed upon the Cross for our salvation. O thou, also, my soul, accompany and follow Jesus, who goes to suffer death for your love, to satisfy for your sins. Tell me, my Jesus and my God, what do you expect from men by giving your life for our sake? St. Bernard answered, 'You expect nothing but to be loved by them: "When God loves, he wishes for nothing but to be loved in return." ' "

St. Alphonsus marvels that our Redeemer has desired to gain our love at so great a cost. How can people not love him? But many will not know him. And many know him but will not love him. "Infinite Love, make yourself known, make yourself loved. Ah, that I could by my blood make you loved by all! But alas that I have lived so many years in the world while I knew you, but loved you little. But now at last you have drawn me to love you by your great goodness", he said. At one time, he relates, he did not truly know Christ and was very unhappy. How much grace he lost! But Jesus was so gracious as to come to him and give the saint the desire to know and love him.

Alphonsus wrote that Jesus' dying for him gave him great confidence. He asks that he never leave off loving Jesus. "My love, my hope," he said, "do not abandon me; make me correspond during the remainder of my life to the especial love that you have borne me. You desire to have me for your own, and I wish to be all to you. I love you, my God, my treasure, my all. I will live and die always repeating, I love you, I love you, I love you."

St. Thomas Aquinas   *November 12*

St. Thomas Aquinas wrote that God created and conserves the world. All is dependent upon him. Creatures are nothing of themselves. "There was nothing and then something was made", he said. All creatures are limited, the Creator is unlimited. All beings other than God have their existence limited by their essence. They are dependent beings, while God alone is an independent being, for there is nothing before him or above him to limit him.

God in creation gives without loss or gain; the creature owes all to him. To create, bring something out of nothing, is an act proper to God alone.

From the notion of creation Thomas passes to conservation and providence. Not only did the Creator create all things in the first place but it is his power that keeps them in existence, or they would instantly perish. Conservation is an extension of creation. "The created world consists of an ordered series of natures which reflect in varying degrees the divine excellence", Thomas said.

Providence, God taking care of all things, is a scheme or order of all that is, in consonance with which all things follow their appointed course. Evil is not created by God; it is an imperfection. God never wills moral evil since it consists precisely in the refusal of a free being to follow what is God's law and one's own best good. God created men free and so they choose good or evil. They choose to follow what God has told them or they can refuse.

The creature by definition is wholly dependent upon God. That is why a person is foolish who feels he has done everything. Pride can make a man think unclearly and can let him attribute to himself that which properly should be attributed to the Creator.

St. Augustine   *November 13*

"The explanation for the goodness of creation is the goodness of God", wrote St. Augustine. He said that there is a hierarchy of created realities, from earthly to heavenly, from visible to invisible, some being better than others, and that the very reason for their inequality is to make possible an existence for them all. For God is the kind of artist whose greatness in his masterpiece is not lessened in his minor works—which, of course, are not significant by reason of any sublimity in themselves, since they have none, but only by reason of the wisdom of their Designer.

St. Augustine wrote, "We ourselves can recognize in ourselves an image of God. Of course, it is merely an image and, in fact, a very remote one. Nevertheless it is an image which by nature is nearer to God than anything else in earthly creation and one that by transforming grace can be perfected into a still closer resemblance.

"For we are, and we know we are, and we love to be and to know that we are. In this trinity of being, knowledge and love there is not a shadow of illusion to disturb us. Without any illusion of image, fancy or phantasm, I am certain that I am, that I know that I am and that I love to be and to know."

Augustine said that skeptics quibble and ask, "What if you are mistaken?" He replies, "Well, if I am mistaken, I am. For if one does not exist he can by no means be mistaken. Therefore, I am, if I am mistaken. And just as I know that I am, I also know that I know. And when I love both to be and to know, then I add to the things I know a third and equally important knowledge, the fact that I love."

Augustine tells us that merely to exist, by the very nature of things, is so pleasant that in itself it is enough to make even the wretched unwilling to die.

St. Augustine   *November 14*

This life is a pilgrimage. We are on a journey to heaven. We men are created to the image of the Creator, St. Augustine tells us. And we are to seek God from whom we came. He sent his only Son to us to show us the way. By following Jesus we will reach eternal life and be with God. In him our existence will know no death, our knowledge embrace no error, our love meet no resistance.

"At present," said the saint, "we are on the way to our final goal, God. With him in heaven there is eternal happiness. In heaven are the holy and faithful angels who never were or ever will be deserters of God, and who were separated by God in the very beginning from those who rejected the eternal light and were turned into darkness."

St. Augustine said, "Since God is the Supreme Being, that is, since he supremely is and therefore is immutable, it follows that he gave being to all that he created out of nothing; not, however, absolute being. To some things he gave more of being and to others less and in this way arranged an order of nature in a hierarchy of beings. Consequently no nature can be contrary to the nature which is supreme and which created whatever other natures have being. Therefore, there is no being opposed to God who is the Supreme Being and Source of all beings without exception."

He wrote, "In Scripture those who oppose God's rule, not by

nature but by sin, are called his enemies. They can do no damage to him, but only to themselves; their enmity is not a power to harm, but merely a velleity to oppose him. In any case, God is immutable and completely invulnerable. Hence the malice by which his enemies oppose God is not a menace to him but merely bad for themselves — an evil because what is good in their nature is wounded. It is not their nature, but the wound in their nature, that is opposed to God."

St. Thomas More   *November 15*

The iron door swung open and St. Thomas More was escorted from the Tower of London. His crime was that he had remained faithful to Christ and would not give in to the false notions of the spoiled, fat and pampered King Henry VIII.

Thomas was dressed in a suit of camelot silk which had been given him and he carried a cross in his hand. His steps were uncertain but his spirits were strong. A woman shouted, "You remember, Sir Thomas, when you were Chancellor you injured me in a wrong judgment." Thomas replied, "Woman, I am now going to my death." He told her he remembered her case and his judgment had been fair.

A man whom Thomas had saved from suicide asked him to help him again. Thomas answered, "Go your way in peace and pray for me and I will not fail to pray for you."

He was in a weakened condition and the stairs to the scaffold were not steady. Thomas said to a soldier, "See me safe up, and as for my coming down let me shift for myself." Even facing death his humor did not leave him. The humble always have a sense of humor.

Thomas on the scaffold was allowed to make a remark. He asked the crowd to pray for him and to bear witness that he was dying "in and for the faith of the Holy Catholic Church". He remained, he said, "the King's good servant but God's first".

He knelt and recited the ancient psalm the *Miserere,* in which the supplicant begs God to forgive his sins. It begins, "Have mercy on me, O God, according to thy great mercy."

As he put his head on the block he moved his beard out of the way, for, he said, "it hath committed no treason."

Thomas More, statesman, literary genius, honest and good, was beheaded. The sad, evil-minded King had triumphed. But St. Thomas More was really the victor, for he went to be with God in heaven and happy forever.

St. Jean de Brébeuf *November 16*

St. Jean de Brébeuf was with the Huron Indians in their village far away from the French settlers. Later he was joined by a second Jesuit. This other priest suffered more than Jean. Having just come from France, he was not used to the Indian ways. He vomited the food given him and suffered from hunger; he ached unmercifully on the long journey from paddling the canoe and from carrying packs in portage. The cool nights made him suffer even more, and the Hurons struck him and growled like animals when he made a mistake. It is a miracle they did not dump him overboard when they were in the middle of the lake.

The two Jesuits had to live in the longhouses with the Indians to be accepted. The air was fetid with urine, decaying food and uncured furs so that these houses smelled like a sewer; they were always filled with smoke, and the fleas and lice were a constant trial. All was dirty, greasy and sticky. During the warm weather the men and boys went naked in the cabins. The older women, after a lifetime of hard work and suffering and cruel treatment, were temperamental and dour-faced. The priests suffered so very, very much to bring Christ to them. Their commitment was all but superhuman.

Father Jean quickly learned the language and spoke with them, but he found it was hard to talk about religion. It was very difficult for them to think of spiritual things. He tried speaking to the women, but having worked in slavish drudgery since early childhood, they were quick to anger and responded with snarling insults. There were times when Jean felt as though he was dealing with wild animals or angry dogs.

Sexual promiscuity abounded; superstition was rampant. And when anything went wrong, the medicine men blamed the Blackrobes. To stay among these people took such strength. How much Father Jean and his companion loved Jesus!

St. Jean de Brébeuf *November 17*

Most of the time Father Jean could only pray and tramp from village to village and try to talk to one or two who were in the mood for listening a little.

But in moving to various villages one always had to be on the lookout for the Iroquois, the dreaded enemy of the Hurons. They were a war-loving tribe and fearsome, and made great trouble for the whole area. When the Iroquois came near, the Hurons became very agitated. Just the rumor that Iroquois were about made them work themselves into a frenzy with hectic dances and blood-curdling cries. And when they captured an Iroquois they tortured him with barbaric cruelty, but their bloody torture was nothing compared to what the Iroquois did when they captured a Huron. For five or six days they would burn a prisoner over a slow fire, pushing red-hot hatchets against his flesh, and cut off parts of his body—and worse.

In his prayers Father Brébeuf offered his life for the salvation of the people he was trying to teach. It would indeed take a miracle to bring them to the faith. The Hurons were lazy, lying, stealing, proud, treacherous: totally uncivilized. They lived in almost complete degradation. But at the same time they were very hospitable. They would share their last food, if necessary, with others. They were generous and kindly to those they liked.

Now Jean, or Echon, was in his third year there and the only priest. The others had gone back. Still he had failed to baptize very many. But he was undeterred. He offered his failure to God.

During that summer the whole northern Huron area suffered a drought. The corn was rotting and there would be a famine the following winter. The women were growing hysterical at the thought of near starvation. And one of the medicine men said it was all because of the Cross above the house of the Blackrobe. So things were made even more difficult for the priest.

St. Jean de Brébeuf   *November 18*

When the drought came and the medicine man blamed the tragedy on the Cross over the longhouse of St. Jean de Brébeuf, an old chief came to the priest and urged him to take down the Cross so it would rain again.

Father Brébeuf replied, "I shall never take down the Cross on which He-who-brings-blessings died." They admired his courage. Next the people came to their Blackrobe and begged him to bring the rain again. He began a novena, told them to pray and gave them a crucifix to kiss—and at the end of the novena the rains came, saving the crop.

Some of the braves became angry with the French. Echon had to be especially careful lest an irrational warrior in his fury would turn his hatred on the priest.

Father Jean de Brébeuf helped where he could. He had baptized only a few. He gave them conditional baptism at the time of their death. Father Jean wrote back to Quebec, "He who comes here has need of much strength and patience. Anyone who decides to come here for any other reason than God, will make a sad mistake." But things did get a little better, and he eventually had thirteen baptized Christians. He said, "May it please our Lord to accept these first few fruits, and give us strength and opportunity to gather more."

In 1649 Father de Brébeuf had been with the Indians for twenty-five years. It was a peaceful day and he was visiting a village. Suddenly savage, blood-curdling shrieks filled the air. The Iroquois had surrounded the village. They captured all. Those who tried to resist they killed. The rest, including Father Jean de Brébeuf, they took prisoner, treating them cruelly at every step.

It was the beginning of the end.

The Iroquois were more animal than human as they danced around their captives like demons. They stripped the priest and the others as naked as themselves. They yelled like hellish maniacs. They then stood on each side and forced their captives to run through their lines, as they brutally beat them. St. Jean de Brébeuf told his fellow prisoners to be brave.

At the end of this excruciating ordeal, the priest huddled among the Hurons praying with them. They shivered in their nakedness, for it had turned cold and windy.

The savages unanimously picked the priest, the white-skinned giant, and made him run up and down as they hit him and leaped on him and broke his bones and chewed his fingers. They dragged him to a torture post. He stumbled to his knees and embraced with his bleeding hands the instrument of his execution. He kissed it reverently before they seized him and tied him to it. He called to the others, "My sons, my brothers, let us lift up our eyes to heaven, let us remember that God is the witness to our suffering, let us die in our faith."

The Iroquois were enraged that they couldn't break him, and it drove them insane. They pushed burning torches into his face and body and into his mouth to keep him from talking. They were frantic because they could not break his courage. They gazed on his burned, blackened face and body in amazement. They hated him but could not keep from admiring his fortitude. Then they poured boiling water on him, and, because he continued to pray, they cut out his tongue. The savages threw him on a platform and scalped him and cut off his feet and drove a spear into his heart.

Because Father de Brébeuf was so brave, a chief rushed forward and cut out his heart and ate it, believing that the courage of this heroic man would pass into his heart.

"When God made man according to his own image, he gave him a soul so endowed with reason and intelligence that it makes man rank higher than all the other creature of the earth", St. Augustine said. God cares for what he creates. He has a special love for man, who can truly love him in return.

Man has a will. He can either love God and be grateful to him or he can ignore him and go his own way. If a man badly directs himself he will end up in despair. If his will is in harmony with God's will he will have peace within. Fear and sadness come when the will of a man is in disagreement with the Maker. But how happy is he who seeks to do as God wishes!

"It is clear then that the man who does not live according to man but according to God must be a lover of the good and, therefore, he hates evil. Since no person is wicked by nature, every man can live according to God.

"The good will is a work of God, since man was created by God with a good will. There can be a falling away from the work of God into man's own works. But in the long run the good triumphs over the evil. It is true, of course, that the Creator permits evil, since men are free", said the saint.

St. Augustine tells us that we can cure a disease or repair a damage only by restoring the nature to health and wholeness. Spiritual sickness is sin. Christ is the divine physician. He can heal the spiritually ill individual.

The sick soul is a slave to sin and vice. Christ came to earth to free us from the slavery of sin and to set us free.

St. Thomas Aquinas *November 21*

The brilliant St. Thomas Aquinas wrote, "To be self-moving is to be alive." Man has life in common with the animal. What distinguishes men from animals is that men have something spiritual, a soul with an intelligence and a free will. Man is the highest form of life on the earth. "Man can know all things and apprehend the immaterial and universal," said Thomas, showing that we have a spiritual source which is called the soul. By our intellect we can know all corporeal things; now if knowledge were in any way corporeal this would not happen, he said, because the particular kind of body it would have to be would prevent it from knowing all else indifferently.

"The intellect knows objects precisely by abstracting from them all that renders them material", he wrote. The intellect removes the object it knows out of space and time and so considers it universally. And the intellect in this action is self-conscious.

"Subsistence means that a thing has a life of its own." Man is subsistent. A human action is not due so much to the soul as to the one being which is composed of soul and body, or form and matter, as Thomas would say.

Because men are free, God gives them rules to guide them, lest they go off on the wrong road. The end of man is eternal happiness with God in his heavenly home. Man must walk the path that goes to the gate of heaven. A thing is made for a certain purpose. Man is made to be a child of God and to go home to eternal joy. Everything acts for a good. The tree tries to be a good tree. Men must strive to be good individuals so that they can reach their goal.

St. Alphonsus Liguori   *November 22*

St. Alphonsus Liguori said, "Jesus was called a lamb because he was dragged into the praetorium of Pilate and then led to death just like an innocent lamb. Therefore John the Baptist called him the Lamb of God. 'Behold the Lamb of God, behold him who takes away the sins of the world.' Jesus is a lamb who suffers and dies a victim on the Cross for our sins. The prophet wrote, 'Surely he has borne our infirmities and carried our sorrows.' Miserable are those who do not love Jesus during their life. On the last day the sight of this Lamb in his wrath will make them say to the mountains, as the Apocalypse says, 'Fall upon us and hide us from the face of him that sits upon the throne, and from the wrath of the Lamb.'

"No, my divine Lamb, if in times past I have not loved you, now I will love you forever. Before, I was blind, but now that you have enlightened me, and have made me know the evil I have done in turning my back upon you, and the infinite love which is due you for your goodness and for the love you have borne me, I repent with all my heart for having offended you, and I love you above all things."

St. Alphonsus said, "O wounds, O blood of my Redeemer, how many souls have you not inflamed with love—inflame my soul also. Ah, my Jesus, continually call to my remembrance your Passion and the pains and ignominies that you have suffered for me, that I may detach my affections from earthly goods and place them all on you, my only infinite good. I love you, Lamb of God, sacrificed and annihilated on the Cross for my sake. You did not refuse to suffer for me, I will not refuse to suffer for you. I will no longer complain of the crosses you send me. Give me the grace to love you more."

St. Alphonsus Liguori   *November 23*

"O God, who shall not have compassion for the Son of God, who for love of men is dying of grief on a Cross?" asked St. Alphonsus Liguori. "He is tormented externally in his body by the innumerable wounds, and internally he is so afflicted and sad that he seeks solace for his great sorrow from the Eternal Father. He calls out, 'My God, my God, why have you forsaken me?'

"His Father, in order to satisfy his divine justice, abandons him, and leaves him to die desolate and despised and deprived of every consolation.

"O desolate death of my Redeemer, you are my hope. O my abandoned Jesus, your merits make me hope that I shall not remain abandoned and separated from you forever. I do not care to live in consolation on this earth; I embrace the pains that you may send me. He is not worthy of consolation who by offending you has merited for himself nothing. It is enough for me to love you, Lord, and to live in your grace. This alone do I obtain from you. Let me never more be deprived of your love. Do not abandon me in my hour of need. I love you, my Jesus, who died abandoned for me. I love you, my only good, my only hope, my only love."

St. Alphonsus quoted St. Francis de Sales, who called the Mount of Calvary the hill of lovers. All love which does not take its origin from the Passion of the Savior is weak. How miserable is the death where there is no love for Jesus!

He said, "Let us stop and consider that this man nailed to the tree of shame is our true God, and that he is here suffering and dying for nothing but the love of us." He said that the immense love Jesus has for us forced him to die.

St. Alphonsus urges us to meditate on Christ crucified. Seeing our Savior in such pain and agony, enduring this horrible death for love of us, we are brought to tears. Christ died for us; we should live for him.

St. Clare of Assisi   *November 24*

St. Francis of Assisi on the way to his death was brought on a stretcher to the convent of St. Clare and her Sisters for a final farewell. There were many tears. They said, "Now who will comfort us in our poverty of this world's goods, and above all in our poverty of spiritual merit? Francis was the lover of poverty who helped us feel rich. O how bitter is this separation, how dire your absence will be!"

When Francis died, the Franciscan superior wrote to all the local superiors, "The loss is common to us all for our true light was the presence of our Brother and Father Francis who directed our steps into the way of peace." This too was the feeling of his Sisters in Christ.

Clare felt alone, but the spirit of Francis was in her heart. She remembered his words to them, "Seeing that by divine inspiration you have become the daughters and handmaids of the Most High, our heavenly Father, and have espoused yourselves to the

Paraclete by choosing to live according to the perfection of the Gospel, I bless you with all my heart."

St. Clare and her Sisters, true to Francis, were ready to suffer the loss of all things for the sake of Christ. They worked with their hands and prayed fervently from their hearts.

Of these nuns it was said, "On the hill of San Damiano there germinated and flowered in the light of the sun the most exquisite virtues of adoring love, self-sacrificing charity and the spirit of prayer that touches the heart of God, the patience that bears the hardest things serenely and joyfully, and that lovely Christian modesty which is the sign of a soul mistress of itself."

Here all hearts were united, all wills bent, bowing before God in praise and glory and thanksgiving.

St. Benedict Joseph Labre   *November 25*

St. Benedict Joseph Labre died a beggar in Rome. This humble, prayerful man, who lived in the eighteenth century, saw more in life than others saw. It disgusted him that so many gave their lives to making money and seeking pleasure. He sought Jesus. He needed little, for he prayed most of the time. Many thought of him as a tramp, but the poor, with their native wisdom, knew he was a saint.

Just being with God in prayer was all he wanted on earth. He did not realize this vocation at once. He attempted many things and failed.

He was a quiet, meditative youth, unable to express himself well, easily misunderstood. But he was always cheerful. He did not take much to study, but he loved the Scriptures. Even as a youth he had liked to help the poor. Often he had emptied his pockets to assist them. But most of all he loved to pray for long periods of time before the Blessed Sacrament.

Benedict lived with a priest-uncle for a time. He was then about eighteen. An epidemic fell upon the city and the uncle and nephew were out every day helping the sick. The uncle took care of their souls. Benedict took care of their bodies. But then in the epidemic the uncle died, and Benedict had no home. He tried different things. He visited monasteries, but none of them suited him. They did not pray enough. It was then that he decided to live alone with God. He would be God's own poor man, depending on whatever people gave him, and praying in church all day. He did this in Rome. He was truly a tramp; he did not bathe very often, his clothes were dirty, he slept in a barn. But how he could pray! And he fasted and abstained continually. He was a hidden saint: sanctity lay beneath his rags.

St. Laurence O'Toole   *November 26*

St. Laurence O'Toole was the Archbishop of Dublin during turbulent times in the twelfth century. When the Normans attacked the city he suffered during the siege and was instrumental in negotiating a treaty.

When Laurence was only ten, in a battle fought by his noble father, he was taken hostage by the enemy. For two years he toiled as a slave until finally his father was able to obtain his release.

He became a monk and in time was elected abbot. He used all the resources of the monastery to aid the hungry when famine struck.

Later he was made Archbishop of Dublin. He was popular with the people but not with many of the clergy because he insisted on reform. He led them by his example in doing penance and praying. On Fridays he ate only bread and water. At night after a weary day with the people he prayed for long periods.

This tall, handsome prelate instructed the people himself and he visited the sick and begged for the poor.

When the Earl of Pembroke, nicknamed "Strongbow", invaded Ireland and advanced on Dublin, the Archbishop met the invaders and tried to stop the fighting, but in vain. He spent his days during the fighting tending the wounded and protecting the innocent from massacre.

He preached that peace of soul comes from helping others. We gain our inspiration for this from Jesus. He feeds and heals our souls. He teaches us that it is the humble who truly do great things. Humility is the foundation of all the other virtues. It is a virtue not of our nothingness, but of God's greatness.

When he was dying someone asked him about making a will. He smiled and said, "God knows I have not a penny in the world."

St. Maximilian Kolbe   *November 27*

St. Maximilian Kolbe was a Polish Franciscan. He was so successful in telling others of Christ that when the Nazis invaded Poland, he was taken to a dreadful concentration camp. There one day some prisoners escaped and the Nazis decided to starve to death ten of the inmates as a lesson to the others. They picked them at random, and one was a family man who wept bitterly for his wife and children. Father Maximilian stepped forward and volunteered to replace the other. He died instead, and even the Nazis were amazed at him.

When Maximilian was a young priest he took seriously the words of Jesus, his final command, "Go out and tell everyone about me." He went to his superior and asked if he could print a little magazine to give away and send out. This was something new for this house and the superior was not enthusiastic. He gave Maximilian permission, but he told him he would have to raise the money himself.

Maximilian went out to the neighborhood houses. He was so embarrassed he walked around the block several times before he got up enough nerve to go up on the porch and ask for money. He was given a few pennies. He went to all the houses there and then to the next block. He finally got enough money to buy an old, hand-cranked printing press. It had to be turned several times to print one page. And thus he put out his first publication. Weaker souls would have given up, but not Maximilian. He truly wanted to tell people about Christ. Some of the other Franciscans made fun of him, but he kept at it. And from that humble beginning before the Nazi invasion he soon had publications reaching a million people. No wonder the invaders thought him dangerous.

Fr. Maximilian worked hard though his health was never good. He kept working to spread the word of God, even when others tried to discourage him. Once a bishop came through the large printing plant and said to Maximilian, "What would St. Francis do if he came here and saw all these expensive presses?" The saint answered, "He would pitch in and help us."

Pope St. Pius X   *November 28*

Pope St. Pius X was a peasant Pope in the early years of this century. He fought against the heresy of Modernism which in his day was trying to undermine the Church. Also, he is known for making it possible for little children to receive Jesus in Holy Communion.

His family was poor. Though the future Pope, Beppo Sarto, was bright, his parents could not afford to send him to high school. The parish priest, however, fortunately was able to arrange things. Beppo went on then to the seminary and became an assistant priest in a village. The pastor was not in good health and the young, energetic priest had to take over many of the duties, which he did gladly. He was very active, helping all. Then he was named a pastor and later a bishop and, before being elected Pope, was the Cardinal Patriarch of Venice. At the papal election in 1903 after Pope Leo XIII died, there were many ballots cast. Gradually the number for Cardinal Sarto increased. He got very restless as he saw this, and he rose and begged the cardinals not to elect him. His voice trembled and he was near tears. After he had spoken he went to pray before the Blessed Sacrament.

That evening several cardinals came to him urging him to accept. Cardinal Sarto only shook his head; over and over he told them how unworthy he was. They told him that God would help him.

Next day he had the largest number of votes. Cardinal Sarto could only say in a low voice, "God's will be done." When he was formally asked if he would accept he was silent for a time but then seemed to gather courage. He was unworthy, he said, but "if this chalice will not pass from me unless I drink it, the holy will of God be done."

Pope Pius X, a saint, was a wonderful gift of God to the Church in those troubled days.

St. Bernard of Clairvaux *November 29*

St. Bernard of Clairvaux wrote, "Believers know well their utter need of Jesus and him crucified; and they, while they embrace and marvel at the love revealed in him, are overwhelmed with shame because they do not pay back, in answer to such love and consolation, even the very little that they are. These easily love God the most, because they understand how greatly they are loved; for he to whom less love is given will himself love less."

The believer is wounded with the dart of love as he sees the Father's only Son carrying his Cross. He sees the Lord of majesty spat upon and stricken, the Fount of life and glory nailed upon the tree, his side pierced by the spear, the insults heaped upon him, surrendering for us at last his precious life. Seeing these things, he feels the sword of love go through his heart. He says, "I am wounded with love. Stay me with flowers, comfort me with fruits, for I am sick with love." And he sees the earth, with thorns and thistles, suddenly break forth with flowers under God's new blessings. His are the words of Scripture, "My heart dances for joy and in my song will I praise him." The fields are full of flowers with which the Lord God has blessed us. For Jesus died for our sins.

God's love is bestowed upon us in abundance. God's chosen shall not lack graces. The memory of his wonderful kindness fills us. With the psalmist he says, "One generation shall praise thy works unto another." Glory be to God and praise and thanksgiving now and forever.

The faithless, stubborn and selfish never know the joy of knowing God.

St. Bernard of Clairvaux

St. Bernard of Clairvaux wrote beautifully of the spiritual life. He quoted Scripture, "I remember God and take delight." There is wonderful happiness and peace and goodness in being with God. Seek then the Lord, he said.

The thought of God is sweet indeed, wrote the saint. And those who think of him hunger for more. Happy are those who hunger and thirst after righteousness, for they shall be filled.

He said, "The faithful soul both yearns for his presence and rests sweetly in the thought of God, and until such a time as a person be fit to see God's glory face to face, he is as God's own dove, and holds himself in waiting." He added, "Out of the memory of your abundant sweetness, Lord, the soul chooses for itself the silver wings of innocence and purity and looks moreover for the day when it will be filled with joy in the light of your countenance and its feathers will shine with purest gold, when it will be received with joy among the saints' bright company in heaven, to share the radiance of their happiness."

St. Bernard wrote that God has given us the singular gift of living in his home in heaven. But what else would you expect to issue from mercy so great and so unmerited as we creatures receive from the good God? When we ponder the love of God for us it is beyond compare, and we can only wonder at his greatness. Surely for love's dear sake we should be most grateful to God. Let us run swiftly to him in prayer. Our love is too small, but we must offer it to him. So great a love as God shows to us can never be paid back. We cannot begin to thank him enough. We never will be able to do so.

Dust that we are, Bernard said, what recompense can we make, even if we give our whole poor selves to him? God was the first to love us, or we would not exist. He is wholly bent on our salvation.

St. Thomas Aquinas wrote that Christians believe in Christ. He is the Son. In the Gospel he called God his Father and the apostles and holy Fathers say in the Creed: "And I believe in Jesus Christ, his only Son." That is, God's only Son.

Heretics have a distorted belief, but authentic followers of Christ are true to the teachings of Christ, the apostles and early Fathers of the Church. Holy Scripture explicitly tells us, as St. John relates, "The only-begotten Son who is in the bosom of the Father, he has declared him." And the words of Jesus, "Before Abraham was, I am." The Nicene Creed states, "Eternally begotten of the Father." And Jesus said, "I am not alone, but I and the Father who sent me are one." The Creed says of Jesus, "God from God, Light from Light." We must believe in God the Son of God the Father, and the Son who is the "Light of the Father who is Light".

St. Thomas writes that since Jesus said, "I and the Father are one", they are one in nature, and, consequently, as the Father always was, so also was the Son; and as the Father is true God, so also is the Son. The Nicene Creed says of Jesus, "true God from true God", and it says of him "begotten, not made", and again, "one in being with the Father".

Thus Christ is the only-begotten of God, and the true Son of God; he has always existed together with the Father; the Person of the Son is distinct from the Person of the Father; the Son is of one nature with the Father. Thus, in the present life we know by faith, but we shall know it by perfect vision in eternal life.

We are reminded of St. Paul, who said that here we see things unclearly, but in the life to come we shall see clearly.

St. Thomas Aquinas   *December 2*

Christ is the Son of God. He became man. "And the Word was made flesh", St. John tells us. He was clothed with flesh and was made manifest and known. The Scripture says, "He was seen on earth and conversed with men." The Apostles' Creed states, "He was conceived by the Holy Spirit, born of the Virgin Mary." St. Thomas Aquinas points out these things. Jesus said, "I came down from heaven, not to do my will, but the will of him who sent me." This shows that he was in heaven. But if he was only a man, and not divine, he would not have been in heaven. He was also a man, for he said, "Handle and see; for a spirit has not flesh and bones, as you see me to have." He was man but also divine, for the angel said to Mary, "The Holy One that shall be born of you shall be called the Son of God."

Jesus was the great Teacher of truth. He told us about God. St. John writes in the Scripture, "No man has ever seen God, the only-begotten Son, who is in the bosom of the Father, he has declared him." Christ made known many things to us which, before he came, were hidden.

Christ gives us new hope. God's Son took our flesh and came to us for our exceeding great good: wherefore he bound himself to us, as it were, by deigning to take a human soul and body and to be born of a Virgin, in order to bestow his Godhead on us, thus becoming man that man might become God, as the Scripture says, "By whom we have access through faith into this grace wherein we stand; and glory in the hope of the glory of the sons of God."

Knowing this, says Thomas, our charity is inflamed, because there is no greater proof of God's love than that God the Creator became a creature for love of us, that our Lord became our brother and that the Son of God became the Son of man. "God so loved the world that he gave his only begotten Son."

St. Alphonsus Liguori   *December 3*

"Ah, my Jesus, if all would stand still and contemplate you on the Cross, believing with a lively faith that you are their God and that you have died for their salvation, how could they live far from you and without your love?" These are the words of St.

Alphonsus Liguori. He said, "All love which does not take its origin from the Passion is weak."

He wrote, "Behold, my Redeemer, to what your love for men has brought you—even to die of sorrow on a Cross, drowned in a sea of grief and ignominy."

He quotes St. Francis de Sales, who said, "Let us contemplate our divine Savior stretched on the cross, as upon the altar of his glory, on which he is dying for love of us. Ah, why, then, do we not in spirit throw ourselves upon him to die upon the Cross with him who has chosen to die there for the love of us? I will die for him. I will hold him, we ought to say; I will never let him go. I will burn in the flames of his love; one and the same fire shall devour this divine Creator and his miserable creature. My Jesus is all mine, and I am all his. I will live and die on his bosom. Neither life nor death shall ever separate me from my Jesus."

St. Alphonsus wrote, "Yes, my dear Redeemer, I hold fast to your Cross; I kiss your pierced feet, touched with compassion and confounded at seeing the affection with which you have died for me. Ah, accept me, and bind me to your feet, that I may no more depart from you, and may from this day forward converse with you alone, consult with you on all my thoughts; in a word, may I henceforth direct all my affections so as to seek nothing but to love you and please you, always longing to leave this valley of danger to come and love you face to face with all my strength in your Kingdom which is the kingdom of eternal love."

Bl. Kateri Tekakwitha   *December 4*

Blessed Kateri Tekakwitha was an Indian girl who loved Christ and who loved to pray.

She was the daughter of an Algonquin mother who was captured by the Mohawks; a chief had taken this captive for his wife. She was a Christian, and few of the Mohawks would have anything to do with the Christians.

Kateri's mother and father died of the "smallpox devil" when the girl was small. She was ill but survived. Her eyes were weakened and her pretty face was scarred for life. She was a quiet girl, and she remembered the beautiful stories her mother had told her about Jesus who suffered so that man could go to heaven, and about his lovely Mother, who was a virgin. After her parents' death she had to live with an uncle and aunt. The aunt was always complaining about her because her poor eyesight slowed her work. She scolded her constantly. Kateri only bowed her head and continued trying to do her work.

In time the French forced the Mohawks to sign a peace treaty which allowed missionaries to go to their villages. Kateri's heart rejoiced. Maybe she could be baptized! But her uncle-chief forbade her to talk to the priests who came. Shyly she served them food, loving their friendly smiles and admiring their self-denial, but she could not tell them what was in her heart. She could not ask for the "Saving Waters".

In time a chapel was built. Kateri prayed to her mother, "Dear Mother, help me. You wanted me to love the Christ and I do. But I know so little of him—help me to learn more."

"Are you coming to the chapel?" a friend asked Kateri. She answered, "I dare not. My uncle has forbidden me."

It made her sad. She was afraid she would never learn about Christ.

Bl. Kateri Tekakwitha   *December 5*

Blessed Kateri Tekakwitha wanted to learn about the Christian faith but her uncle hated the missionaries and would not let her. When her friend asked her to come to the chapel, Kateri sadly said she was not permitted to do so.

"Oh, you must go. Tomorrow is Christmas and the crib will be so beautiful."

Kateri knew she couldn't and she was heartsick. Imagine her amazement then when her uncle told her she was to go to Christmas Mass at the chapel! As it turned out, the Blackrobes insisted all the families attend the Midnight Mass, and the uncle was afraid to insult the powerful French. Kateri was happy beyond words.

In the chapel a feeling of peace came to her heart. She felt she was home at last. The children sang like heavenly angels. Kateri could not take her eyes off the crib and the Baby. And there, looking so sweetly on him was his Mother. Even the animals looked on the Child with love.

Her uncle continued to hate the Christians. He and her aunt badly mistreated Kateri.

Then in the winter the Mohawk war chief came back to the village praising Christ. No one could believe it. He told what had happened to him. He was in a terrible snowstorm and was starving. He wandered and came upon a lone hut in a forest. An old Oneida squaw lived there alone. She fed him and gave him shelter. He mocked the old woman's Christian faith, but she answered him with such good sense he decided to talk to the Blackrobe who taught her. From this missionary he learned about the Christ and came back to tell his people.

Then one day Kateri hurt her foot in the field. The Blackrobe came to visit her. Here at last was her opportunity. She poured out her longing to know Jesus. The priest was amazed at the beauty of her soul among these pagans.

Bl. Kateri Tekakwitha   *December 6*

Blessed Kateri Tekakwitha was baptized. The uncle was afraid to oppose this because of the war chief. Kateri was so happy.

Her aunt ordered her to go to the field and work on Sunday. The girl said, "I cannot—it is the Lord's day—I will work extra tomorrow." Her aunt was doubly angry. She said, "Those who do not work, do not eat. You do not eat today."

Things went from bad to worse. The priest thought she should go to the Christian Indian village, but Kateri knew her uncle would never allow it. However, she slipped away one day when her uncle was gone and her ill-tempered aunt was drunk.

Her uncle heard of it and he and a band of braves tried to intercept her on the long journey north to Montreal. She and her companions often had to hide. Her uncle came very close, but did not find them. They walked most of the long journey. But finally one happy day they came to a village with a Cross. It was where the Christian Indians lived in peace. It was called St. Francis Xavier of the Sault.

The priest who knew Kateri sent a letter with her to the Blackrobe of this village. He wrote, "You will soon know what a treasure I have sent you. May she profit in your hands for the glory of God!"

That night when she went to sleep Kateri for the first time was not afraid. She rejoiced that she was no longer surrounded by superstitious, uncivilized pagans. She told herself, "Now I can live close to Christ." It was something she had always dreamed of.

The Indians at this Christian village were good and kind. One priest said, "For my own part, I find more pleasure among these Indians in a single day than among the French in many months." And Kateri was the most devout of them all. She often visited the chapel; she frequently said the Rosary. And when she went to Holy Communion she wept for joy.

Here she died. After her holy death, people could not believe what happened. The pockmarks had disappeared from her face and she was beautiful again.

St. Alphonsus Liguori   *December 7*

"We see that Jesus Christ willed to appear in the world as a guilty and accused man, hanging on the Cross to deliver us from eternal malediction", said St. Alphonsus Liguori.

Jesus accepted all the pain he suffered, and in doing so he obtained pardon for our sins, he wrote. These graces come to us in his help to overcome temptations, in his consolations and compassionate feelings, in the light he gives us and in the call of his love.

In a bath of his own blood Jesus saved us. Jesus bought our salvation with his blood.

"What great things the martyrs have done in giving their lives for God, while this God has humbled himself to the death of the Cross for their love. To render a just return for the death of a God, it would not be sufficient to sacrifice the lives of all", Alphonsus said.

He went on to tell how tender and full of unction were the words of St. Francis de Sales. Francis wrote, "Nothing forces and presses the soul of man so much as love. If a man knows that he is loved by anyone, he feels himself forced to love him; but if a peasant is loved by a lord, he is still more strongly forced; and if by a monarch, how much more so. Know, then, that Jesus, the true God, has loved us so far as to suffer death, even the death of the Cross for us. Is not this to have our hearts put under a press, and to feel them squeezed and crushed so as to force out our love with a violence which is all the stronger for being so loving?"

St. Alphonsus uses the words of St. Paul, "The charity of Christ presseth us." He explains that Paul meant to say it is not so much the thought of all that Christ has suffered for us that should constrain us to love him, as the thought of the love that he has shown us in wishing to suffer so much for us.

Immaculate Conception   *December 8*

This winter feast in honor of the Blessed Mother, the Immaculate Conception, reminds us that she was the greatest of all creatures. She never had any sin in her entire life. She was so beautiful in soul that God chose her to bring Jesus into the world.

Mary is a wonderful example for us all. We cannot pray as she prayed, but it was, we know, because of her fervent prayers that she was so pleasing to God. Her humility made Mary realize that we are here in the world to praise God. We are nothing of ourselves. She knew well that she was God's lowly handmaid, but she knew also that if one were humble—that is, honest—God raises him up. As Jesus said, "In my Kingdom the first shall be last and the last shall be first." Jesus, the Master, washed the feet of his disciples.

Mary did no great things when she was here in the world, but with a heart of gold she was forever assisting her neighbors in need. We are sure that if anyone was sick in Nazareth, she was there. And she did whatever she could. Nothing was too lowly for her. She was thoughtless of self. The needs of others were what mattered.

Mary was made the Queen of Heaven. She did not ask for this. She did not like honors and titles for herself. Her whole life was helping others to know her Son as she knew him. But she accepted the queenship because she knew that in this way she could be of greater help to us, her children, here on earth.

The Blessed Mother loves us with a mother's love. She cares for us very much. She wants to take care of us, if only we will pray to her so she can come to our assistance. She never fails her children who pray to her.

St. Thomas Aquinas   *December 9*

"We are encouraged to keep our souls pure inasmuch as our nature was ennobled and raised through being united to God to the extent of being assumed into union with a Divine Person; wherefore after the Incarnation he became our brother." These are the words of St. Thomas Aquinas. He went on to say that men ought to bear their exaltation in mind and, in consideration thereof, should disdain to debase themselves and their nature by falling into sin. For this reason, Thomas recalled that St. Peter said, "He has given us most great and precious promises; that by these you may be made partakers of the divine nature, flying the corruption of that concupiscence which is in the world."

"Thereby is inflamed our desire of going to Christ. Thus a man whose brother is a king in a far-distant country will have a great longing to go to him, to be with and stay with him: wherefore seeing that Christ is our brother, we should long to be with him and to be united to him", said Thomas. He mentions St. Paul, saying that he desired "to be dissolved and to be with Christ". This same desire should be with us as we reflect on the Incarnation. Christ became man, God with us.

Not only did Jesus live among us, he died for us. Why did he suffer so? He wanted to redeem us from our sins and he wanted to show us how very much he loves us. By dying, Christ diminished our weakness. And he gained for us the graces we need to go to heaven. Sin no longer has as much power over men. Grace strengthens us. We are able to overcome temptations with the help of Jesus. We are able to arise from our sins. What a great and tremendous blessing is Jesus' dying on the Cross for us.

St. Thomas Aquinas   *December 10*

"He shall be led as a sheep to the slaughter and shall be dumb as a lamb before his shearer", the prophet said of the holy one who was to redeem us. St. Thomas Aquinas tells us that Jesus could have escaped this agony and death, but he did not will to escape. Christ suffered greatly on the Cross. The Scripture says, "Oh, all you that pass by the way, attend and see if there be any sorrow like unto my sorrow." All this Jesus suffered patiently. Great was Christ's patience upon the Cross.

"If you seek an example of humility, look on the crucifixion", Thomas said. "Although he was God, he chose to be judged by Pontius Pilate and to suffer death. The Master chose to die for his servants. If you seek an example of obedience, follow him who was made obedient to the Father even unto death. If you seek an example for contempt for earthly things, follow him, the King of kings and Lord of lords, in whom are the treasures of wisdom; and see him on the Cross, despoiled, derided, spat upon, scourged, crowned with thorns, served with gall and hyssop, dead.

"Take no account of your apparel for they parted his garments among them; nor of honors, since he suffered himself to be jeered at and scourged; nor of rank, since they fixed a crown of thorns and placed it on his head; nor of pleasures, since in his thirst they gave him vinegar to drink." St. Augustine said, "The man Christ despised all earthly things in order to teach us to despise them." This is a reflection of the words in the Epistle to the Hebrews, "Who, having joy set before him, endured the Cross, despising the shame".

334

Since Jesus laid down his life for us, we should not deem it a hardship to suffer for his sake.

St. Thomas à Becket

St. Thomas à Becket as a young man was a friend and companion of the wild-living English king, Henry II. The king was constantly fighting with the Archbishop of Canterbury, who defended the Church against the desire of the monarch to rule it. So when the old Archbishop died, Henry thought it would be a wonderful idea to have his friend Thomas as archbishop.

Thomas said, "Don't do this to me." The king said that this would be an ideal appointment. He stated, "You are my closest friend and you will see to it that the Church obeys the king." Thomas continued to object, but to no avail. The king as always had his way.

But as Archbishop, Thomas changed. He lived a life of prayer and penance. And with even more fervor than his predecessor he defended the Church against the King taking over. Soon these two old friends were clashing. They locked horns constantly. In time their differences became so pronounced that Becket was forced into exile. He had to flee to France. There he lived in a monastery, growing in grace. Then a truce was reached and Thomas returned. But the peace did not last for long. The king felt betrayed by his former close friend. One day he shouted loudly, "Is there no one to rid me of this troublesome prelate?"

Four of his knights heard these words and took them literally. Shortly after Christmas they went to the Cathedral at Canterbury. The knights approached the Archbishop and threatened him. Thomas was not frightened. He said simply, "Here I am, no traitor, but Archbishop and priest."

The knights drew their swords. Thomas said, "I am ready to die." He covered his face and called aloud to God. They rushed up to him and hacked this great martyr to death with their swords.

St. Thomas Aquinas, the Angelic Doctor, was like St. Dominic "ever joyous in the sight of men". He remembered faithfully the presence of God. He said, "Be assured that he who walks faithfully in God's presence, and who is ready to give an account of his actions, will never be parted from Him by yielding to sin."

Prayer was for him the very breath of his life. Frequently he urged the maxim of St. Augustine, "He knows how to live rightly, who has learned to pray properly." Father Reginald, his faithful secretary, said that his great and uplifting writings Thomas owed less to the power of genius than to the efficacy of his prayers. Before studying, lecturing, reading, writing or dictating, he began by shutting himself up in secret prayer: he prayed with tears, so as to obtain from God understanding and light. When he encountered a difficulty, he had recourse to prayer.

His devotion to the Blessed Mother was dear and deep. He wrote, "Mother of him who created all things, this day and all the days of my life I commend to you all my actions, so that through your prayers they may all be ordered according to the will of your beloved Son, our Lord Jesus Christ. Lady most holy, be my helper and comforter against the attacks of the ancient foe, and all my enemies. Amen."

The year 1273 he stopped writing, before reaching his fiftieth birthday. He said, "I can do no more." Father Reginald urged him to go on. "Father, why do you leave unfinished this great work, which you have undertaken for God's glory and the enlightenment of the world?" Thomas said that he had had a vision of heaven and "all that I have written seems to be only like a handful of straw."

He died not long after. And then for all eternity he saw the greatness of God.

St. Teresa of Avila said, "The chief happiness which seems to me to be in the Kingdom of heaven, among many other sources of joy, is this, that there no account is made of any earthly thing; but there is a repose, a glory in the Blessed, a rejoicing that all rejoice, a perpetual peace, a great satisfaction in themselves; and this comes to them, because they see all the inhabitants sanctify and praise God, and bless his name, and that none offend him. All love him, and the soul herself minds nothing else but to love him, and she cannot forbear loving him because she knows him. And so we should love him in this world, did we know him, though not in such perfection and with such steadfastness: but we should love him in a manner different from what we do now, did we once know him."

Our divine Master wishes our petitions. He told us to ask God for help. In this life we are still at sea and on a journey, in exile, and we need divine assistance. There are seasons when our Lord places those who are weary of traveling in a state wherein the powers are tranquil, and the soul is quiet; wherein, as it were by signs, he makes them clearly understand how sweet that is which our Lord gives to those whom he brings to his Kingdom; and on those to whom this is given he bestows certain pledges, that by means of them they may conceive great hope of being enabled to enjoy eternally, what they are allowed only to sip in this world.

St. Teresa says that in some Christ already begins to give his Kingdom here, in order that they may truly praise and sanctify his name and endeavor that all men may do the same. He sets the soul at peace.

The great St. Teresa of Avila states that Jesus wishes us to give to his Father what he offered himself. "Thy will be done on earth as it is in heaven." The soil of our souls is barren, but there is a great blessing in this prayer of one sentence.

St. Teresa said, "O my Lord, what a great consolation is this to me, that you would not leave to so bad a will as mine the accomplishing or not accomplishing of your will. Were the accomplishment of your will in heaven and on earth in my hands, what a condition should I be in. I therefore now freely give all to you, for I have tried, and this by long experience, I know what gain is obtained by resigning my will to yours. O my friends, what a great benefit is acquired here. O what a great loss, when we do not perform what we promise God in the Our Father, respecting what we offer him."

She said that our Lord knows what everyone can bear and so he acts accordingly. Our Lord has a greater love for us than we have. He highly values what we give him and he desires to reward us amply. He acts conformably to the love he has for us. To them that love little, he gives little. For her part, she said, she thought that the rule of being able to bear great or little is that of love. We should freely give God our will so that his will may be done.

St. Teresa wrote that we must ask the Lord that we will accomplish his will. How powerful is this prayer and what a gift we give to God who has done everything for us. When we pray thus it induces the Almighty to become one with our baseness: it transforms us into him, and unites the Creator with the creature. Consider well that this is the way to gain the affection of Christ. Then God instructs us how and by what manner we are to serve him. This is what matters most in the spiritual life.

St. Paul   *December 15*

"But Saul, still breathing threats of slaughter against the disciples of the Lord, went to the high priest and asked him for letters to the synagogues at Damascus, that if he found any men or women belonging to this Way, he might bring them in bonds to Jerusalem." This the Acts of the Apostles tells us about St. Paul.

"And as he went on his journey, it came to pass that he drew near Damascus, when suddenly a light from heaven shone round about him; and falling to the ground, he heard a voice saying to him, 'Saul, Saul, why do you persecute me?' And he said, 'Who are you, Lord?' and he said, 'I am Jesus, whom you are persecuting. It is hard for you to kick against the goad.' And he, trembling and amazed, said, 'Lord, what will you have me to do?' And the Lord said to him, 'Arise and go into the city, and it will be told you what you must do.' Now the men who journeyed with him stood speechless, hearing indeed the voice, but seeing no one. And Saul arose from the ground, but when his eyes were opened, he could see nothing. And leading him by the hand, they brought him into Damascus. And for three days he could not see, and he neither ate nor drank.

"Now there was in Damascus a certain disciple named Ananias, and the Lord said to him in a vision, 'Ananias'. And he said, 'Here I am, Lord.' And the Lord said to him, 'Arise and go to the street called Straight and ask at the house of Judas for a man of Tarsus named Saul. For behold he is praying, and he has seen a man named Ananias come in and lay his hands upon him that he might recover his sight.' But Ananias answered, 'Lord, I have heard from many about this man, how much evil he has done to your saints in Jerusalem. And here too he has authority from the high priests to arrest all who invoke your name.' But the Lord said to him, 'Go, for this man is a chosen vessel to me, to carry my name among nations and kings and the children of Israel. For I will show him how much he must suffer for my name.' "

And Ananias laid his hands on him; he recovered his sight and was baptized. Later he became the great St. Paul.

St. Ignatius of Antioch   *December 16*

St. Ignatius, the Bishop of Antioch, wrote to Polycarp, "who is bishop of the Church of Smyrna—or rather who has God the Father and the Lord Jesus Christ for *his* bishop". He told Polycarp that he was well pleased with his "godly mind, which is fixed . . . on an immovable rock". He said, "I exhort you, clothed as you are with the garment of grace, to speed on your course and exhort all others to attend to their salvation."

He went on, "Do justice to your office with the utmost solicitude. Be concerned about unity, the greatest blessing. Bear with all, just as the Lord does with you. Have patience with all charity, as indeed you do. To prayer give yourself unceasingly; beg for an increase in understanding; watch without letting your spirit flag. Speak to each one singly in imitation of God's way. Bear the infirmities of all, like a master athlete. The greater the toil, the greater the reward."

Bishop Ignatius wrote that you can expect little thanks in this world, but a wonderful reward awaits us. One must not be upset by those who are against us. We must always teach the truths of Christ, no matter what. "Look for him who is above all time—the Timeless, the Invisible, who for our sake became visible, the Impassible, who became subject to suffering on our account and for our sake endured everything."

The Bishop of Antioch told the Bishop of Smyrna not to neglect the widows. After the Lord, he must be their guardian. Be calm and patient. Do not treat servants with a haughty air, but neither should they have airs. On the contrary, for the glory of God he should be of service to all.

Let all in the Church toil together, Bishop Ignatius said. Suffer together, rest together since you are stewards in God's household, his servants. The servant must serve. Let your baptism be your armor; your faith, your helmet, your love, your spear.

St. Ignatius of Antioch   *December 17*

"Avoid the noxious weeds. Their gardener is not Jesus, because they are not the planting of the Father. Do not be deceived if a man runs after a schismatic. He will not inherit the Kingdom of God. If a man chooses to be a dissenter, he severs all connection with the Passion", said the early Christian bishop St. Ignatius of Antioch. Tradition has it that he was appointed by St. Peter as the Bishop of Antioch.

St. Ignatius wrote, "I extol Jesus Christ, the God who has granted us wisdom. Be thoroughly trained in unshaken faith."

He told the people, "You have been nailed, as it were, to the Cross of the Lord Jesus Christ both in body and soul; be well established in love through the Blood of Christ. . . . He was nailed to the Cross in the flesh for our sake—of whose fruits we are, in virtue of his most blessed Passion. Through the Resurrection, he raised a banner for all times for his saints and faithful followers that they might be united in a single body, that is, his Church." St. Ignatius continued, "All these sufferings, assuredly, he underwent for our sake, that we might be saved."

He wrote, "Some disown Jesus through ignorance. Let no one be deceived. Even the heavenly powers and the angels in their splendor must either believe in the Blood of Christ, or else face damnation. Let no rank puff up anyone; for faith and love are paramount—the greatest blessings in the world. Observe those who hold erroneous opinions concerning the grace of Jesus Christ which has come to us, and see how they run counter to the mind of Christ!"

He stated, "Let no one do anything touching the Church apart from the bishop. Let that celebration of the Eucharist be considered valid which is held under the bishop or anyone to whom he has committed it. Thus everything you do will be proof against danger and will be valid."

St. Cyril of Jerusalem   *December 18*

St. Cyril, Bishop of Jerusalem in the fourth century, wrote, "Christ was truly crucified for our sins. And should you wish to deny this, the visible place itself, the blessed Gologotha, refutes you in the name of him who was here crucified. He was crucified not for his own sins, but that we might be freed from ours. He was despised and buffeted by men at that time as man, but was acknowledged as God by creation. For the sun, seeing its Master dishonored, was darkened and trembled, not enduring the sight."

He said that Jesus was laid in a rock tomb. And Jesus who was buried rose again on the third day. After he had risen he was seen by his disciples. The eleven apostles were witnesses of his Resurrection, testifying, not with words meant to please, but contending for the truth of the Resurrection even unto torture and death.

"When Jesus had completed the patient course of his teaching, he returned to heaven. He was reunited to the Father. Now this Christ who was crucified is worshipped in all parts of the world. We proclaim the Crucified and the demons tremble. Let us not be ashamed of the Cross of Christ", Cyril said. "Seal it openly on your brow. Make this sign when eating and drinking, when rising up and lying down. For he who was crucified on the Cross is now in heaven. The Cross is sacred because we were saved from sin by it. His Father, when Jesus ascended into heaven, said, 'Sit at my right hand until I make your enemies your footstool.'

"This Jesus who ascended will come again from heaven to judge the world. Look to Christ, the only-begotten Son of God, who will appear to all at his coming like lightning and the splendor of light."

St. Teresa of Avila   *December 19*

St. Teresa of Avila said that our good Jesus knows our weakness. He understands our difficulties. We can trust him because he is so merciful. We cannot accomplish our objective, the salvation of our soul, without his help. At times we do not understand the Divine Will. We should accept it. It is for the best for us.

It is God's will that we should praise him. It is his will that we should help our neighbor. We do this with his help. What would become of us, if we did not pray?

Say to the Father, "Thy will be done." This is the perfect prayer. The good God who sees our necessities, for he knows us better than we know ourselves, will give us what we need. He will not always give us everything we want, for sometimes what we want is bad for us. God who loves each of us with a great love will not give us things to do us harm, no more than a mother would do this to her child.

We receive so much from the good God. We should be thanking him daily, we can never thank him enough. If we are to have love and courage, we must ask him for it.

When we say, "God's will be done", we are bowing to a better judgment. God is infinitely wiser than we are. The humble know this very well. The proud in their blindness will never admit it. The child is supposed to do what his father tells him; we expect him to know that his father is wiser than he is. And God is so much wiser than we are; our minds are like a grain of sand and his is like the majestic ocean. Surely anyone who thinks will know that to follow God is the wisest thing that he can do.

How foolish the person who follows himself. It is like "the blind leading the blind and both fall into the pit".

Praise God, thank him, do his will, ask for his mercy and he will come to your assistance.

St. Clare of Assisi   *December 20*

St. Clare of Assisi was the most faithful disciple that St. Francis had. When Francis was dying he thought of Clare and her Sisters and sent them "sweet words of comfort like a song for their consolation and edification, knowing them to be greatly afflicted by his suffering. Because he could no longer visit them he called upon them to ever praise the Lord to whom men owe their whole love." He reminded them of their calling, of their vows of poverty and obedience, and of the gratitude they should feel for the alms by which they lived. "Should a Sister ask for anything that is denied her," he said in his last letter, "let her suffer this patiently for love of the Lord, who lacked so many things in this life, and sought in vain for consolation."

Francis said, "Every privation a Sister suffers in this life will be counted to her as martyrdom; and even should her health suffer, let her forgive the injury with all her heart." He said that Brother Body must be spared if he is to stand the burden of the spiritual life; he exhorted them to inner mortification, to gentleness, compassion and mutual charity, and with this he sent his last blessing.

The Sisters could hardly bear the thought that they would not see him again, and this was especially true of Clare. They remembered Francis saying, "I, little Brother Francis, desire to follow the life and poverty of our most high Lord Jesus Christ, and his holy Mother, and to persevere therein until the end. And I beseech you, my Sisters, and I counsel you that you live also in this most holy life of poverty. And be greatly careful of yourselves lest by the teaching and counsel of anyone you in any way or at any time draw away from it."

At the very end Francis said, "Go and tell Sister Clare to put aside all sorrow and sadness, for though she cannot see me now, yet before her death she and her Sisters shall see me and have great comfort through me."

St. Clare of Assisi   *December 21*

Someone at the convent saw a bright and marvelous light in the sky and before the messenger arrived the Sisters knew that Sister Death had opened the gate. "Francis, poor and humble, entered rich into heaven", they said.

Francis was gone, but St. Clare carried on. And he did often comfort her, as he said he would. She wrote to a new Sister in another convent: "I have learned, my dear Sister, that by the grace of God you have renounced the world. This has filled me with gladness, and I greatly admire the generosity of your resolution, and the great fervor with which you are setting out along the path of perfection. I pray you to keep faithful to the divine Bridegroom to whom you have consecrated yourself; and be sure that your efforts will be rewarded with the crown of immortality. The period of trial is short; that of the reward unending. Do not let yourself be discouraged by the splendor of the world which will pass like a shadow; do not be deceived by appearances that are false. It is true the devil will tempt you with bad suggestions; but be strong, shut your ears to him and you will put him to flight.

"Beware, beloved, that you are not overthrown by adversity,

and that your heart does not swell with pride in prosperity, for the sign of faith is to make us humble in success, and unmoved by failure. Give to God what you have vowed to him, give it with gentle care, and he will know how to repay your sacrifices. Lift your eyes continually to heaven, for it is heaven that calls to you to take up your cross and follow Jesus Christ who precedes you. With the whole strength of your soul love God who is infinitely adorable, and his divine Son who deigned to be crucified for our sins. Meditate on his Passion and on the sufferings of his holy Mother beneath the Cross. Watch and pray. Apply your strength to finish the good work you have begun."

St. Alphonsus Liguori   *December 22*

St. Alphonsus Liguori wrote about the first Christmas, saying, "The Eternal Word had no other end in becoming man than to inflame us with divine love. Let us ask for the light of Jesus Christ and his most holy Mother to be more grateful for his coming."

Man in the beginning, he said, rebelled against God. And so men then lived in the world in pain and misery. To rescue us God sent his divine Son into the world.

The Angel Gabriel appeared to Mary, asking her if she would accept God's Son to be her Son, so he could redeem us. Mary said Yes. Jesus then made his entry into the world in all humility and obedience, saying, "Since, O my Father, men cannot make atonement to thy offended justice by their works and sacrifices, behold me, thy Son, now clothed in mortal flesh, behold me ready to give thee in their stead satisfaction with my sufferings and with my death!"

So then for us miserable creatures and to captivate our love, God deigned to become man. So much has God done in order to be loved by us.

St. Alphonsus wrote, "Man does not love me, God would seem to say, because he does not see me. I wish to make myself seen by him and converse with him and so make myself loved."

The divine love for us is so great, so wholehearted, so extreme.

God said, "I have loved you with an everlasting love." But it was difficult for men to realize his great love. It truly appeared, however, when the Son of God showed himself a little one on a bundle of straw in the stable. The Scripture says, "The goodness and kindness of God our Savior appeared." God showed us his singular love. The world had seen the power of God in creation; it had seen his wisdom in the governance of the world; but only after the Incarnation did it see how great is the mercy of God.

St. Alphonsus Liguori   *December 23*

St. Alphonsus Liguori said that before God was seen by men on earth, they could not truly conceive of the divine goodness. But when God took mortal flesh, appearing as man, the greatness of his benignity was made plain to all.

Following the rebellion of Adam and Eve, man was unable to return to God alone, so God came to earth in search of man. St. Alphonsus quoted St. Augustine who said, "Because we could not go to the Mediator, he condescended to come to us."

Men are drawn by love. Christ manifested the tremendous love of God. To do this the Eternal Word became man, to draw to himself by such a show of affection—a love stronger than which could not possibly be found—God's love for men. Our Redeemer showed his love for us, which is beyond words.

St. Alphonsus told of the holy Franciscan Father to whom the lovely Infant Jesus appeared. The holy friar always longed to hold the beautiful Baby in his arms. One day the sweet Child allowed him to do so, as if to show that Jesus is a prisoner of our love.

In coming to earth Jesus made himself a prisoner of our love. He has such a prodigious amount of love for us that he seems unable to do otherwise. In many ways God shows his love, but no more clearly did he exhibit the excess of his bounty than by becoming man to redeem us, to teach us the way of salvation and to procure for us the life of grace.

St. Thomas Aquinas wrote, "In Christ, mercy itself came down to those who were in sin, truth to those wandering out of the way and life to those who were dead."

The Incarnation is purely the effect of the surpassing love that God bears for man.

St. Alphonsus Liguori *December 24*

St. Alphonsus Liguori cited the writing of St. Thomas Aquinas, who in speaking of the Incarnation wrote, "This proceeded from the very great love God has for man." Christ was born to us because of God's immense charity. In no instance has God so clearly manifested his loving charity to men as when he was made man. Here the depth of the divine love shines forth so greatly. The Son of God came searching for man, while man foolishly was fleeing from God.

God came from heaven to arrest, as it were, ungrateful man in his flight from him, Alphonsus said. It is as if he had said, "O man, behold, it is nothing but the love of you that has brought me to earth to seek after you. Why do you flee me? Stay with me, love me, for I so greatly love you." Why are we so cold to Christ?

St. John Chrysologus told us that Jesus is shivering, a little Baby in a damp cavern, but he is fire and flames for us; he supplies us with a flame of love that rivers of water shall never quench.

It is not enough that divine love made us to his own image and likeness in creating us, but he must also himself be made to our image in redeeming us. "God is made our brother", said St. Augustine.

St. Alphonsus wrote, "It was an immeasurably greater humiliation for God to become man than if all the princes of the earth and all the angels and saints of heaven had been turned into a blade of grass." He quoted St. Bernard, who said that the more God humbled himself for us in becoming man, so much the more has he made his goodness known to us. "The smaller he has become by humility, the greater he has shown us his love." No wonder St. Paul said, "The charity of Christ urges us."

Christmas

In the beginning was the Word,
   and the Word was with God;
   and the Word was God.
He was in the beginning with God.
All things were made through him,
   and without him was made
   nothing that was made.
In him was life,
   and the life was the light of men.
And the light shines in the darkness;
   and the darkness grasped it not.
There was a man,
   one sent from God,
   whose name was John.
This man came as a witness,
   to bear witness to the light,
   that all might believe through him.
He was not himself the light,
   but was to bear witness to the light.
It was the true light
   that enlightens every man
   who comes into the world.
He was in the world,
   and the world was made through him,
   and the world knew him not.
He came unto his own,
   and his own received him not.
But to as many as received him
   he gave the power of becoming sons of God;
   to those who believe in his name:
Who were born not of blood,

nor of the will of the flesh,
nor of the will of man,
but of God.
And the Word was made flesh,
and dwelt among us.
And we saw his glory—
glory as of the only-begotten of the Father—
full of grace and of truth.

—St. John the Evangelist

St. Ignatius Loyola

December 26

St. Ignatius Loyola said that God looked upon the earth and saw what darkness was here. So the Second Person of the Holy Trinity was sent to bring light, to save the human race. The angel announced to Mary this good news, and she, lovingly, consented to be the Mother of the Savior. The angel went to the house of Mary in Nazareth to ask if God might become man so that we may love him and follow him.

The world was in chaos and turmoil. There was sin and evil everywhere. People were weeping and troubled. There was such blindness among the people. Souls were sinning and being lost.

Then at Nazareth the angel greeted our Lady, most pure and beautiful of souls. Here was light in the black night of the world.

Most men at that time acted and lived like animals, killing, full of cruelty, blasphemy and hatred. God said, "Let us work for the redemption of all." He sent his messenger to Mary, and then, "in the fullness of time" the Baby was born in Bethlehem.

Joseph and Mary had to make the arduous, long journey to Bethlehem because of the census. It was most difficult, and then when they arrived there there was no room for them. And so Jesus, our Savior, was born in a cave. But though the place was poor, Mary and Joseph were happy. For the Redeemer was born.

On the journey they had been cold and hungry and thirsty and weary, but now they rejoiced. Jesus' holy Mother held him warmly and tenderly in her loving arms. She smiled sweetly as she looked at him and so found great peace. The love and holiness of this Child, the beautiful fragrance and wonderful goodness made her heart supremely happy.

St. Bernard of Clairvaux *December 27*

St. Bernard of Clairvaux wrote, "In the struggles and combats of every day, which are at no time wanting to those who live close to Christ, whether it be of the flesh, the world or the devil, so that the life of man on earth is a continual warfare, as you experience incessantly in your own selves, let us take time to think of the joy of the coming of Christ."

Let the image of God as man rise before you. Look upon Jesus at his birth and let him animate your soul to the love of holiness and drive away fleshly vices; let him put to flight temptations and calm your desires. "I consider", Bernard wrote, "that a principal cause why God, who is invisible, willed to render himself visible in the flesh, and to dwell as a man among men, was to draw, in the first place, to the salutary love of himself all the affections of men."

Jesus descended from heaven. As St. Paul said, "Jesus, . . . though he was in the form of God, did not count equality with God a thing to be grasped, but emptied himself, taking the form of a servant, being born in the likeness of men."

We truly confess in the Creed Christ to be God and man. In the Incarnation God came down to us, he who "has borne our griefs and carried our sorrows". Being a man he knew by personal experience the miseries of men and so was compassionate. As a man he learned obedience. The Epistle to the Hebrews states, "He learned obedience by the things which he suffered." In this manner also he learned human mercy.

His mercy was shown in the beginning as he blessed the shepherds for coming to the cave of Bethlehem. These men of little learning were humble and when they saw the Baby in Mary's arms they bowed down and honored him. We must do the same.

St. Alphonsus Liguori said, why are we ungrateful? Why do many ignore Jesus? Has anyone ever loved you as he loves you? He has such a love for you that to release you from eternal death he died for you. To save you he gave his heart's blood, even to the last drop. He endured a most terrible death with horrible torture. He died the death which you justly deserved. But he died in your stead. He died for you. And in so doing he washed our sins from us with his very blood. "Greater love than this has no man than that he lay down his life for another."

Yes, said St. Gregory Nazianzen, because in no other way could he better show forth the divine love than by abasing himself, taking upon himself the greatest misery and ignominy that men ever suffer on this earth. St. Gregory said, "God could not otherwise declare his love for us than by descending for our sakes to what was most low." Richard of St. Victor added that man, who had the boldness to offend the majesty of God, needed the intervention of the most excessive humiliation in order to expiate his guilt: "For the expiation of the sin, the humiliation of the highest to the lowest was necessary."

St. Alphonsus quoted St. Bernard who said that to raise us up, God lowered himself.

This began at the first Christmas when God became a little Baby in a manger in a cave. We must respond with love and gratitude unless our hearts are made of stone. St. Augustine said, "Lift yourself up and praise God." He said that if we are humble Christ comes to us.

St. Alphonsus said that God resists the proud and does not listen to them, but when we are humble, and bow before the Baby of Bethlehem, he cannot deny his graces to us.

St. Augustine   *December 29*

As we approach the New Year, St. Augustine gives us new hope.
He wrote, "Who can measure the happiness of heaven, where no
evil at all can touch us, no good will be out of reach; where life is
to be one long laud praising God, who will be all in all; where
there will be no weariness to call for rest, no need to call for toil,
no place for any energy but praise. Of this I am assured whenever
I read or hear the sacred song: 'Blessed are they that dwell in thy
house, O Lord: they shall praise thee for ever and ever.' Every
fiber and organ of our imperishable body will play its part in the
praising of God. On earth these varied organs have each a special
function, but, in heaven, function will be swallowed up in felicity,
in the perfect certainty of an untroubled everlastingness of joy."

St. Augustine said that all our being will swell, in every fiber,
into a great hymn of praise to the supreme Artist who has
fashioned us, within and without, and who, by this and every
other element of a magnificent and marvelous order, will ravish
our minds with spiritual beauty.

He continued, "The movements of our bodies will be of such
unimaginable beauty that I dare not say more than this: There
will be such poise, such grace, such beauty as become a place
where nothing unbecoming can be found. Wherever the spirit
wills, there, in a flash, will the body be. Nor will the spirit ever
will anything unbecoming either to itself or the body."

In heaven we will be home, for God's home is our home, and
we will be happy, warm, loving and generous, and we shall
rejoice forever.

St. Augustine   *December 30*

"In Heaven", wrote the great St. Augustine, "all glory will be
true glory, since no one could ever err in praising too little or too
much. True honor will never be denied where due, never be
given where undeserved, and, since none but the worthy are
permitted there, no one with unworthy ambition will seek glory.

Perfect peace with reign, since nothing in ourselves or in any others could disturb this peace. The promised reward of virtue will be the best and the greatest of all possible prizes—the very Giver of virtue himself, for that is what the prophet meant, 'I will be the source of every satisfaction, more than any heart can rightly crave, more than life and health, food and wealth, glory and honor, peace and every good'—so that God, as St. Paul said, 'may be all in all'. He will be the consummation of all our desiring—the object of our unending vision, of our unlessening love, of our unwearying praise. And in this gift of vision, this response of love, this paean of praise, all alike will share, as all will share in everlasting life."

St. Augustine said, "But now who can imagine, let alone describe, the ranks upon ranks of rewarded saints, to be graded, undoubtedly, according to their variously merited honor and glory." He continued, "Yet there will be no envy of angel for archangel—for this is one of the great blessednesses of this blessed City of God. The less rewarded will be linked in perfect peace with the more highly favored, but lower could no more long for higher than a finger of the body could want to be an eye. The less endowed will have the high endowment of longing for nothing loftier than their lower gifts."

St. Augustine   *December 31*

"The souls in bliss will still possess the freedom of will, though sin will have no power to tempt them", said St. Augustine in speaking of heaven. "They will be more free than ever—so free, in fact, from all delight in sinning as to find, in not sinning, an unfailing source of joy. By the freedom which was given to the first man, who was constituted in rectitude, he could choose either to sin or not to sin; in eternity, freedom is that more potent freedom which makes all sin impossible."

This great Christian writer went on, "Such freedom, of course, is a gift of God, beyond the power of nature to achieve. For it is one thing to be God, another to be a sharer in the divine nature. God, by his nature, cannot sin, but a mere sharer in his nature must receive from God such immunity from sin. It is proper that, in the process of divine endowment, the first step should be a freedom not to sin, and the last a freedom even from the power of sin."

St. Augustine tells us that in heaven "the memory of our previous miseries will be a matter of purely mental contemplation, with no renewal of any feelings connected with these experiences— much as learned doctors know by science many of those bodily maladies which, by suffering, they have no sensible experience. All ills, in fact, can be forgotten.

"Heaven, too, will be the fulfillment of that Sabbath rest foretold in the command: 'Be still and see that I am God.' This indeed will be that ultimate Day of Rest that has no evening and which the Lord foreshadowed in the account of creation. We too will have a Day of Rest when we shall be filled with God's blessing and remade by his sanctification. In the stillness of that rest we shall see that he is the God of all.

"Only when we are remade by God and perfected by a greater grace shall we have this eternal stillness." This we will enjoy in heaven forever.

FEAST DAYS

All Saints'	November 1
All Souls'	November 2
Alphonsus Liguori	August 1
Angela Merici	January 27
Anthony of Padua	June 13
Augustine	August 28
Basil the Great	January 2
Benedict	July 11
Benedict Joseph Labre	April 16
Bernadette	April 16
Bernard of Clairvaux	August 20
Bonaventure	July 15
Catherine Labouré	November 28
Catherine of Siena	April 29
Charles Borromeo	November 4
Clare of Assisi	August 12
Columban	November 23
Cyprian	September 16
Cyril of Jerusalem	March 18
Dominic	August 8

Edmund Campion	December 1
Elizabeth Ann Seton	January 4
Frances Xavier Cabrini	November 13
Francis de Sales	January 24
Francis of Assisi	October 4
Francis Xavier	December 3
Gertrude	November 16
Gregory of Nyssa	March 9
Ignatius Loyola	July 31
Ignatius of Antioch	October 17
Jean de Brébeuf	October 19
John Bosco	January 31
John Chrysostom	July 13
John of the Cross	December 14
John Vianney	August 8
Joseph	March 19 May 1
Kateri Tekakwitha	July 14
Laurence O'Toole	November 14
Martin de Porres	July 25 November 3
Mary, Mother of God	January 1 March 25 May 31 August 15 October 7 December 8
Maximilian Kolbe	August 14

Patrick	March 17
Paul	June 29
Peter	June 29
Peter Claver	September 9
Peter Julian Eymard	August 3
Philip Neri	May 26
Pius X, Pope	August 21
Rose Philippine Duchesne	November 18
Teresa of Avila	October 15
Thérèse of Lisieux	October 1
Thomas à Becket	December 29
Thomas Aquinas	January 28
Thomas More	July 9
Vincent de Paul	September 27

INDEX OF READINGS

Bernard of Clairvaux	March 15
	April 6
	May 5, 8, 30
	June 16
	July 5–6
	August 12, 14, 21, 28–31
	September 1
	October 2, 27–28
	November 29–30
	December 27
Bonaventure	February 15, 18
	March 3, 13
	April 7, 30
	May 19
	June 13–15
	July 13–17
Catherine Labouré	April 9–11
Catherine of Siena	February 1–2
	April 16, 19–20, 24
	September 7, 27
Charles Borromeo	January 21–22
	February 4
Christmas	December 25
Clare of Assisi	April 26
	September 3, 18
	October 1
	November 24
	December 20–21
Columban	April 27–28
Cyprian	April 14, 21
	May 15–16
Cyril of Jerusalem	May 18, 22, 26
	December 18

Dominic	February 3
	April 29
Edmund Campion	May 9–10
Elizabeth Seton	January 23, 26–28
	September 11–13, 15, 24
	October 17
Frances Xavier Cabrini	August 23, 27
	September 8–9
Francis de Sales	January 1, 6, 11
	February 5
	March 22
	April 8
	June 11–12, 17–19
	October 6
	November 7–8
Francis of Assisi	February 13–14, 19
	March 4–5, 12
	April 25
	May 11, 20–21, 25
	June 10
	July 18
	September 2
	October 11
Francis Xavier	May 6–7, 13–14, 23–24
	June 21–22
	July 31
	September 26
	October 12–13
Gertrude	January 9, 31
	April 3, 17
	May 29
	July 21
	August 6
Gregory of Nyssa	June 24

Ignatius Loyola	January 20
	February 10–12, 20–25
	June 25
	September 28
	December 26
Ignatius of Antioch	March 20
	December 16–17
Jean de Brébeuf	September 25
	October 14–15, 21–22
	November 16–19
John Bosco	June 29–30
	July 1
John Chrysostom	July 11–12
John of the Cross	January 3, 5, 13, 16
	February 6–7, 27
	July 2, 20
	October 5
	November 3–4, 6
John Vianney	January 24–25
Joseph	March 19
Kateri Tekakwitha	December 4–6
Laurence O'Toole	November 26
Martin de Porres	July 25
	August 1, 22
Mary, Mother of God	March 25
	May 1–3, 31
	August 15
	October 7
	December 8
Maximilian Kolbe	November 27

Patrick	March 17 September 6, 20
Paul	December 15
Peter Claver	September 30 October 10, 16
Peter Julian Eymard	July 23, 27 August 10, 17 September 14 October 8 November 5, 9
Philip Neri	January 30 March 6 April 2, 22 May 28 July 24
Pius X, Pope	November 28
Rose Philippine Duchesne	September 21–23
Teresa of Avila	January 2 March 21 April 12–13 July 8–9 August 11 August 24–26 September 29 October 4, 31 December 13–14, 19
Thérèse of Lisieux	January 12, 14–15 February 9, 26 March 1, 14 May 4, 12 June 26 October 9

Thomas à Becket	December 11
Thomas Aquinas	January 4,7
	February 8
	March 18
	April 18
	May 27
	June 7, 9, 20, 27–28
	July 28–30
	August 9
	September 4, 16
	October 3, 24, 29–30
	November 12, 21
	December 1–2, 9–10, 12
Thomas More	January 17
	March 2, 29
	April 23
	May 17
	June 6
	July 4
	August 8
	September 10
	November 15
Vincent de Paul	January 18–19
	March 9, 16
	April 4, 15
	June 1–3